Chinese Wushu Fundamental Training

中國武術基礎訓練

Yajun Zhuang

Wushu, Originated in China
But Belongs to the World
武術源於中國, 屬於世界

I dedicated this book to
my family
friends
my students

In the 1980s, the Author Practiced Wushu in China

In 1984, the Author Showed a Backward Somersault of the Long Fist in Hui Yin, China

Practiced Drunken Boxing, in Huai Yin 1985

I

Practiced Swordplay at Huai Yin Normal University in 1986.

Practiced Mantis Boxing, in Nanjing 1988

In the 1980s, Author Worked as a Wushu Coach in Huaiyin, Jiangsu Province, China

In the 1990s, Author Worked as a Wushu Coach in Nanjing, Jiangsu Province, China

From 1999 to 2002, the Author was the Guest Coach of Dutch Wushu National Team

2011 Performance by the Author and the Students
at the China Spring Festival Gala in Baton Rouge, LA, USA

The Students Represented the USA Team in the 13th Pan American Wushu Championships in Brazil, 2022

The Students were Awarded Gold Metals in the 4th Pan America KungFu Championship Held in Canada 2023

Wushu Fundamental Training in Adult Class

Performing the Basic Skills of Wushu in the Community

Contents

Acknowledgement   XI

Forward   XIII

Part 1 Wushu Basic Skills

Chapter 1 Jiān - Bì – Gōng
Shoulder and Arm Training Exercises   3

1.   Yà Jiān, 'Shoulder Stretch'   4
2.   Chí Gùn Zhuǎn Jiān, 'Holding a Stick and Rotating the Shoulder'   6
3.   Shǒu Dǎo Lì, 'Handstan   8
4.   Sǒng Jiān Chén Jiān, 'Shrugging and Sinking Shoulders'   10
5.   Kāi Jiān Hé Jiān, 'Opening and Closing Shoulder'   11
6.   Dān Bì Rào Huán, 'Single-Arm Circle'   11
7.   Shuāng Bì Rào Huán, 'Circle Both Arms '   14
8.   Pū Bù Lūn Pāi, 'Circle Arms and Slaps the Ground with a Crouch-Stance'
    18

Chapter 2 Tui - Gōng
Leg Training Exercises   24

1.   'Yà Tuǐ' or 'Leg Stretch'   25
2.   'Bān Tuǐ' or 'Leg Holding'   40
3.   'Pī Tuǐ' or Leg Splitting   46

Chapter 3 Yao - Gong
Waist Training Exercises   64

1.   'Qián Fǔ Yāo,' 'Forward Bend,'   64
2.   'Shuǎi Yāo,' 'Waist Forward and Backward Bend with Arm Swing'   66
3.   'Huàng Yāo,' 'Sway Waist'   67
4.   'Níng Yāo, "Twist Waist'   69
5.   'Fān Yāo,' 'Flip Over the Waist Exercise'   71
6.   'Shuàn Yāo,' 'Circle Waist'   72
7.   'Xià Yāo,' 'Bridge'   74

Chapter 4 Zhan Zhuang Gong Fu
Standing Post Kung Fu   80

Sì-Píng-Mǎ-Bù-Zhuāng or Four-Level Horse Stance Standing Post   83
Gōng-Bù-Zhuāng or Bow Stance Post   85
Xū - Bù-Zhuāng or Empty Stance Post   86

Part 2 Wushu Basic Technique

Chapter 5 Basic Movements (1)
Shǒu Xíng Shǒu Fǎ - Hand Form and Hand Technique   91

Shǒu Xíng or Hand Form   91
Shǒu Fǎ or Hand Techniques   96

Chapter 6 Basic Movements (2)
Bù Xíng Bù Fǎ - Footwork Stances and Footwork   129

Bù Xíng or Stances   129
Bù Fǎ or Footwork   138

Chapter 7 Basic Movements (3)
Zhǒu Fǎ - Elbow Techniques   148

Chapter 8 Basic Movements (4)
Tuǐ Fǎ - Leg Techniques   155

Zhí Bǎi Xìng 'Tuǐ Fǎ, Straight Swinging Leg Techniques   155
Qū Shēn Xìng Tuǐ Fǎ, Flexion and Extension Leg Techniques   175
Sǎo Zhuǎn Xìng Tuǐ Fǎ, Sweeping-Rotating Leg Techniques   181
Jī Pāi Xìng Tuǐ Fǎ, Slap Kick Leg Technique   188

Chapter 9 Basic Movements (5)
Píng Héng or Balance   193

Lasting Balance   193
Non-Persistent Balance   206
How to Practice 'Balance' Movement in Wushu Routine   208

Chapter 10 Basic Movements (6)
Tiao Yue - Jump   211

1. 'Dà Yuè Bù Qián Chuān', Giant Leap Forward   212
2. 'Téng Kōng Jiàn Tàn', Aerial Snap Kick   218
3. 'Téng Kōng Fēi Jiǎo,' Jumping, Front Straight Kick   231

4. 'Téng Kōng Bǎi Lián,' Jumping Lotus Kick   239
5. Téng Kōng Xuànfēng Jiǎo, Jump Tornado Kick   252
6. Cè Kōng Fān, Aerial Cartwheel or Cartwheel Roll   260
7. Xuán Zi, Butterfly kick   267
8. 'Xuán Zi Zhuàn Tǐ,' Butterfly-twist   276

Chapter 11 Basic Movements (7)
Die Pu Gun Fan - Tumbling   281

1. Qiǎng Bèi, Side-Diving Roll Forward   279
2. Lǐyú Dǎtǐng, Carp Flipping Up   287
3. Wū Lóng Jiǎo Zhù, Black Dragon Coiling Around a Pole   294
4. Zai Bei, Straight Forward (Backward) Falling   298
5. Pū Hǔ, Pounce on the tiger   301

Appendix
Physical Fitness Training Methods for Wushu Jumping Movements   303
1. Vertical Jumps   303
2. Jump Squats   304
3. Split Squat Jumps   304
4. Knees Tuck Jumps   305
5. Box jump   306
6. Hurdle jumps   308
7. Frog jumps   309
8. Burpees   310
9. Heels Raises   311
10. Heels Raise with Dumbbells   312
11. Leg Raises   313
12. Push Up   314
13. Hanging Knees Raise   315
14. Hanging Legs Raise   316
15. V Sit-Up   317

Chapter 12
Combination Movement Practice   321

The Combination of 'Stance' Movement Exercises   321
1. The Combination of 'Bow Stance' and 'Horse Stance'   321
2. The Combination of 'Empty Stance,' and 'Crouch Stance'   332
3. The Combination of 'Empty Stance,' 'Crouch Stance' and 'Rest Stance'
                                                                          335
4. The Combination of 'Rest Stance' and 'Horse Stance'   346

5. The Combination of 'Cross-Legged Behind,' 'Sitting,' and 'Bow Stance'
    350
6. A Combination of 'Five Types of Stances' or 'Five Stances Fist'   354

The Combination of 'Leg Technique' Exercises   367
1. The Combination of 'Inside Kick' and 'Front Straight Kick'   367
2. The Combination of 'Pat Foot' and 'Side Sole Kick'   375
3. The Combination of 'Front Sweep Kick' and Back' Sweep Kick'   382

The Combination of 'Balance' Exercises   387
  'Back Cross-Legged Balance' and 'Swallow Balance'   387
  'Raised Knee Balance,' 'Kick into Sky,' and 'Look at the Moon Balance' 393

The Combination of 'Jumping' Exercises   398
  'Jump Front Straight Kick' and 'Crouch Stance   398
  'Jump Lotus Kick' and 'Split'   404
  'Jump Tornado Kick' and 'Horse Stance'   409

References
About Author

Acknowledgement

Creating a book is a journey that relies on the support and contributions of numerous individuals and organizations. I am deeply grateful to all those who played a pivotal role in bringing 'Wushu Fundamental Training' to fruition.

First and foremost, I extend my heartfelt gratitude to my family for their unwavering encouragement and understanding throughout this endeavor.

I sincerely thank my dedicated students, Sharon O'Brien, Michael Buscemi, Edwin Scott Hackenberg, and Ryan M. Bergeron, for their invaluable assistance in writing this book. I would also like to express my gratitude to my friend Chongyang Man for his contributions in taking pictures and editing the illustrations used in the text.

I also want to acknowledge the valuable resources I have utilized in this work, primarily the Wushu pictures from various Wushu websites. These resources have significantly enriched the quality and depth of my book, and I have duly cited and attributed them.

Furthermore, I want to acknowledge the sources of knowledge and inspiration, including 'General Sports College Teaching Materials,' 'Specialized Sports College Teaching Materials Volume 1,' and 'National Wushu Training Material Volume 1,' which have made substantial contributions to the content of this book.

Lastly, I am deeply grateful to the readers and learners who will embark on this journey with 'Wushu Fundamental Training.' Your pursuit of excellence in Wushu is a testament to the enduring spirit of this martial art.

Finally, I extend my heartfelt thanks to everyone who contributed to this book in various ways, whether through their expertise, feedback, or encouragement. Your contributions have enriched this work and made it a better reflection of the ideas and themes it aims to explore. Your contributions are deeply appreciated.

Yajun Zhuang
Baton Rouge, Louisiana
2023

Forward

In the world of Chinese Wushu, where grace seamlessly intertwines with power, technique harmoniously melds with discipline, and tradition effortlessly fuses with innovation, a fundamental truth cherished by all Wushu practitioners emerges: the journey commences with mastering the basics. 'Wushu Fundamental Training,' this book, is my testament to the profound significance of establishing a rock-solid foundation in the art of Wushu.

In the expansive and intricate realm of Chinese Wushu, the fundamentals serve as the heartbeat, the core that pulses through every graceful movement, every precise strike, and every fluid form—whether it is a simple 'hand form' or a complex 'jump' and 'combination movement.' These fundamentals are not mere starting points; they are the bedrock upon which the entire structure of Wushu is constructed.

But why are these fundamentals so crucial? What is the essence of this treasure trove of Wushu wisdom? How do you embark on this journey, and what are the basic building blocks that will lead you to mastery? These questions lie at the very heart of 'Wushu Fundamental Training.'

As you peruse these pages, you will embark on a voyage of self-discovery—an expedition that delves deep into the heart of Chinese Wushu. Whether you are a novice taking your initial steps on this enlightening path, a seasoned practitioner aspiring to refine your skills, or perhaps a Wushu teacher, this book will serve as your steadfast guide and reference.

This book starts from the targeted Wushu 'stretches' that enhance flexibility to the foundational Wushu 'stances,' from the intricate 'footwork' to the graceful 'hand forms,' from the precise 'hand techniques' to the mighty 'leg techniques,' and from the agility required in 'jumps,' 'balances,' and 'tumbling' to the seamless blending of 'combination movements.' Each of these elements constructs the sturdy foundation of your Wushu journey. You will also delve into forms that encapsulate the essence of Wushu skills and explore the philosophical principles that inspire this art. Along this path, you will gradually uncover the time-honored Wushu training secrets passed down through generations. These secrets are not meant to remain concealed but to be shared, practiced, and treasured.

Prepare to immerse yourself in the wisdom and artistry of Chinese Wushu. Prepare to acquire both the physical techniques and the mental and spiritual facets that make Wushu a holistic way of life. Brace yourself for a transformative journey that will shape your body, mind, and soul.

To facilitate easy learning from this book, the author has meticulously divided the extensive domain of 'Wushu Fundamental Training' into two essential components: 'Basic Skill Training' and 'Basic Technique Training.'

The section dedicated to unarmed hand training embarks on a comprehensive journey aimed at enhancing various aspects of the body through the infusion of fundamental skills and techniques. This systematic approach expedites the development of Wushu's distinct physical attributes while promoting standardization, establishing correct posture, fostering technique mastery, addressing any irregular physical development, and significantly reducing the risk of injuries during practice. Moreover, it lays a solid foundation for exploring barehanded forms and weapon routines, enhancing overall athletic prowess.

The first picture captures Evan Zhuang at the start of his Wushu journey at the tender age of 5. The second picture, taken six years later, showcases the same movement but with the remarkable progress and transformation achieved through dedicated fundamental training.

Throughout the entire book, the author seamlessly amalgamates wisdom and insights gleaned from a plethora of teaching sources, including 'General Sports College Teaching Materials,' 'Specialized Sports College Teaching Materials Volume 1,' and 'China National Wushu Training Material Volume 1.' These sources, complemented by the author's invaluable personal teaching and training experience, along with years spent as a Wushu referee, converge to create a comprehensive learning resource. For each movement, the author employs an approach that delves into intricate details, refines key points, and offers effective teaching strategies, methods, and gentle reminders to rectify common errors. This multi-dimensional approach ensures that readers and learners can effortlessly grasp the essence and intricacies of each movement.

At its core, this book provides a robust and practical path for aspiring Wushu practitioners, especially those taking their initial steps on this enlightening journey. It all begins with wholeheartedly embracing the fundamental framework of each movement, coupled with a sincere commitment to understanding the author's teaching intentions through diligent practice. As practitioners wholeheartedly commit to this path, they will gradually achieve a harmonious fusion of mind and body. While it's acknowledged that readers may not grasp all the fundamental concepts, essentials, and requirements outlined in this book entirely at first, the author firmly believes that continued study and practice will ultimately illuminate these details.

In China, there's a proverb: 'A towering skyscraper rises from level ground.' This adage underscores the idea that even the tallest building must be constructed from the ground up, with a solidly laid foundation. It metaphorically signifies that all things come into existence from nothing, emphasizing that everything should commence from the basics and progress from small to large, from low to high. It conveys the notion that remarkable achievements often have humble and basic beginnings, underscoring the importance of establishing a strong foundation before aiming for great heights. Chinese Wushu training also adheres to natural principles to attain its ultimate goal, allowing practitioners to progress from a basic to an advanced level, particularly in 'Competitive Sports.' This principle holds true for 'Contemporary Wushu' as well.

As we discussed earlier, fundamental training forms the cornerstone for achieving the ultimate goal in Wushu, enabling practitioners to progress from a basic to an advanced level. Here are key reasons why fundamental training in Wushu is indispensable:

(1) Establishing a Strong Foundation: Just as a skyscraper requires a solid foundation to stand tall, Wushu practitioners need fundamental training to construct a robust base for their practice. It provides the essential groundwork for developing advanced techniques and skills.
(2) Holistic Development: Fundamental training in Wushu focuses on enhancing various facets of the body, including flexibility, strength, speed, stamina, balance, and coordination. It ensures that practitioners cultivate a well-rounded set of physical attributes, laying the foundation for comprehensive skill development.
(3) Standardization and Correct Posture: Fundamental training fosters standardization and helps practitioners establish correct posture and technique. This standardization is not only crucial for performing movements accurately but also for ensuring safety during practice.
(4) Technique Mastery: Fundamental training empowers practitioners to master the core techniques of Wushu. These techniques serve as the building blocks for more advanced movements and forms.
(5) Foundation for Advanced Study: It serves as the cornerstone for delving into advanced aspects of Wushu, including barehanded forms and weapon routines, while elevating overall athletic prowess.

As you embark on your journey through 'Wushu Fundamental Training,' remember that you are not merely learning Chinese Wushu but embracing a legacy, a heritage, and a philosophy. You are becoming part of something ancient and eternal that transcends time and borders. May this book be your guide, companion, and source of inspiration as you venture into this beautiful, challenging, and rewarding path into the heart of Chinese Wushu.

May this book serve as a guiding star for all who embark on the magnificent journey of Chinese Wushu, illuminating the path toward proficiency, mastery, and the timeless wisdom of this ancient art form.

Yajun Zhuang
Baton Rouge, Louisianan
2023

Part 1
Wushu Basic Skills
武術基本功

The book you are reading primarily focuses on the 'Chang Quan' or 'Long Fist' category, which is the central practice method in Chinese Wushu. Within this category, the 'Basic Skills' are extensively explored, essential for establishing a solid foundation in Wushu practice. These 'Basic Skills' encompass many physical, technical, and psychological qualities vital to the practice of Wushu.

The 'Basic Skills' consist of a comprehensive series of strategies and techniques to develop various aspects of the human body, both internally and externally. Traditional Chinese Kungfu philosophy emphasizes the cultivation of internal Qi, focusing on harnessing and channeling the body's vital energy. Simultaneously, it emphasizes external training to strengthen the muscles, bones, and skin, fostering strength, flexibility, and jumping ability.

These 'Basic Skills' form the building blocks for progressing in Wushu practice. They provide the foundation for mastering advanced techniques and forms, enabling practitioners to perform with precision, power, and grace. Diligent training in the 'Basic Skills' helps practitioners develop a strong mind-body connection, improve overall fitness, and cultivate discipline and focus.

The study of 'Wushu Basic Skills' goes beyond physical training; it also involves understanding Chinese martial arts' underlying principles, concepts, and philosophies. This holistic approach ensures practitioners develop physical prowess and gain deeper insights into the art and its cultural significance.

Through consistent practice and dedication to the 'Basic Skills,' practitioners can unlock their full potential and embark on a rewarding journey of self-discovery and personal growth in Wushu.

One crucial aspect of Wushu practice is the significant emphasis on muscle stretching. The human skeletal structure serves as the framework for the body, with tendons playing a critical role in connecting and supporting the bones. When tendons become contracted, it can lead to joint stiffness, resulting in restricted and awkward movements. Moreover, if tendons are not regularly stretched, the power generated by the muscles cannot be efficiently transmitted when striking targets.

Conversely, regular stretching of tendons naturally opens up the joints, allowing for increased mobility. When tendons contract and relax, it contributes to loosening the bones and promoting fluid movement. Nurturing tendons requires a harmonious combination of Qi, blood circulation, nutrients, and protection. Nerves and blood vessels provide the necessary support for healthy tendon function.

The human body relies on 72 bones to support its structure, with the knees and ankles bearing the heaviest weight (Basically, the bones of the human body have the role of supporting the body, in which the bony tissue and cartilage tissue are part of the human connective tissue. Most adults have 206 bones, and newborns have about 300 bones). Therefore, it is crucial to regularly stretch the bones and tendons to enhance flexibility and reduce the risk of injury. This practice elongates the limbs and waist, enabling a more comprehensive range of motion. Basic leg skills are fundamental introductory courses in Wushu, emphasizing the importance of developing strength, flexibility, and stability in the lower body.

Practitioners can improve flexibility, joint mobility, and muscular coordination by prioritizing stretching exercises. It also helps prevent muscle imbalances and promote proper alignment, leading to more efficient and powerful movements. Integrating stretching routines into Wushu training is essential for maintaining optimal physical condition and ensuring longevity in practice.

Before embarking on Wushu practice, it is crucial to properly warm up the body with exercises that enhance blood and Qi circulation, reducing the risk of potential injuries. While different Wushu schools may have unique styles, they all prioritize fundamental aspects such as stretching, waist bending, kicking, arm rotations, and chest expansion. Developing flexibility in the legs, shoulders, and waist is compulsory for beginners in Wushu. Cultivating flexibility and suppleness in these areas is essential to prepare for more advanced movements, including splits, high kicks, jumps, balances, and weapon forms. This concept, known as 'softness within hardness,' is a fundamental principle in Wushu, emphasizing the importance of flexibility.

The 'Basic Skills' in Wushu encompasses hand forms, hand techniques, stances, footwork, shoulder stretching, waist stretching, leg stretching, jumps, balances, tumbling, and combination movements. These foundational elements are integral to Chinese Wushu training and teaching, serving as the cornerstone for further advancement. While different Wushu schools may have their specific techniques, the practice methods for the 'Basic Skills' are generally consistent across various styles.

By focusing on the 'Basic Skills' and its components, practitioners can develop a strong foundation in Wushu, laying the groundwork for more complex and advanced techniques. Mastering these fundamental skills is essential for building strength, coordination, and precision in executing Wushu movements. Whether practicing in different schools or styles, the 'Basic Skills' remains a fundamental and unifying aspect of Wushu training.

Chapter 1
Jiān - Bì - Gōng
肩臂功
Shoulder and Arm Training Exercises

The objective of shoulder and arm training is to improve shoulder ligament flexibility, expand the range of motion, and concurrently develop arm strength. This training enhances upper limb agility, promotes relaxation, and improves rotational capabilities. It is valuable for mastering various 'Hand Techniques,' especially those involving movements above the head, such as 'Flash Palm in Lifted Knee Balance' or 'Frame Palm, Punch in Front Cross-Legged Balance.' Please refer to the figure below.

'Flash Palm in Lifted Knee Balance' 'Frame Palm, Punch in Front Cross-Legged Balance'

Insufficient shoulder flexibility and pull strength can impede the spread of upper limb movement and limit supporting power, ultimately resulting in a hunched back, lowered head, and stiffened body. The main practice methods of arms and shoulder training exercises to prevent these issues include shoulder stretching, arms circling, and arms swinging. Incorporating these exercises into your fitness routine can improve your overall flexibility and range of motion while building strength and agility in your upper body.

3

1. Yà Jiān or Shoulder Stretch

'Ya' (壓) has a meaning of pressing and signifies the application of force from above.

'Ya Jian,' (壓肩) is shoulder stretching, called 'Pressing Shoulder Downward' in English, is a vital component of arms and shoulder training. It consists of a series of exercises specifically designed to stretch and improve the flexibility of the muscles and ligaments in the shoulder joint, ultimately enhancing the range of motion. These stretching exercises involve gentle movements that target the muscles and ligaments surrounding the shoulder joint.

Regular shoulder stretching helps to alleviate tension, improve posture, and enhance overall shoulder mobility. It mainly benefits Wushu practitioners as it prepares the shoulder for the intricate 'Hand Techniques' and movements required in Wushu.

Practice Method 1:

- Stand with your feet together or slightly wider, facing a wall bar or a specific object about one meter away. Grasp the wall bar with your hands and keep a firm footing with your feet on the ground. Begin by gently bending your upper body forward, aiming to keep your chest stretched and lower back pressed down.
- Simultaneously, shift your hips inward, creating an angle of approximately 90 degrees between your torso and legs.
- Using your body weight as resistance, engage your shoulders by alternately raising and lowering them (Figure 1.1).

When stretching, it should begin with light pressure on the shoulders and gradually increase the intensity of the stretch. This gradual progression allows for a safer and more effective stretching experience, helping to prevent any potential discomfort or injury.

Figure 1.1

4

Practice Method 2:

This stretching exercise involves two people standing face to face, with each person holding their partner's shoulders.

- Begin by extending the shoulders and legs. The movement consists of pressing down and pulling backward while maintaining a comfortable level of pressure (Figure 1.2).

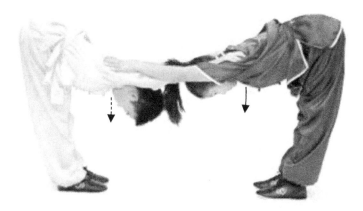

Figure 1.2

When performing this exercise, it is important to communicate with your partner and ensure that both individuals feel comfortable and safe throughout the stretching process. Adjust the pressure and intensity of the stretch according to your partner's feedback and limitations to prevent any potential strain or discomfort.

Practice Method 3:

To achieve a deeper shoulder stretch, you can involve a partner to assist you (Figure 1.3). Here's how to perform this stretching:

- Have your partner stand beside you. Position yourself in a comfortable stance with your feet together. Relax your shoulders, keep your arms stretched, and hold the wall bar.
- Your partner should gently press down on your shoulders or upper back, applying a controlled and comfortable amount of pressure to stretch your shoulder muscles.
- Hold the stretch for a few seconds while maintaining a relaxed and steady breathing pattern.

Communicate with your partner throughout the stretch to ensure it remains comfortable and does not cause any pain or discomfort. Remember, it is important to perform this stretch with a partner who understands the proper technique and can apply the appropriate amount of pressure. If at any point you feel pain or excessive discomfort, stop the stretch.

Figure 1.3

Key Points:

(1) When performing the stretch, focus on relaxing your shoulders and extending your arms and legs. This will help create a more effective stretch.

(2) Apply pressure to the shoulder area while performing the stretch. Start with a gentle force and gradually increase it from minor to larger movements.

(3) The duration of the practice should be based on your physical condition. Aim to continue the stretching until you feel your shoulders have warmed up, which typically takes at least 2 minutes.

(4) Remember to listen to your body and adjust the intensity of the stretch based on your comfort level. It's important to avoid any sharp or excessive pain during the stretching exercise.

2. Chí Gùn Zhuǎn Jiān or Holding a Stick and Rotating the Shoulder

'Chí' (持) refers to holding or grasping, while 'Zhuǎn' (轉) stands for rotating or turning. The term 'Gùn' (棍) is translated as stick, staff, or cudgel in English. In the International Wushu Federation, the formal term used is 'Cudgel,' but in America, many Wushu practitioners prefer to use the term 'staff' instead of 'Cudgel.'

'Holding a Stick or a Staff and Rotating the Shoulders' is an effective way to stretch and increase the range of motion in your shoulder. Here are the instructions for performing this exercise:

6

Practice Methods:

- Start by standing with your feet shoulder-width apart or feet together. Hold a stick with both hands, adjusting the distance between your hands based on the condition and flexibility of your shoulders. The grip should be firm but not tight.
- Use your shoulder as an axis or pivot point and swing your arms forward and backward over your head. The stick should move in a smooth and controlled motion.
- As you swing the stick forward, your arms should extend in front of your body, reaching as far as possible without causing strain or discomfort.
- Swing the stick backward, bringing it behind your head and down towards your back. Again, perform this motion within a comfortable range of motion.
- Repeat the swinging motion of the stick forward and backward for the desired number of repetitions or as advised by your instructor. Focus on maintaining proper form and a smooth rhythm throughout the exercise (Figure 1.4).

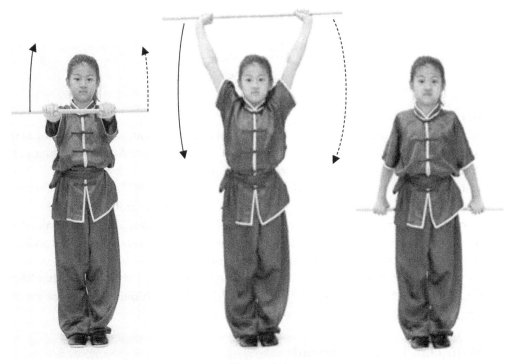

Figure 1.4

Alternatively, if you have a partner or someone available to assist you, you can ask them to stretch your shoulders (Figure 1.5). Your partner will hold your arms and gently pull your shoulder and upper limbs backward to assist in stretching the shoulder muscles. Effective communication with your partner is crucial to ensure that the pressure applied remains comfortable and does not cause any pain or discomfort.

7

Figure 1.5

Key Points:
(1) When performing the 'Holding a Stick and Rotating the Shoulder' exercise, focus on keeping your arms fully extended throughout the movement. Avoid stiffening your shoulder muscles and aim for a smooth and fluid motion.
(2) Maintain a consistent distance between your hands on the stick and avoid altering it during the exercise. This will help ensure a balanced and controlled movement.
(3) If you have someone assisting you in stretching your shoulders, it is crucial to communicate effectively and work together safely. Be clear about your comfort level and avoid excessive pulling or straining of the shoulders.
(4) For optimal effectiveness, the distance between your hands on the stick should be narrower than the width between your shoulders. This positioning allows for a more targeted and effective stretch of the shoulder muscles.

3. Shǒu Dǎo Lì or Handstand

In English, 'Shǒu' (手) translates to hand, 'Dǎo' (倒) signifies fall or reverse, and 'Lì' (立) refers to stand. Consequently, it is rendered as a 'Handstand,' signifying a movement where the body reverses its position, with the hands supporting a standing posture, akin to a gymnastic maneuver.

A handstand is a fundamental skill in gymnastics and Chinese Wushu that requires balancing the body in a stable, vertical position on the hands. To perform a basic handstand, follow these instructions:

Practice Methods:

- Begin in a standing position. Place your hands on the ground, shoulder-width apart, fingers spread wide and facing forward.
- Lean forward slightly and kick one leg into the air, using the other to push off the ground. Aim to create a straight line from your hands to your elevated leg.
- As your kicking leg reaches the top, bring your second leg up to meet it, aligning your body into a straight and vertical position. Keep your arms and legs fully extended. Balance on your hands, engaging your core muscles to help stabilize your body. Maintain a straight posture and focus on a fixed point in front of you to assist with balance.
- To support during practice, you can touch the wall with your feet or have a trusted individual hold your legs (Figure 1.6).
- Hold the 'Handstand' for as long as possible, gradually building your strength and endurance. Remember to breathe steadily throughout. To exit the 'Handstand,' slowly lower one leg back to the ground, followed by the other leg.
- Repeat the handstand as desired, maintaining proper form, balance, and control.

Figure 1.6

It is crucial to exercise caution and prioritize safety when practicing 'Handstands.' Always warm up your body before attempting any acrobatic movements to reduce the risk of injury. Begin with the support of a spotter or by practicing against a wall until you feel confident and comfortable with your balance and form.

Key Points:

(1) Extend your chest, raise your head, and stretch your waist while straightening legs. This helps maintain proper body alignment and balance during the 'Handstand.'

(2) Keep your hands still and grounded on the floor to maintain stability and balance. Avoid excessive movement or shifting of your hands.

(3) As a beginner, start by holding the 'Handstand' for a shorter duration, such as a minute, and gradually increase the time as you build strength and confidence.

(4) Once you feel comfortable and have developed sufficient strength and balance, you can try practicing 'Handstands' without the support of walls or assistance. However, always ensure you are in a safe environment and have proper supervision if needed.

4. Sǒng Jiān Chén Jiān or Shrugging, Sinking Shoulders

The term 'Song' (聳) in English means 'shrug' originally. It has the same pronunciation as 'Sǒng' (松), meaning 'relax,' but is spelled differently. 'Chén' (沉) refers to sinking or dropping down.

• Stand straight with your feet together and place your fists on your waist.

• Raise your shoulders towards your ears as high as possible without straining.

• After holding the raised position for a moment, relax and gently drop or sink your shoulders towards the ground, allowing them to feel heavy.

• Repeat this movement alternately, lifting and lowering your shoulders in a controlled manner. Focus on maintaining an upright head position and keeping your chest relaxed throughout the exercise (Figure 1.7).

Figure 1.7

5. Kāi Jiān Hé Jiān or Opening and Closing Shoulder

'Kāi' (開) means open, while 'Hé ' (合) means closing or gathering.

In medical terminology, opening and closing the shoulder, also known as shoulder abduction and adduction, can help improve shoulder mobility and flexibility, relieve tension, and improve the range of motion in the shoulders.

Practice Methods:
- Stand up straight with your feet together and your arms at your sides. Place your fists on your waist, elbows pointing towards your back.
- Roll your chest inwards, bringing your shoulder forward and towards the midline of your body. Open your chest by extending your shoulder back, moving it away from the midline of your body (Figure 1.8).
- Repeat these movements alternately, rolling your shoulder forward and then extending them back in a controlled manner.
- During the exercise, maintain an upright head position without tilting it forward as your shoulder stretches back. Additionally, ensure that your shoulder does not elevate when it moves inward.

Figure 1.8

6. Dān Bì Rào Huán or Single-Arm Circle

'Dān' (單) means single or individual, and 'Bì' (臂) means arm. 'Rào' (繞) means to wind around or surround, and 'Huán'(環) means ring. However, the term 'Rào Huán' refers to 'Winding Around the Ring' or 'Winding a Circle' with arms in the context of Wushu.

11

The 'Single-Arm Circle,' also known as the 'One-Arm Circle,' is an exercise that enhances shoulder mobility and flexibility. By performing circular movements with the arm, this exercise helps improve the range of motion and alleviate tension in the upper body. Here's how to properly execute the single-arm circle exercise:

Practice Method 1: Forward Circle (using the right arm as an example):

- Stand in a left bow stance, with your left foot positioned forward and your right foot placed back. Rest your left palm on your left knee while putting your right arm on your right side behind your body. Ensure your right palm faces downwards and is parallel to your right leg. Keep your gaze straight ahead (Figure 1.9 (1)).
- Extend your right arm and swing it forward, upward, and backward in a circular motion on your right side (Figure 1.9 (2), (3)) (4).

Figure 1.9 (1) Figure 1.9 (2)

Figure 1.9 (3) Figure 1.9 (4)

This movement is called a 'Forward Circle.' Repeat this movement several times while maintaining a straight arm and focusing on maintaining control throughout the exercise.

During practice, focus on drawing a smooth circle with your arm while keeping it straight. Engage your core muscles to maintain balance and stability in your stance.

Practice Method 2: Backward Circle (using the right arm as an example):

- Start from the left bow stance with your left foot forward and right foot back. Place your left palm on your left knee and extend your right arm forward (Figure 1.10 (1)).
- Swing your right arm backward, upward, and then forward, drawing a circle on your right side in the opposite direction of the 'Forward Circle' movement (Figure 1.10 (2), (3) (4)), This movement is known as a 'Backward Circle.'

Figure 1.10 (1)   Figure 1.10 (2)

Figure 1.10 (3)   Figure 1.10 (4)

- Repeat this movement several times as desired, ensuring your arm remains straight and maintains control throughout.

During practice, it is beneficial to alternate between the forward and backward circle movements, giving equal attention to both arms. Focus on keeping your arm straight, drawing smooth circles, and engaging your core muscles to ensure balance and stability in your stance.

Key Points:
(1) To maintain balance and stability during the exercise, engage your core muscles. This will help stabilize your body and support the movement of your arm. Keep your back of your body straight throughout the training.
(2) Keep your head up and your gaze forward. This will help ensure that the circle you're drawing with your arm is vertical. Avoid leaning or tilting your body.
(3) As you raise and extend your arm to the side, keep it straight without bending your elbow. This will maximize the benefits of the exercise by improving shoulder mobility and flexibility.
(4) Start by rotating the arm in a slow and controlled manner. Gradually increase the movement speed as you become more comfortable and confident. Remember to maintain control throughout the exercise.

7. Shuāng Bì Rào Huán or Circle Both Arms

'Shuāng' (雙) refers to double or both in English.

In Wushu, the 'Circle Both Arms' is frequently utilized as a warm-up exercise or integrated into a more comprehensive routine. This maneuver entails a fluid, circular motion of the arms, designed to harmonize and invigorate the body's energy. Practicing the 'Circle Both Arms' can yield several benefits, such as enhancing arm, shoulder, and upper back flexibility and mobility. It also fortifies arm and shoulder muscles, which can serve as a preventive measure against injuries and contribute to improved overall physical performance. Furthermore, the circular arm movement stimulates blood circulation and energy (Qi) flow throughout the body, fostering a profound sense of relaxation and inner tranquility.

(1) Qián Hòu Rào Huán or Back and Forth Circle

'Qián' (前) is the front, and 'Hòu' (后) is the back.

'Back and Forth Circle,' also known as 'Front-Back Circle,' is a dynamic exercise that involves circular arm movements in both the front and back directions.

Practice Methods:
- Start by standing upright with your feet shoulder-width apart. Raise your right arm above your head and extend your left arm forward (Figure 1.11 (1)). Initiate a circular motion with your left arm, starting from the front, moving it upward toward the back, and then bringing it down along a vertical path to the front. Concurrently, perform

a similar circular movement with your right arm, originating from the top, moving it backward, then downward to the forward again, and finally up to the top. Essentially, you are tracing a backward circle with each arm individually Figure 1.11 (2), (3)). The correct method involves using your waist as an axis and moving both arms in a straight line as if you were pedaling a bicycle wheel up and down in turn.

- Perform several repetitions in this direction. After completing several repetitions, switch directions and circle in the opposite direction.

Figure 1.11 (1)   Figure 1.11 (2)   Figure 1.11 (3)

During the exercise, focus on maintaining a relaxed yet engaged posture. Keep your core muscles active and your movements controlled. Perform the circles smoothly and coordinated, aiming for fluidity and symmetry between your arms.

Key Points:
(1) Coordinate arm movements with waist rotation to ensure both arms move forward and backward simultaneously, creating two tilted circles in front of your body.
(2) Maintain straight arms throughout the exercise to enhance flexibility and mobility in the arms, shoulder, and upper back.
(3) Practice proper breathing techniques by inhaling deeply as you circle your arms forward and exhaling as you circle them backward. This synchronization of breath and movement strengthens the mind-body connection and promotes relaxation.
(4) Engage your core muscles to provide stability and support during the movement.

(2) Zuǒ Yòu Rào Huán or Left and Right Circle

'Zuǒ' (左) refers to the left, and 'Yòu' (右) to the right. 'Left and Right Circle' indicates circling your arms straightly successively from left to right or from the right to the left along a vertical circular path in Wushu practice.

Practice Methods:

- Stand with your feet shoulder-width apart and lift your arms to the right first. Straighten your right arm and place your left hand close to the inside of your right armpit, with all fingers pointing upwards. Turn your head towards your right hand (Figure 1.12 (1)).
- Swing your arms up from right to left in a vertical circular motion, simultaneously turning your head to the left. End in a mirrored version of the original posture (Figure 1.12 (2)). Hold this position briefly, then swing your arms down and back to the original place (Figure 1.12 (1)).
- Repeat the exercise several times in the same direction, and then switch to the opposite direction.

During practice, focus on maintaining relaxed shoulders and elbows, allowing your arms to swing naturally. Maintain a stable stance with your feet firmly planted on the ground, and keep your gaze focused on your hands as they move in a circular motion. Following these instructions, you can effectively enhance flexibility, promote relaxation, and improve arms, shoulders, and upper body coordination.

Figure 1.12 (1)   Figure 1.12 (2)

Key Points:

(1) Ensure that your shoulders and elbows are fully relaxed during the 'Left and Right Circle' exercises to facilitate free and fluid arm movement.

(2) Keep your body upright and maintain a straight posture while exercising.

(3) Throughout the exercise, maintain a stable stance with your feet firmly planted on the ground. Avoid any unnecessary twisting of your body, bending of your knees, or moving your feet, as it can impact your balance and the quality of your movements.

(4) Keep your attention on your hands as they move in a circular motion. This focus will help you maintain proper form, balance, and full engagement in the exercise, leading to more effective results.

(3) Jiāo Chā Rào Huán or Cross Circle

'Jiāo Chā' (交叉) translates to 'Cross' in English, and the 'Cross Circle' is a Wushu exercise designed to improve coordination, balance, and agility. This exercise involves coordinating opposite-direction movements of both arms, enhancing left-right coordination and overall body control. Additionally, it promotes relaxation and inner calm by stimulating blood flow and energy circulation. The 'Cross Circle' can increase flexibility and mobility in the shoulders and upper back while strengthening the arm and shoulder muscles, reducing the risk of injuries, and enhancing physical performance.

Figure 1.13 (1)   Figure 1.13 (2)   Figure 1.13 (3)

Practice Methods:

- Start by standing upright with your feet shoulder-width apart or slightly wider. Raise your arms straight overhead while keeping your shoulder relaxed (Figure 1.13 (1)).
- Initiate the exercise by circling your right arm in a vertical motion. Move it forward, then down, and finally backward. Simultaneously, swing your left arm back, down, and forward to the top of your body. Both arms should swing alongside your body simultaneously but in opposite directions (Figure 1.13 (2), (3)).
- After completing several repetitions in one direction, reverse the direction of the arm movements and repeat the exercise.
- Maintain an upright posture and ensure your feet remain firmly planted throughout the exercise for stability and balance.

Key Points:

(1) Employ your waist as the central axis to drive the motion of your arms during the 'Cross Circle' exercise. This will contribute to maintaining agility and flexibility throughout your entire body.
(2) Keep your arms and shoulders straight in a relaxed state throughout the exercise. The circular motion should flow smoothly, devoid of any stiffness or tension.
(3) When performing the circular motion, maintain a vertical plane, with the front arm slightly crossing over the centerline, while ensuring your movements are fluid and well-balanced.
(4) Avoid unnecessary movements such as shifting your feet or leaning your body in any direction while performing the 'Cross Circle.' Concentrate on preserving stability and control in your stance.

8. Pū Bù Lūn Pāi or Circle Arms and Slaps the Ground with a Crouch-Stance

'Pū' (仆) refers to falling forward, lying prostrate; 'Bù' (步) means step, pace; ' Lūn' (掄) means swing; and 'Pāi' (拍) stands for clap, tap, or beat.

The 'Circle Arms and Slaps the Ground with a Crouch-Stance' technique, also known as 'Black Dragon Coils to Strike' (烏龍盤打), is a dynamic Wushu maneuver that harmonizes circular arm movements with a crouched stance and ground slapping. This technique is designed to improve body coordination, enhance agility, and boost overall power. Here are the instructions:

Practice Methods:

Begin by standing with your feet slightly wider than your shoulder-width apart. Raise your arms to shoulder height on both sides of your body. Ensure that your shoulders are relaxed, and elbows are lowered. Keep your gaze fixed straight ahead (Figure 1.14 (1)).

Movement 1: Rotate your body to the left, transitioning into a left bow stance. Lean your upper body forward and circle your right arm down in front of you. Simultaneously, place your left palm on the inside of your right elbow. Keep your focus on your right hand during this movement (Figure 1.14 (2)). Allow your right arm to follow a natural arc to the left and downward as you turn.

Figure 1.14 (1)

Figure 1.14 (2)

Movement 2: Rotate your body to the right, shifting into a right bow stance. Circle your right arm upward and to the right, while at the same time, swing your left palm down to the left. Maintain your gaze on your right hand (Figure 1.14 (3)). Ensure stability and refrain from unnecessary up and down movements of your body.

Figure 1.14 (3)

Movement 3: Proceed with the sequence by turning your body to the right, pivoting towards the rear. Simultaneously, circle your right arm down behind your body, while swinging your left arm to the front of your head. Maintain your gaze towards your right hand (Figure 1.14 (4)). While twisting your upper body to the right, fully extend your arms. You may slightly lift your left heel to aid in the turn while ensuring balance is maintained. Keep your focus fixed on your right hand throughout this movement.

Figure 1.14 (4)

Movement 4: Following the previous movement, rotate your body to the left and lower yourself into a right crouching stance. Circle your right arm from behind, moving it upward, to the right, and then downward. As your right arm reaches the inside of your right leg, straighten it out and slap the ground with your right palm. Simultaneously, circle your left arm downward, to the left, and then upward. Maintain your gaze directed towards your right hand (Figure 1.14 (5)).

Figure 1.14 (5)

Important Note: Movements 1 to 4 constitute a complete, continuous sequence. While breaking them down into teaching segments can be helpful for learning, the ultimate goal is to master the movements and execute them seamlessly as a fluid sequence without any interruption.

During your practice sessions, be sure to alternate between the left and right directions, as shown in Figure 1.15 (1) (2) (3) (4). This alternating approach is essential for training both sides of your body and achieving balanced development.

Figure 1.15 (1)   Figure 1.15 (2)

| Figure 1.15 (3) | Figure 1.15 (4) |

Key Points:

(1) Utilize your hands to guide the movement of your elbows and shoulders. Ensure that your arms follow a vertical circle, moving from left to right or right to left. This alignment is crucial for maintaining proper form and maximizing the movement's effectiveness.

(2) The power and coordination of this technique primarily originate from your waist. Use your waist to initiate the twisting motion and generate speed and force in your right arm as it contacts the ground during the crouching stance.

(3) Remember that this movement is in place, so there's no need to move forward or backward. Concentrate on expanding the range of your movements and coordinating the actions of your waist and upper limbs. Avoid standing rigidly and allow your feet position to adjust as your waist twists naturally.

(4) Maintain a steady gaze on your leading hand throughout the sequence. This prevents your head from dropping and your chest from collapsing, ensuring proper alignment and balance throughout the movement.

(5) The bow stance mentioned in the practice of this movement is not standard, just a transitional step; it is flexible, allowing for adjustments to a higher or lower position depending on your physical condition or needs.

Emphasizing Shoulder Stretching is Crucial
for Several Compelling Reasons in Wushu Practice

Range of Motion:

Shoulder stretching significantly enhances the upper body's range of motion, leading to greater flexibility and mobility. This is pivotal in Wushu, which demands various intricate arm movements like punches, strikes, blocks, and sweeping motions. Improved shoulder flexibility empowers practitioners to execute these techniques with precision, extended reach, and fluidity.

Technique Execution:

Proper shoulder flexibility is a prerequisite for executing Wushu techniques correctly. Many advanced movements, including flips, jumps, and aerial techniques, heavily rely on strong and flexible shoulder muscles. Adequate shoulder flexibility allows for the correct positioning and extension of the arms during these movements, thereby enhancing power, control, and aesthetics.

Injury Prevention:

Shoulder stretching plays a critical role in preventing injuries during Wushu training. Well-stretched and properly warmed-up shoulder muscles are less susceptible to strains, tears, and overuse injuries. Consistent shoulder stretching helps maintain healthy muscle tissue and reduces the risk of shoulder-related injuries, such as rotator cuff strains or shoulder impingements.

Posture and Alignment:

Shoulder stretching contributes significantly to improved overall posture and alignment in Wushu. Well-aligned shoulders promote a more upright and balanced stance, facilitating superior weight distribution and stability. It also optimizes the positioning of the arms and upper body, thereby enhancing the efficiency and effectiveness of movements.

Coordination and Fluidity:

Flexible shoulders are pivotal for better coordination and fluidity in Wushu movements. Seamlessly transitioning between techniques and integrating arm movements is essential for a polished and captivating performance. Shoulder stretching empowers practitioners to achieve superior coordination between the upper and lower body, resulting in more harmonious and synchronized movements.

Strength and Power:

While primarily focused on flexibility, shoulder stretching also contributes to enhancing the strength and power of shoulder muscles. Through stretching exercises, practitioners can develop increased muscular endurance, stability, and power. This translates into more potent strikes, quicker arm movements, and an overall improved performance in Wushu.

In summary, prioritizing shoulder stretching in Wushu practice is paramount for optimizing range of motion, technique execution, injury prevention, posture and alignment, coordination, and overall strength and power. Regular inclusion of shoulder stretching exercises in training routines not only minimizes the risk of injuries but also aids in achieving greater proficiency and mastery in Wushu.

Chapter 2
Tui - Gōng
腿功
Leg Training Exercises

'Leg Training' is central to Wushu practice, given its pivotal importance in combat effectiveness. A well-known Wushu proverb underscores this significance, stating, 'The hands are like two hinged doors for protection, but success in fighting all depends on the leg's skills' (手是兩扇門全憑脚打人). This proverb underlines the critical role of 'Leg Techniques' in combat scenarios. According to Chinese Wushu's philosophy, kicking constitutes 70% of attacks, whereas hand strikes contribute only 30%.

Engaging in 'Leg Technique' training offers a multitude of advantages. It enhances the flexibility of leg ligaments and muscles, strengthening the lower limbs' power. Furthermore, practical legwork refines basic stances, footwork, and balance while boosting leg movements' power and speed.

Standard training methods for 'Leg Techniques' encompass a range of exercises, including leg stretching, leg swinging, splits, kicks, and holding positions. Consistent practice of these techniques yields several benefits, including:

Improved Stability: Leg training enhances the stability of leg movements, allowing practitioners to maintain balance and control during complex maneuvers.

Enhanced Flexibility: Regular leg stretching and swinging exercises improve leg muscle and ligament flexibility, enabling high kicks and dynamic movements.

Increased Strength: Strengthening leg muscles through leg techniques contributes to overall lower body strength, enabling more powerful kicks and strikes.

Refined Kicking Skills: Training leg techniques hones the precision and effectiveness of kicks, enabling practitioners to execute them with accuracy and speed.

Better Stance and Footwork: Leg training refines fundamental stances and footwork, promoting better posture and maneuverability during Wushu routines.

Combat Effectiveness: As kicking is a predominant component of Wushu attacks, leg training directly improves one's combat effectiveness, making them a more formidable martial artist.

Leg training is an essential pillar of Wushu practice, deeply rooted in its combat philosophy. Emphasizing 'Leg Techniques' fortifies lower limb strength and flexibility and refines fundamental skills, contributing to improved balance, power, and speed. By regularly incorporating leg training exercises, practitioners can elevate their martial arts capabilities and become more proficient in Wushu.

1. Yà Tuǐ or Leg Stretch

'Yà Tuǐ' (壓腿) originally means 'pressing leg' or 'leg stretch.'

'Pressing Leg' or 'Leg Stretch' involves one leg supporting the body's weight while the other remains straight, with the heel resting on an elevated surface. During this exercise, the upper body can be gently bent forward, or both hands can be directed downward toward the knee. This movement elongates the ligaments of the ankle, knee, and hip joints, as well as the muscles at the back of the leg. Additionally, 'Leg Stretching' aids in increasing the range of motion in the hips (mainly in the Kua or crotch in English). 'Leg Stretching' encompasses 'Front Straight Leg Pressing Stretch,' 'Side Leg Stretching,' and 'Back Leg Stretching.' The instructions for each exercise are as follows:

(1) Zhèng Yà Tuǐ or Front Straight Leg Pressing Stretch

The term 'Zhèng' means the 'front' in English.

The 'Front Straight Leg Pressing Stretch' (正壓腿) involves placing the heel of one leg on a surface and then pressing the body forward.

To perform this stretch correctly, ensure that every part of your body is facing forward, including your face, the front of your body, the front of your supporting leg, toes, and stretching heel.

The key point is to avoid bouncing or jerking during the stretch, as this can lead to injury. It's essential to perform the stretch in a controlled and smooth manner. Additionally, never force your body to stretch beyond its limits. Respect your body's boundaries and gradually increase your flexibility with consistent practice. Listen to your body, and if you experience any pain or discomfort, stop immediately. In other words, stretching should feel challenging but not painful.

Practice Method 1: Hào Tuǐ (using the right leg as an example)

'Hào Tuǐ' (耗腿), also known as the 'Consuming Leg' or 'Exhausting the Leg' in English, is an exercise specifically designed to stretch and strengthen the hamstring muscles, which are located at the back of the thigh. Here's how to perform this exercise effectively:

- Start by positioning yourself against a wall bar or any object of a specific height, with your feet together.
- Place your right heel on the object while hooking your right toes inward, facing your body. This position helps to extend and stretch your right hamstring effectively.
- Rest your palms on your right knee and gently contract your right hip slightly inward. This action helps you maintain stability and engages the muscles in the hamstring region.
- Keep your upper body upright and maintain good posture throughout the exercise.
- Hold this position for a duration that suits your flexibility level. You can perform it as a static stretch, holding the position, or engage in static stretching exercises that specifically target the hamstring muscles, which is why it is called 'Consuming.'

The goal of 'Hao Tui' is to improve the flexibility and strength of the hamstring muscles, ultimately enhancing overall leg function (Figure 2.1).

Figure 2.1

Practice Method 2: Hamstring Stretching (using the right leg as an example)

The 'Hamstring Stretching' exercise you described aims to improve flexibility and stretch the muscles at the back of the thighs. Engage your core muscles by activating them and tucking your hips in. This will help maintain stability and proper alignment throughout the exercise. Here are the steps involved:

- Following the correct posture for the 'Leg Stretch' mentioned above.
- Slowly bend your waist forward but keep your upper body straight to reach down towards your right foot. As you do this, use your hands to press down on your right knee gently. This action will help deepen the stretch in your right hamstring muscles.
- Hold the stretch for 20-30 seconds or until you feel a moderate stretch in your right hamstring (Figure 2.2).
- Avoid bouncing or jerking motions and remember to breathe deeply and relax into the stretch.
- Slowly release the stretch and return to an upright position.
- Repeat the stretch on the other leg, following the same steps and requirements.

This exercise helps lengthen and loosen the hamstring muscles, promoting flexibility and reducing the risk of muscle tightness or injuries.

| Figure 2.2 | Figure 2.3 |

Practice Method 3: Touching Toe with the Elbow (using the right leg as an example)
- Extend your right leg in front of you.
- Slowly lean forward, reaching your right leg with your upper body. As you reach forward, use your right hand to press your right knee or use your left hand to grab your right foot, hooking it inward. This action helps deepen the stretch.
- Slightly twist your upper body to the right, aiming to touch your right toe with your left elbow. This additional twist can further engage the hamstring muscles and promote a deeper stretch.
- Maintain this position for some time, allowing the stretch to be held. Breathe deeply and try to relax into the stretch (Figure 2.3).
- Release the stretch and return to the starting position.
- Repeat the stretch on the other leg, following the same steps and requirements.

Practice Method 4: Reaching the Head (using the right leg as an example)
- Hold the sole of your right foot with both hands.
- Slowly bring your right foot towards your head, aiming to touch your right toe with your forehead (Figure 2.4).
- Maintain this position for a while, feeling the stretch in your hamstring and calf muscles.
- Focus on breathing deeply and relaxing into the stretch.
- Release the stretch and return to the starting position.
- Repeat the stretch on the other leg, following the same steps and requirements.

Figure 2.4   Figure 2.5

Practice Method 5: Advanced Stretching (using the right leg as an example)

- Hold the sole of your right foot with both hands and gradually bring your right foot towards your face, aiming to touch your right toe with your nose (Figure 2.5), mouth, and eventually your chin.
- Maintain this position for a while, feeling the stretch in your hamstring and calf muscles. Take slow and controlled breaths.
- If you require assistance or find it challenging to reach the desired position, you can ask your teacher or teammates for help (Figure 2.6).
- Release the stretch and return to the starting position.
- Repeat the stretch on the other leg, following the same steps.

When performing this advanced stretching exercise, it's crucial to approach it cautiously and only attempt it if you have sufficient flexibility and experience. Avoid forcing or straining your muscles, and never push beyond your limits. If you feel any pain or discomfort, release the stretch immediately.

Figure 2.6

Remember to alternate between stretching your left and right legs to maintain balance and flexibility on both sides. Incorporating advanced stretching exercises into your routine can help improve flexibility, promote muscle health, and enhance overall physical performance.

In addition to stretching your legs on the wall bar, you can also sit on the ground or simply stand for practice.

Seated Toe Touches

- Sit on the floor with your legs extended in front of you. Ensure your legs are straight and your toes point upward as far as possible without bending your knees.
- Keep your head aligned with your spine and place your hands on your thighs.
- Slowly bend forward from your hips, sliding your hands down towards your ankles, and then hold your feet. Focus on maintaining a flat back position throughout the movement (Figure 2.7).
- Reach as far as you comfortably can, feeling a stretch in the back of your legs. Hold this position for 15-30 seconds, breathing deeply and allowing the muscles to relax and lengthen. Slowly return to your starting position by sitting back up.
- Repeat the movement 2-4 times, gradually increasing the depth of the stretch with each repetition.

Figure 2.7

Standing One-Legged Hamstring Stretch (using the right leg as an example)

- Stand on your left leg and find your balance. Adjust the bend in your left knee based on your comfort level. Extend your right leg before you, keeping your toes pointing upward as far as possible.
- Use both hands to hold your right foot, gripping it firmly. Slowly bend forward at the hips while maintaining a straight back, aiming to touch your head, nose, or mouth with your right foot. Feel the stretch in the hamstring muscles behind your right thigh. You may also feel a stretch in your calf.
- Hold the stretch for 15 to 30 seconds, focusing on breathing deeply and relaxing into the stretch (Figure 2.8).
- Release the stretch and return to an upright position. Repeat the stretch three times, gradually increasing the depth of the stretch with each repetition.

- Repeat the entire sequence using your other leg as the working leg.

In Chinese Wushu, this movement is known as 'Kiss the Boot,' which conveys the idea of reaching for your desired goal or aspiration as if going to kiss it.

Figure 2.8

Attention Must be Paid to the Following Keys When Practicing

Persistence and Hard Work: 'Leg Stretching ' requires consistent effort and dedication, especially as you progress in your training. It is common to experience leg and hip pain, like long-distance runners. However, this process is necessary for Wushu practice. To prepare for 'Leg Stretching,' it is essential to warm up properly, focusing on movements that engage the waist, groin, legs, and ankles. Warming up increases muscle temperature, which is important for the extension of ligaments. Additionally, relaxing the body's muscles and reducing muscle viscosity promotes leg flexibility.

Progression from Light to Heavy: When stretching your legs, it is crucial to gradually increase the pressure on the ligaments, tendons, and muscles. Start with light pressure and gradually intensify it over time. Avoid applying excessive force from the beginning, as it can lead to leg pain and injuries. Begin with gentle stretches and gradually increase the intensity as your body adapts and becomes more flexible.

Progression from Low to High: It's essential to raise the height of your leg during stretching exercises incrementally. Begin by positioning your foot at waist height and gradually progress to reaching your toe with your mouth or chin. As you advance, continue to elevate your leg by placing it on an object at chest height. Maintain this progression until you can confidently position your foot at shoulder height or above your head. This systematic approach effectively challenges and enhances flexibility while prioritizing safety and control (Figure 2.9).

Figure 2.9

Progression from Static to Dynamic: It is recommended to start with static stretching, such as the 'Consuming Leg' method, as it allows for gradual elongation of the ligaments, tendons, and muscles. Avoid applying excessive elongation in the beginning, as it may not achieve the desired effect and can potentially lead to ligament damage. After holding the stretch for a while (static), gradually introduce dynamic stretching by applying vibrating pressure on the leg. Remember that progress takes time, so avoid rushing and be patient in your practice.

Consistency in Training: Practice regularly and avoid missing training sessions. Consistency is key to achieving progress in leg flexibility. Treat each day of training as an opportunity to improve. Missing a day of training is like wasting ten, so make it a habit to practice consistently.

Recommended Practice Duration: Aim to practice each leg for 15 minutes every day. Children can achieve success in leg flexibility within a year, while adults may require two years or more to increase their leg flexibility gradually. Remember that individual progress may vary, so be patient and focus on your own journey.

(2) Cè Yà Tuǐ or Side Leg Stretch

'Cè' (側) means side.

The 'Side Leg Stretch' (側壓腿) and 'Front Straight Leg Pressing Stretch' methods have similarities and distinct differences. In the 'Side Leg Stretch,' the body is oriented sideways, with one shoulder facing the wall bar. This results in the support leg, foot, face, and the front of the body turning 90 degrees outward while facing the same direction. To execute this stretch accurately, follow these steps using the left leg as an example:

Practice Methods:

- Stand with your left shoulder facing the wall bar and place your left heel on it. Your right toe should point outward at a 90-degree angle with the wall bar. Ensure that your right knee, navel, and nose align in the same direction as your right toe. Slightly inwardly rotate your left hip and hook your left toes toward your left ear. Raise your right palm above your head and place your left hand on your right chest (Figure 2.10). Straighten both legs, lift your waist, and slightly open your right hip. Ensure that your right foot is parallel to the wall bar.
- Grasp your left foot with your right hand and aim to touch your left foot with your head, progressing from the forehead to the left ear (Figure 2.11).
- Following these steps will help you achieve the correct posture for the 'Side Leg Stretch.' It is important to note that this stretch differs from the 'Front Straight Leg Pressing Stretch,' which involves a different body position and technique.

Figure 2.10   Figure 2.11

Similarly, you have the option to perform the 'Side Leg Stretch' while sitting on the floor or standing on the floor. These variations provide flexibility in your practice and allow you to choose the most comfortable and suitable position for your stretching routine.

Side-Seated Toe Touches (using the left leg as an example):

- Begin by sitting on the floor with your right leg bent inward, positioning the outside of your right leg on the floor. Extend your left leg to the left side, pointing your left toes upward while keeping your left knee straight.
- Maintain an upright seated position with your head aligned with your spine. Raise your right hand and place your left hand on your right chest (Figure 2.12 (1)).
- Activate the muscles on the right side of your torso and gradually lean your upper body from the right hip towards the left, allowing your left shoulder to face your left leg. Simultaneously, extend your right hand downward to reach your left toe or grasp your right foot (Figure 2.12 (2)).
- Hold this stretched position for 15-30 seconds, then release and return to your initial sitting posture. Repeat the stretch 2-4 times for optimal results.
- Repeat the entire sequence using your other leg as the working leg.

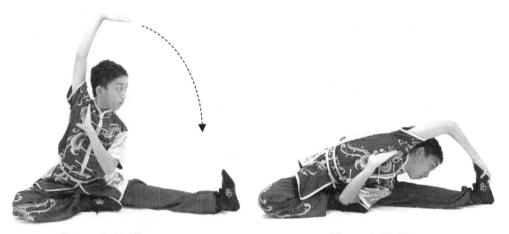

Figure 2.12 (1)   Figure 2.12 (2)

Standing One-Legged Hamstring Side Stretch (using the left leg as an example):

- Begin by standing with your right leg and adjust the degree of bend in your knee to suit your comfort level. Extend your left leg to the left side with your toes pointing upward. Reach down and securely grasp your left foot with your right hand, while placing your left hand on your chest. Essentially, your left shoulder faces the left leg.
- While maintaining your balance, gently lean your upper body to the left side, aiming to reach as far as possible until your head touches your left foot (Figure 2.13).
- Maintain this stretched position for 15 to 30 seconds, concentrating on feeling the stretch in your left hamstring. Repeat this stretch three times.

- After completing the stretches on the left side, replicate the entire sequence with your other leg.

Figure 2.13

The key point of the 'Side-Legged Stretch' is akin to that of the 'Front Straight Leg Pressing Stretch.' The primary distinction lies in the orientation of the stretching and assisting movements, which are executed on the side of the body. The higher stretching and assisting motions are depicted in Figures 2.14 and 2.15.

Figure 2.14

Figure 2.15

(3) Hòu Yà Tuǐ or Leg Stretches to the Rear

'Hòu' refers to backward.

'Leg Stretches to the Rear' (后壓腿), primarily focus on stretching your lower back, emphasizing flexibility in the waist. Here is the correct posture to practice this stretch, using the left leg as an example:

- Begin by positioning the back of your left foot against the wall bar with your palms on your waist and hold this position for a few moments.
- Gently lean your upper body backward, tilting it slightly (Figure 2.16).
- Continuously move your lower body back and forth in a controlled manner, enhancing the stretch.

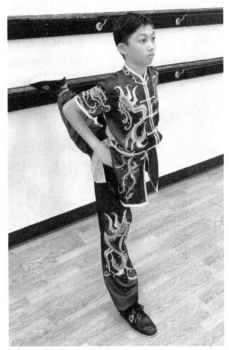

Figure 2.16

Practice Method 1: Stretching Backward in a Sitting Position

- Start by sitting on the floor with your upper body held upright. Extend your left leg behind you while bending your right knee in front, with the outside of your leg touching the ground. Place your palms beside your body (Figure 2.17 (1)).
- In this position, maintain your posture and gently lean back slightly for a few moments (Figure 2.17 (2)).
- When leaning your body backward, ensure that you avoid twisting your shoulders. Keep your body straight with your extended back leg, aiming to reach your head towards your back leg if possible.

Figure 2.17 (1)   Figure 2.17 (2)

Practice Method 2: Stretching Backward in a Standing Position
- Place the back of your left foot against the wall bar positioned behind you. Extend your right hand and hold onto the wall bar in front of you while moving your right foot forward slightly. Maintain this posture briefly.
- Gradually lean your upper body backward and create a subtle rocking motion in your lower body by shifting it back and forth for a duration (Figure 2.18).

Figure 2.18

Practice Method 3: Splitting Backward in a Standing Position
In a similar manner, position the back of your left foot against the wall bar behind you and firmly grasp the wall bar in front of you with both hands. Extend your right foot forward as far as your flexibility allows (Figure 2.19).

Figure 2.19

Keep an upright upper body and gently tilt it backward. Hold this position for as long as you comfortably can.

Practice Method 4: Help

If needed, you can enlist the assistance of your teacher or teammate. However, it's essential to prioritize safety during this collaborative effort. Adjust the force your partner applies, ranging from light to heavy (Figure 2.20).

Figure 2.20

(4) Pū Bù Yà Tuǐ or Crouch-Stance Leg Stretch

'Crouch-Stance Leg Stretch' (仆步壓腿), is an effective exercise for stretching the hamstrings and lower back. It is also beneficial for enhancing flexibility in the inner thigh and hip joints.

Practice Method 1: Press the Knee with One Hand (using left leg as an example):

- Start by fully squatting down with your right leg. Rotate your right toes outward at approximately 45 degrees. Extend your left leg to the left side with your left toes pointing upward.
- Place both palms on your right knee (Figure 2.21), or if preferred, position your left palm on your left knee while holding your right knee with your right hand (Figure 2.22).
- Gradually tilt your upper body gently to the left side, aiming to reach down towards your left foot. Go only as far as your flexibility allows. You should feel a stretch along the right side of your body and your left leg.

Figure 2.21   Figure 2.22

- Maintain this stretched position for 15-30 seconds. Remember to breathe deeply and slowly during the stretch.
- Now, execute ten gentle vibrations up and down with your left leg. This can help to further stretch and loosen the muscles in your leg.
- After completing the vibrations, relax for a moment. Repeat the entire stretch sequence on the other leg (Figure 2.23, 2.24). Tilt your upper body gently to the right side, maintain the stretch for 15-30 seconds, and then perform ten gentle leg vibrations with your right leg.

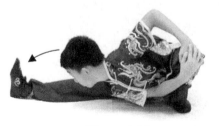 

Figure 2.23   Figure 2.24

Pressing the knee with one hand can indeed be helpful in enhancing the stretch and deepening the effect on the targeted muscles. However, it's crucial to maintain a gentle and controlled pressure to avoid any strain or discomfort. Remember to perform these stretches slowly and gently without forcing your body into uncomfortable positions. It's important to listen to your body and stop if you feel any pain.

Practice Method 2: Hold Foot with Both Hands (using the left leg as an example):
- Begin by squatting down entirely with your right leg. Move your right toes outward about 45 degrees and extend your left knee on the left while turning your left toes inward about 90 degrees. Ensure that both soles of your feet are rooted into the ground and avoid lifting either side of your feet off the ground.
- Lean your upper body as far to the left as possible and tightly grasp the outside of your left foot with your hands.
- Hold this position for 15-30 seconds, then vibrate your upper body towards the left foot until you feel slight tension in your left leg (Figure 2.25).
- Repeat the stretch with your right leg (Figure 2.26). The movement is the same as the left crouch-stance leg stretching.

Holding the foot with both hands can be an effective way to deepen the stretch and improve flexibility. Make sure to perform this action gently and gradually to avoid any strain or discomfort.

Figure 2.25   Figure 2.26

Key Points (using the left crouch stance as an example):
- Activate and strengthen your left leg while firmly grounding the outside edge of your left foot, turning 90 degrees inward.
- Focus on drawing the back of your left thigh toward your left ankle to achieve a deep stretch in your inner thigh and hamstring.
- Keep your upper body upright and in a straight line as you twist to the left, leaning as far as your flexibility allows toward your left foot.
- Be vigilant about keeping your right heel and the outer edge of your right foot on the ground and ensure that your right knee remains in proper alignment, avoiding inward rotation.

2. Bān Tuǐ or Leg Holding

'Bān' (搬) in this context means to hold or grip in English. 'Bān Tuǐ' (搬腿) originally means 'Holding the Leg.'

'Leg Holding,' also known as 'Assisted Stretching,' is an exercise that involves gripping the foot and stretching it forward or upward with the aid of hands or a partner. The primary goal of this exercise is to enhance leg flexibility, increase the range of hip motion, and strengthen the legs' lifting capacity. The practice methods include front holding, side holding, and back holding. Here are the action instructions:

(1) Front Leg Holding

Practice Method 1: Hold Leg with Bent Knee (using the right leg as an example):

- Stand with your left leg straight and lift your right knee as high as possible towards your chest. Hold onto your right foot with your left hand and support your right knee with your right hand (Figure 2.27).
- Ensure that your body remains upright, your head is held high, your chest is lifted, and you slightly grasp the ground with your left toes. Sink Qi to Dntian.
- Hold this position for a while and maintain your balance, and then switch to your right leg and repeat the exercise (Figure 2.28).

Figure 2.27   Figure 2.28

Practice Method 2: Hold the Foot with a Stretched Knee

- Grasp the outside of your right foot with your left hand and extend your right leg forward, stretching your right knee. Allow the outside of your right foot to move as far forward as possible, aiming to reach the height of your waist or over (Figure 2.29).
- Place your right fist on your right waist and maintain a straight gaze ahead. Hold this posture briefly before transitioning to your left leg (Figure 2.30).

| Figure 2.29 | Side | Figure 2.30 |

If you find it challenging to stretch your legs independently, don't hesitate to seek assistance from your teacher or teammates. Here, the author gives you two options: One approach is to have one person stand while another lies on their back and supports your leg, aiding in the stretching process.

Standing Position (using the right leg as an example):
- Begin by adopting a straight standing posture with your back, shoulder, and heels aligned against the wall.
- Your teacher or teammate should position their left hand on your right heel while placing their right hand on your right knee.
- Slowly lift your right leg, with the goal of bringing it as close to your forehead as possible while keeping your toes in contact with the wall.
- During the exercise, pay close attention to avoiding the opening of your right hip; instead, engage and contract it inward.
- Furthermore, ensure continuous contact between your back and the wall throughout the duration of this practice (Figure 2.31).

Figure 2.31

Lying Position (using the right leg as an example):

- Begin by lying on your back with your hands resting at your sides and your knees fully extended.
- One person should gently hold and apply slight pressure to your left foot and knee, while another person holds your right ankle.
- Gradually, raise your right leg from the front, striving to bring it as close to your forehead as possible while allowing your toes to maintain contact with the floor.
- Throughout this practice, be vigilant in avoiding the opening of your hip; instead, engage and contract it inward.
- Furthermore, ensure that your entire back maintains contact with the ground during the entirety of the exercise (Figure 2.32).

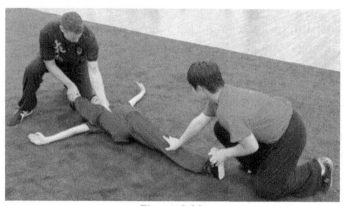

Figure 2.32

(2) Side Leg Holding

Practice Method 1: Single Hand (using the left leg as an example):

- Start by standing upright with your right foot planted firmly on the ground while raising your left leg and bending your left knee, extending it out to the side.
- Extend your left hand to the inside of your calf, securing a firm grip on your left ankle, and use your right hand to grasp the outside of your left foot (Figure 2.33).
- Gradually elevate your left leg to the side of your head while ensuring that the sole of your left foot points up. Extend your right hand above your head and maintain a straight waist. Your goal is to fully extend your left knee and move your left leg as far back as possible, away from your left shoulder (Figure 2.34).
- Hold this position for 15-30 seconds, then switch to the exercise with your right leg (Figure 2.35). Be sure to sustain your balance throughout the entire exercise.

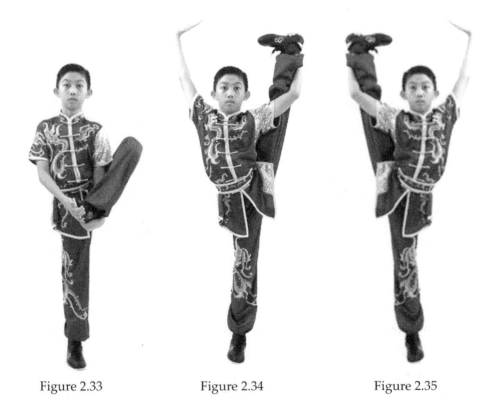

| Figure 2.33 | Figure 2.34 | Figure 2.35 |

Practice Method 2: Double Hands (using the left leg as an example)

- Stand upright on your right leg, bend your left knee, and lift your left leg. Hold your left ankle from the inside of your calf with your left hand and the outside of your left foot with your right hand (Figure 2.33).
- Lift your left leg towards the top of your head using both hands, with the sole of your left foot pointing up. Extend your left knee and move your left leg as far back as

possible from your left shoulder. While practicing, gently pull your left leg inward with your hands to straighten it as much as possible, keeping it close to your body.

- Ensure your waist, spine, and tailbone remain straight, maintaining proper posture in a straight line from top to bottom (Figure 2.36).
- Maintain this stance for a moment, concentrating on sustaining your balance. Now, replicate the exercise with your right leg (Figure 2.37).

Figure 2.36   Figure 2.37

In addition to performing 'Leg Stretches' independently, it's also beneficial to seek assistance from your teacher or teammates when necessary. Their support can help you achieve a deeper stretch safely. For instance:

Lying Position (using the right leg as an example):
- Begin by lying on your back with your hands placed beside your body and your knees fully extended.
- One should apply moderate and stable pressure to your left foot and knee, offering support without causing discomfort. Simultaneously, another person should grasp your right ankle and gently lift your right leg toward the right side of your head until your toes make contact with the top.
- During this practice, keep your hips contracted inward and ensure that your entire back and the back of your left leg maintain contact with the ground (Figure 2.38).

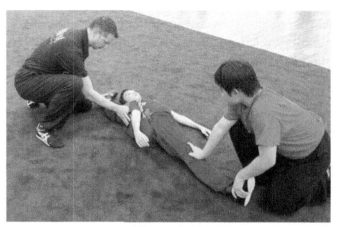

Figure 2.38

Standing Position (using the right leg as an example):
- Begin by standing upright with the left side of your shoulder against the wall. Your teacher or teammate should support your right heel with their right hand while placing their left hand on your right knee. Gradually elevate your leg toward the right side of your head until your toes make contact with the wall.
- Throughout this exercise, concentrate on engaging your hips inward and sustaining contact between the side of your left shoulder and the wall. This emphasis on alignment and stability is crucial for an effective stretch (Figure 2.39).

Figure 2.39
45

(3) Rear Leg Holds (using the right leg as an example):

- Locate a wall bar or a sturdy object at an appropriate height that you can hold onto.
- Stand upright with your left leg serving as the supporting leg, and have your teacher or partner support your right leg from behind. Keep your right knee and foot fully extended.
- Slightly lean forward, and as your teacher or partner applies gentle pressure to your right leg, carefully arch your upper body backward. Alternate between practicing with each leg (Figure 2.40).
- While executing the stretch, pay attention to keeping your back leg straight and open. Maintaining alignment between your shoulders and hips ensures they are in the same plane. Slightly elongate your waist and push backward as far as your flexibility allows. Hold this position for a duration to intensify the stretch.

Figure 2.40

3. Pī Tuǐ or Leg Splitting

'Pī' (劈) means split or cut apart. 'Pī Tuǐ' (劈腿) can be translated as 'Split Legs' in English.

'Leg Splitting' encompasses a range of 'Leg Techniques' that involve performing different types of splits. The primary goal of split training is to increase hip flexibility and expand the range of motion in your legs. To achieve this, split training can be supplemented with 'Leg Stretching' and 'Holding' exercises. There are three primary methods for split training: vertical splits, center splits, and drop splits. Below are instructions for each method:

(1) Shù Chā or Vertical (Side) Splitting

'Shù' (竖) here refers to 'vertical,' while 'Vertical Splitting' (竖叉) involves stretching one leg to the front of the body and the other leg to the back of the body. The name of the 'Vertical Split' is determined by the leg extending ahead of the body. For example, if the left leg is facing forward, it is called the left split. Here are the correct movements to perform 'Vertical Splits' (using the left leg as an example):

- Place your hands on both sides of your body or raise your arms beside your body.
- Separate your legs into a straight line, with one leg (left) extending forward and the other leg (right) extending backward.
- Press the back of your left leg onto the ground while the inside of your right leg touches the ground.
- Keep your gaze straight ahead and maintain proper alignment (Figure 2.41).

Remember to engage your core muscles during the 'Vertical Split,' maintain a straight posture, and avoid any excessive strain. Gradually increase the depth of your split over time and practice consistently to improve your flexibility.

Figure 2.41

Practice Method 1: The Bow-Arrow Stance Stretch (using left leg as an example):
- Begin by assuming a left bow-arrow stance, with your left foot on the ground and your right knee bent far behind, keeping your back toes on the floor.
- Place your left hand on your left knee and your right hand on the right floor and twist your upper body to the left as far as possible.
- Keep your chest and back straight and vertical, maintaining proper alignment.
- Slowly push your hips towards the floor while keeping your left knee aligned with your left toes. Repeat this movement 5-10 times, focusing on the stretch and maintaining control (Figure 2.42).
- Repeat the same steps with your right leg, assuming a right bow-arrow stance, and perform the hip-pushing movement (Figure 2.43).

Figure 2.42   Figure 2.43

Practice Method 2: Forward and Backward Split (using left leg as an example):
- Hold your left foot with both hands, maintaining a secure grip. Slowly bend forward from the waist, strive to make contact between your abdomen, chest, and head with your left leg, and if possible, reach your left toes with your head. Maintain this position for 10-15 seconds, feeling the stretch in your hamstrings and groin (Figure 2.44).
- Be mindful not to lower your head excessively. Instead, use your chin to gaze toward your front toes or keep your neck neutral.

Figure 2.44

- Next, lean your upper body backward while using your hands for balance, supporting yourself with them. Gently arch your back and hold this position for 10-15 seconds, experiencing the stretch in your hips, lower back, and thighs (Figure 2.45).

Figure 2.45

- Repeat these steps with your right leg, ensuring both sides receive equal attention and stretching.

It's vital to tune into your body, progress only as far as it feels comfortable, and refrain from forcing movements. Regular practice and correct technique can gradually enhance your flexibility in 'Vertical Splits.'

Practice Method 3: Splitting with Elevated Object (using left leg as an example):

- Position your left heel on a stable object, such as a block or step, ensuring that your legs form a straight line both forward and backward. Keep your left toes pointing upward.
- Maintain balance and stability by supporting the ground with both hands, or placing them on either side of your left foot (Figure 2.46). Keep your upper body upright and well-aligned. Engage your core muscles to enhance stability. Hold this position for 10-15 seconds, sensing the stretch in your inner thighs and groin area.

Figure 2.46

- Alternatively, you can perform a gentle bouncing motion to your left leg, allowing it to relax and oscillate a few times (Figure 2.47).

Figure 2.47

- Next, hinge forward from your waist to bring your abdomen and chest in contact with your left leg. Alternatively, you can strive to touch your head to your left toes while using your hands to hold your left foot for support (Figure 2.48). Hold this position for 10-15 seconds, focusing on the stretch in your hamstrings and lower back. Remember to align your head with your spine and avoid excessive neck flexion.

Figure 2.48

- Afterward, lean your upper body backward while placing your hands beside the ground for support (Figure 2.49). Hold this position for 10-15 seconds, feeling the stretch in the front of your hips, lower back, and thighs.

Figure 2.49

- Repeat the same steps with your right leg, ensuring equal attention and stretching on both sides (Figure 2.50, 2.51, 2.52, 2.53).

Figure 2.50

Figure 2.51

Figure 2.52   Figure 2.53

Practice Method 4: High Leg Split Practice (using the left leg as an example):

- Begin by positioning your left heel on a wall or an object slightly higher than your head level, ensuring that your left toes point inward. Hold the wall bar or just wall with both hands, placing them on either side of your left foot to maintain balance and stability (Figure 2.54).

Figure 2.54

- Extend your right foot as backward as possible, aligning it straight with your left leg. While in this position, you can introduce gentle vibrations with your left leg, allowing it to relax and oscillate a few times. This can help release tension and deepen the stretch.
- Next, hold your left foot with your hands and, while hinging forward from your waist, bring your abdomen and chest into contact with your left leg. Alternatively, work towards touching your head to your left toes. Maintain this position for 10-15 seconds, concentrating on the stretch in your hamstrings and lower back (Figure 2.55).

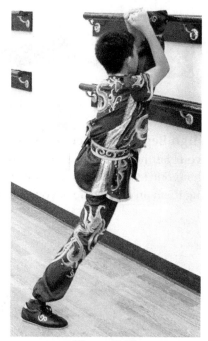

Figure 2.55

Key Points:

(1) Always start with a proper warm-up and incorporate dynamic stretches to prepare your muscles for 'Split' practice. This helps prevent injuries and enhances flexibility.

(2) Understand that developing flexibility and achieving a 'Split' is a gradual process. Stay consistent in your practice and work slowly towards deeper stretches and an increased range of motion.

(3) Focus on deep and mindful breathing during your stretches and strive to relax your muscles. Avoid sudden or jerky movements that could strain your muscles. Allow your body to ease into the stretch gradually.

(4) Avoid pushing your body too hard or forcing yourself into a 'Split ' position that causes pain or discomfort. Always respect your body's limits and progress at a pace that suits you.

(5) Over time, gradually increase the intensity and duration of your 'Split' practice. This will help your body adapt safely and improve your flexibility.

(6) If you have any concerns or questions about 'Split' training, consider consulting a professional trainer or coach. They can provide personalized guidance, correct your form, and offer modifications tailored to your specific needs.

- Repeat these same steps with your right leg, ensuring proper alignment and balance throughout the exercise (Figure 2.56 and 2.57).

| Figure 2.56 | Figure 2.57 |

(2) Héng Chā or Center Splitting

The term 'Héng' (橫) generally means 'horizontal,' but in this context, it denotes the concept of the center or midpoint. 'Center Splitting,' also known as 'Side Splits' or 'Straddle Splits,' is a stretching practice designed to improve the flexibility of the inner thighs and legs.

- Begin by extending your legs to the sides as far as is comfortable. Keep your knees pointing upward or slightly inward, and ensure your toes are pointing forward or slightly upward.
- Place your hands on the ground in front of you for added support or keep them positioned beside your body for better balance. Ensure that both legs are fully straight and evenly extended to the sides. Keep your feet straightened and maintain contact between the inner edges of your feet and the ground (Figure 2.58).

- Maintain an upright and straight back, engaging your core muscles to provide stability. Relax your shoulders and focus on deep, steady breathing throughout the stretch.
- Hold the 'Center Split' position for 15-30 seconds or longer if comfortable. As you gain flexibility, you can gradually increase the duration of the hold.
- Slowly bring your legs together and stand up to release the stretch.
- Repeat the 'Center Splitting' exercise for several sets, gradually working towards a wider split over time.

Figure 2.58

Practice Method 1: Seated Butterfly Stretch

The 'Seated Butterfly Stretch' effectively stretches and prepares the groin and inner thigh muscles for 'Center Splits.' Here's a breakdown of the practice method:

- Begin by sitting on the floor with your legs extended in front of you. Bend your knees and bring the soles of your feet together, allowing your knees to fall out to the sides. Keep your heels as close to your groin as comfortable.
- Hold your feet with your hands, gripping your toes or ankles. You can use your thumbs to gently apply pressure on the inner arches of your feet (Figure 2.59).
- Maintain an upright posture with your back straight, avoiding any slouching. While keeping your spine aligned, hinge forward from your hips. Lower your chest toward your feet, guiding your elbows toward your knees. This movement helps intensify the stretch in your groin and inner thighs.
- You can gently apply pressure with your elbows or palms to your inner thighs or knees, encouraging your knees to move closer to the floor while maintaining proper form and alignment (Figure 2.60). It's crucial not to force the stretch or go beyond your comfort level. The goal is to feel a gentle pulling and tension in the groin area.
- Hold the stretch for 20 to 30 seconds while taking deep breaths and allowing yourself to relax into the position. As you continue to breathe, you may find that you can sink deeper into the stretch with each exhalation.

Figure 2.59   Figure 2.60

- Slowly release the stretch and return to the starting position with your legs extended.
- Repeat the seated butterfly stretch several times to promote relaxation and gradual deepening of the stretch.

Remember to prioritize smooth and controlled movements throughout the stretch. Avoid any bouncing or the use of excessive force, as these actions can potentially lead to injury or overstretching. If you ever encounter pain or discomfort, gently release the stretch and make any necessary adjustments. With consistent practice and patience, you will gradually enhance your flexibility over time.

Practice Method 2: Seated Center Stretch Forward
- Sit on the floor with your legs spread apart as wide as possible. Keep your upper body upright and engaged. Place your hands down in front of you on the floor, with your fingers pointing forward. You can adjust the position of your hands to find what feels most comfortable for you (Figure 2.61).

Figure 2.61

- Slowly and gradually leaning forward from your hips. Aim to bring your chest closer to the floor while maintaining a straight back and avoiding any spine rounding. Concentrate on elongating your torso.
- As you lean forward, progressively allow your chin to move forward, leading the way. Do not bend your knees or enable the inside of your thighs to leave the floor, as this could cause your hips to protrude. Maintain neck alignment and prevent unnecessary strain (Figure 2.62).

Figure 2.62

- Progress to a depth in the stretch that feels comfortable, experiencing a gentle pulling sensation in your inner thighs and groin. Avoid pushing yourself too aggressively or attempting to force the stretch beyond your current level of flexibility. The objective is to feel a moderate stretch, not to experience pain.
- After moving your body and arms forward, maintain the stretch for a few seconds, focusing on deep and controlled breathing. Subsequently, release the stretch slowly and return to the starting position.
- Repeat the stretch several times, progressively working towards a deeper stretch with each repetition. Over time, you may notice an increased range of motion and the ability to reach further towards your legs.

Practice Method 3: Wide Leg Stretch (using the right leg as an example):
- Sit on the floor with your legs spread apart as wide as possible. Keep your upper body upright and engaged (Figure 2.61).
- Turn your upper body to the right, facing the right leg. Your torso should be aligned with the leg you are facing. This helps to target the inner thigh muscles and prepare them for the stretch.
- Reach your right hand or both hands towards your right foot and bend your waist as much as possible to the right side. Aim to bring your upper body closer to your right leg but avoid lowering your head or hunching your back. Keep your back straight and maintain good posture throughout the stretch (Figure 2.63, 2.64).

Figure 2.63

Figure 2.64

- As you bend towards the right leg, you should feel a stretch in your inner thighs and groin area. Avoid pushing yourself too far beyond your current flexibility level.
- Hold the stretch (Figure 2.64) for 20 to 30 seconds, focusing on deep, controlled breathing. Relax into the stretch and allow your muscles to gradually release and lengthen. If the stretch becomes too intense or uncomfortable, ease off slightly.
- After holding the stretch on the right side, release the stretch and return to the starting position (Figure 2.61). Then, repeat the same steps on the left side. Turn your upper body to the left, reach towards your left foot, and bend your waist to the left side (Figure 2.65, 2.66).

Figure 2.65,   Figure 2.66

- Repeat the stretch on both sides for a few rounds, gradually working towards a deeper stretch over time. As you continue to practice, you may find that your range of motion increases and you can reach further towards your legs.

Practice Method 4: Side Stretch (using the left leg as an example):

- Sit on the floor with your legs spread apart as wide as possible. Keep your upper body upright and engaged (Figure 2.61).
- Raise your right arm towards the ceiling, lengthening your right side. As you exhale, bend your upper body towards the left side. Reach your right hand towards your left foot to touch it or get as close as possible without straining. Allow your left arm to naturally lower towards the ground or rest on your left leg (Figure 2.67, 2.68).

| Figure 2.67 | Figure 2.68 |

- As you bend to the left side, you should feel a stretch along the right side of your body, from your hip to your fingertips. Focus on lengthening your right side and avoid collapsing or rounding your shoulders.
- Hold the stretch for 20 to 30 seconds, breathing deeply and allowing your body to relax into the stretch.
- After holding the stretch on the left side, slowly release the stretch and return to the starting position. Then, repeat the same steps on the opposite side. Raise your left arm, bend to the right side, and touch your right foot with your left hand (Figure 2.69, 2.70).

| Figure 2.69- | Figure 2.70 |

- Repeat the side stretch on both sides for a few rounds, gradually working towards a deeper stretch over time. As you continue to practice, you may find that your range of motion increases and you can reach further towards your feet.

Practice Method 5: Frog Stretch

- Start by lying face down on the floor. Extend your arms forward and bend your legs, positioning them on the floor like a frog. Spread your knees as wide as your current flexibility allows and turn your feet outward with the soles facing backward (Figure 2.71).

Figure 2.71

- To enhance the stretch, gently shift your hips backward toward your heels while keeping your knees in a wide position. Gradually lower your upper body onto your forearms, resting your weight on them. This adjustment will increase the stretch in your hips and inner thighs.
- Once you've found a comfortable position, hold the stretch to the extent you can comfortably tolerate it. You can introduce gentle vibrations into the position to further intensify the stretch. While in the frog stretch, slightly shift your hips forward and move your abdomen with gentle rocking motions. This may cause some discomfort in the ligaments but aim to maintain the stretch as much as you can tolerate for approximately one minute. Afterward, continue with gentle vibrations and pressure for an additional five minutes.
- Throughout the stretch, concentrate on deep breathing and relaxation. Take slow, deep breaths to release tension and encourage your muscles to relax. Strive to balance intensity and comfort as you hold the stretch and incorporate vibrations.
- As with any stretching routine, starting gradually and respecting your body's limitations is essential. Over time, you can work on increasing the stretch duration and the depth of your hip and inner thigh opening. However, avoid pushing yourself too forcefully or attempting to force the stretch beyond your current capabilities.

Assisted 'Center Split Stretch'

Assisted stretching can significantly enhance your leg flexibility. Here's how to perform an assisted 'Leg Stretch' while lying face-up and face-down:

(1) Face Up:
- Begin by lying on your back on the floor. You can have your hands under your head or at your sides. Extend your knees and separate your legs as wide as your current flexibility allows.

- Your assistant should kneel in front of you, facing you. They should position their palms on the inside of your knees or calves, ensuring a firm yet comfortable grip. The assistant's placement should enable them to apply moderate and stable pressure to your legs.
- As you relax, your assistant gently presses your legs toward the floor (Figure 2.72). The objective is to increase the stretch in your inner thighs and hips gradually. Communication with your assistant is crucial throughout the process; provide feedback regarding the pressure level and your comfort.

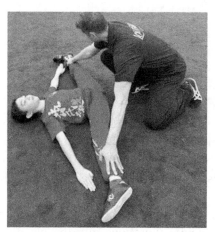
Figure 2.72

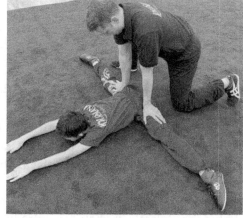
Figure 2.73

- Safety should always be a top priority during assisted stretching. The pressure applied by your assistant should be controlled and should not cause any pain or discomfort. Your assistant should attentively monitor your responses and adjust the pressure accordingly.
- Hold the stretch in the downward position for a comfortable duration, typically around 20 to 30 seconds. Subsequently, release the pressure gradually and repeat the stretch a few times, allowing your muscles to adapt and relax further.

(2) Face Down:
- Lie face down on the floor, supporting yourself with your palms, elbows, or stretch your arms forward. Extend your knees and separate your legs by spreading them to the sides as wide as your current flexibility allows.
- Your assistant should kneel behind you and place their palms on your hips or outside your thighs. Their position should provide stability and control during the stretch.
- With your assistant's guidance, slowly press your legs downward toward the floor, aiming to bring your legs into a straight line. The assistant should apply moderate and stable pressure to facilitate the stretch in your inner thighs and hips (Figure 2.73).
- Safety is paramount during assisted stretching. The pressure applied by the assistant should be controlled and should not cause any pain or discomfort. Communicate

with your assistant about the pressure level, and they should adjust accordingly to ensure a safe and effective stretch.

- Hold the stretch in the downward position for a comfortable duration, typically around 20 to 30 seconds. Gradually release the pressure and repeat the stretch a few times, allowing your muscles to relax and adapt to the stretch.

(3) Diē Chā or Falling Split

'Diē' (跌) means 'fall down' in English, while the 'Falling Split' (跌叉) is a dynamic movement where the practitioners transition from a jump movement into a vertical split position (Figure 2.74).

It is frequently employed in Contemporary Wushu Competitive routines to elevate the difficulty level and perform visually captivating sequences with other movements, such as 'Tornado Kicks,' 'Lotus Kicks,' or 'Butterfly Twists.' The 'Falling Split' requires a strong command of vertical splitting and is typically performed by advanced-level practitioners. The key to this maneuver is propelling yourself off the ground with your feet and seamlessly transitioning into the split position while maintaining precise control and balance throughout the sequence.

Figure 2.74

The Butterfly Twists 720 Degrees Connecting into 'Vertical Split' is a Spectacular Wushu Move Performed by the Renowned Chinese Athlete Wu Zhao Hua

In Competitive Wushu Competitions, precise execution of the 'Falling Split' technique is crucial, and specific requirements and deduction points are applied to ensure proper alignment and form. Deviations from the prescribed technique may lead to deduction points. Here are the typical requirements and deduction points associated with the 'Falling Split':

(1) Incorrect Foot Position: If the sole of the front foot turns inward, causing the toe of the front foot to touch the ground, deduction points will be assigned.

(2) Rear Leg Bent: The rear leg should remain fully extended and straight. Any bending of the rear leg at an angle of 45° or more will result in deduction points.

Wushu athletes must adhere to these requirements to showcase proper technique and maximize their scores in competitive routines. Judges meticulously assess the execution of the 'Falling Split' based on these criteria and assign deduction points accordingly.

Stretching the legs is of utmost importance in Wushu training for several significant reasons:

(1) Flexibility and Range of Motion:
Stretching the leg muscles helps improve flexibility and increases the range of motion in the lower body. Wushu requires a wide array of 'Leg Techniques,' such as high kicks, splits, and deep stances. Adequate flexibility in the legs allows practitioners to perform these techniques with greater ease, precision, and control. It also helps prevent muscle strains and injuries by allowing the muscles to move through their full range of motion without resistance or limitation.

(2) Execution of Techniques:
Stretching the legs directly impacts the execution of various Wushu techniques. By improving leg flexibility, practitioners can achieve higher kicks, deeper stances, and more fluid movements. The increased range of motion allows for greater extension and extension of the legs, leading to enhanced aesthetics, balance, and power in techniques. Stretching also improves the overall quality and accuracy of kicks, jumps, and sweeps.

(3) Injury Prevention:

Regular leg stretching plays a crucial role in injury prevention during Wushu training. Flexible leg muscles are less prone to strains, pulls, and tears. By maintaining good flexibility, practitioners reduce the risk of overstretching or injuring the muscles and connective tissues in the legs. Stretching also helps alleviate muscle imbalances, which can lead to compensatory movements and potential injuries.

(4) Balance and Stability:

Stretching the legs contributes to improved balance and stability in Wushu practice. Flexible leg muscles allow for better weight distribution and weight shifting during stances and dynamic movements. This enables practitioners to maintain stability, control, and proper alignment while performing techniques. Enhanced balance and stability not only improve the quality of movements but also reduce the risk of falls or instability during challenging Wushu routines.

In conclusion, stretching the legs is essential in Wushu training to improve flexibility, increase the range of motion, enhance technique execution, prevent injuries, promote balance and stability, and elevate overall performance. By incorporating regular leg stretching exercises into training routines, practitioners can optimize their physical abilities and excel in the practice of Wushu.

Chapter 3
Yāo - Gōng
腰功
Waist Training Exercises

The foundation of 'Body Technique' in Wushu training is rooted in the development of the waist, with a particular focus on strengthening and refining the waist area. The waist serves as a pivotal connection point between the upper and lower body and is regarded as the core of the human body. Several expressions in Wushu highlight the significance of waist training, such as 'Without practicing the waist, achieving high-quality skills is impossible' (練武不練腰,終究藝不高), and 'A moving waist makes footwork agile like a snake.' The waist is often referred to as the 'master' and 'upright axis,' underscoring its crucial role in Wushu training.

To cultivate and enhance waist skills, various methods are employed, encompassing bending, swinging, swaying, twisting, rolling, circling, and bridging. Here are detailed instructions for each of these movements:

1. Qián Fǔ Yāo or Forward Bend, Forward Stretch

'Qián' (前) refers to the front, 'Fǔ' (俯) means to bow down or face down, and 'Yao' (腰) stands for the waist, indicating the area above the crotch (hip) and under the ribs in the middle of the body. 'Qian Fu Yao' (前俯腰) signifies the action of bending the waist forward.

Preparation Posture:

Start by standing with your feet together. Cross your fingers above your head, inhale deeply, and extend your arms with palms facing upward. Maintain an upright posture with your head up, chest out, and gaze straight ahead (Figure 3.1). Generally, you should stretch your arms upward as far as possible, as if supporting the sky with your palms, feeling your armpit areas extending and opening.

Practice Method 1: Palms Reach
- While keeping your upper body straight, exhale and gradually bend at the waist, lowering your torso forward.
- Allow your palms to contact the ground in front of you (Figure 3.2). Keep your legs straight throughout this movement.
- Hold the stretch for a few seconds, focusing on feeling the stretch in your lower back and hamstrings.
- Inhale as you slowly return to the starting position.
- Repeat this movement several times, emphasizing controlled and rhythmic breathing while maintaining a smooth motion.

Practice Method 2: Leg Reach

- Begin by assuming the Preparation Posture (Figure 3.1), keeping your hands crossed. Then, bend at your waist, gradually lowering your upper body forward until your palms touch the ground (Figure 3.2).
- Release your hands from the crossed position and gently pull to bring yourself closer to your legs, allowing you to feel the stretch in your hamstrings and lower back. Tighten your grip on your ankles with your hands (Figure 3.3). Keep your legs straight and avoid any sudden or jerking movements. Hold the stretch for a few seconds, focusing on deepening the stretch without overexerting yourself.
- Slowly release the stretch and return your upper body to the starting position.
- Repeat this movement several times, allowing your body to relax deeper into the stretch with each repetition.

| Figure 3.1 | Figure 3.2 | Figure 3.3 |

Practice Method 3: Waist Bend Side

- Start from the 'Preparation Posture' above mentioned.
- Bend your waist to the left side, reaching down towards the ground with your palms while keeping your legs straight (Figure 3.4). Hold the stretch for a few seconds, feeling the stretch on the right side of your waist and torso.
- Slowly return to the starting position, maintaining control and stability.

- Repeat the movement on the right side, bending your waist to the right and reaching down towards the ground with your palms (Figure 3.5). Hold the stretch for a few seconds on the right side of your waist and torso.
- Alternate between the left and right-side bends, focusing on maintaining proper posture with a straight chest, waist, and tucked hips. Remember to avoid moving your feet while bending to the side and emphasize a smooth and controlled motion.

Figure 3.4   Figure 3.5

2. Shuǎi Yāo or Waist Forward and Backward Bend with Arm Swing

'Shuǎi' (甩) means to throw away or swing firmly with the arms. 'Shuǎi Yāo' (甩腰) originally refers to using your waist as an axis and moving it forward and backward with your arms. The range of motion of this exercise depends on your physical condition and can be either large or small.

Practice Methods:
- Standing with your feet shoulder-width apart, maintaining a straight and aligned posture. Ensure your legs are straight and engage your core muscles for stability.
- Start the movement by bending your waist forward, allowing your upper body to lean forward from the hips. Simultaneously, swing your arms forward and downward, extending them in front of your body (Figure 3.6).
- Slowly reverse the motion by straightening your waist and bending it backward as far as possible. Swing your arms back, open your shoulders, and extend your arms behind you (Figure 3.7).
- Ensure a smooth and controlled motion throughout and avoid any jerky or sudden movements. Feel the stretch in your chest, shoulders, and the front of your body as you extend your arms and open your shoulders.
- Coordinate the movement of your waist and arms, creating a fluid and flexible motion.
- Repeat the forward and backward bend with arm swing several times, focusing on maintaining proper form and control.

Figure 3.6   Figure 3.7

- Repeat the forward and backward bend with arm swing several times, focusing on maintaining proper form and control. Breathe deeply and rhythmically throughout the exercise, syncing your breath with the movement.
- As you become more comfortable and flexible, you can gradually increase the range of motion and speed of the movement.

3. Huàng Yāo or Sway Waist

'Huàng' (晃) means to sway or shake, while in Wushu, 'Huàng Yāo' (晃腰) refers to swinging your upper body from left to right. Generally, you can bend your waist forward or downward, then twist the upper body to move.

Practice Methods:
- To begin the 'Sway Waist' exercise, stand with your feet shoulder-width apart or slightly wider. Lift your arms out to the sides of your body and extend them fully. Keep your gaze forward (Figure 3.8).
- Lean forward, lowering your head, and rotate your upper body as if twisting a rope, trying to turn it as far to the right as possible. Swing your arms along with your upper body, letting them follow the direction of your movement. While swinging to the right, stretch your left arm toward your right foot as far as possible, extending your right arm upward in a straight line with your left arm (Figure 3.9).
- Hold the stretch for a moment and then return to the starting position (Figure 3.8).

- Repeat the movement, leaning forward and turning your upper body to the left. Swing your arms along with your upper body, extending your right arm towards your left foot as far as possible (Figure 3.10).
- Hold the stretch for a moment and return to the starting position.

Figure 3.8

Figure 3.9

Figure 3.8

Figure 3.10

Key Points:

(1) Maintain a straight line with your extended arms throughout the movement.

(2) Keep your chest straight and extend your abdomen as you sway.

(3) Allow your waist to move naturally and let your body swing with elasticity.

(4) Focus your gaze on the direction of your body's movement to enhance coordination.

(5) Perform the movement in a controlled manner, avoiding any jerking or abrupt motions.

(6) Practice with smooth and fluid motions, gradually increasing the range of motion as your flexibility improves.

4. Níng Yāo or Twist Waist, Waist Turning Exercise

'Níng' (擰) means to twist or wring in English, and the motion resembles twisting a rope. 'Níng Yāo' (擰腰) is a regular and conventional movement in Chinese Wushu. Generally, most moves in the Wushu routine use the waist as an axis and involve internal twisting. Some people refer to this as 'twisting the waist like a snake,' where the shape resembles Dantian's inner turn. This motion is more common in Contemporary Wushu Competition Routines 'Swordplay and Spearplay.'

Preparation Posture (using the left turn as an example):

To begin by standing upright with your left leg and raise your right knee in front of your body. Point your right toe downwards. Extend your right arm to the right, palm facing down. Bend your left elbow and place your left forearm horizontally on your chest with your palm facing down. Look towards your right (See Figure 3.11).

Figure 3.11

69

Practice Method 1:
- Keep your upper limbs still (left arm on your chest, right arm extended to the right).
- Lean your upper body to the right as far as possible. Extend your right leg to the left side and cross your right foot to the outside of your left foot while bending your left knee.
- When you extend your right leg to the left, try to stretch your right arm to the right as if you want to touch something with your right hand.
- Look to the right hand (Figure 3.12).

Practice Method 2:
- To continue the sequence, use your waist as the axis and twist it, rolling your upper body over to the left, while keeping your right leg lifted to maintain parallel alignment with your waist.
- Continue extending your right arm and right leg as much as possible. Maintain focus on your right hand throughout the movement (Figure 3.13).
- Practice this movement alternately with the first movement, repeating several times on each side.
- Remember to keep your upper limbs still during the first movement and maintain a smooth and fluid motion throughout the sequence.

Figure 3.12   Figure 3.13

Key Points:
(1) Engage your core muscles for stability and control during the movements. Maintain proper posture and alignment throughout the exercise.
(2) Focus on twisting your waist and using your waist as the axis for the movements. Extend your limbs as much as possible while maintaining comfort and control.
(3) Keep your gaze directed towards your moving hand to enhance coordination and focus. Perform the exercise in a controlled manner, gradually increasing the range of motion as your flexibility and strength improve.

(4) The 'Waist Twist' or 'Waist Turning' exercise helps develop flexibility, coordination, and strength in the waist area, promoting overall body control and mobility.

5. Fān Yāo or Flip Over the Waist Exercise

'Fān' (翻) means flipping, rolling, and turning over in English. 'Fan' and 'Fān Yāo' (翻腰) both involve a waist-turning motion in Chinese Wushu routines.

Preparation Posture (using the left turn as an example):
Start by crossing your legs, take your right leg in front and left leg in the back, and squat down to form a right 'Rest Stance.' Keep your upper body upright and aligned. Extend your right arm to the right side, with fingers pointing up. Bend your left elbow and place your left hand close to your right chest. Look toward the right (Figure 3.14).

In the Chinese 'Beijing Opera,' many roles, such as 'Huadan' (花旦 lively girl), 'Qingyi' (青衣 virtuous female), 'Xiao Sheng' (小生 young male), and 'Wusheng' (武生 martial male), incorporate this movement into their performances.

Figure 3.14

Practice Methods:
- To perform this exercise, begin by leaning your upper body slightly forward. Initiate the roll-over motion by flipping your upper body to the left and backward along the horizontal axis.
- During the movement, extend your arms and swing your left hand first, followed by your right hand, in a proper sequence. Keep your arms moving in a downward, leftward, upward, and rightward motion, resembling the turning of a wheel.
- The waist acts as the axle of the wheeling motion, with your arms moving in a straight line.
- Continue the roll-over motion until your arms and palms reach the opposite posture in a left rest stance (left leg in front and right leg in the back).
- Practice alternating the legs in the front and back during the exercise (Figures 3.15 and 3.16).

71

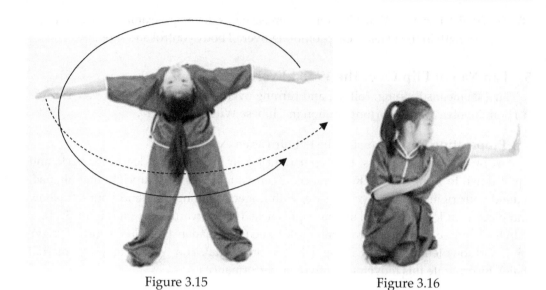

| Figure 3.15 | Figure 3.16 |

Key Points:

- Lean your upper body slightly forward before flipping it to the left-back along the horizontal axis.
- Engage your core muscles for stability and control. Coordinate the movement of your arms and waist to create a smooth and fluid motion.
- Visualize your arms and palms moving in a circular path, resembling a wheel turning.
- Focus on using your waist as the axis and maintaining a straight line with your arms.

6. Shuàn Yāo or Circle Waist

'Shuàn Yāo' (涮腰) is a specific technique in Chinese Wushu, typically employed to enhance the flexibility and agility of the waist. This movement may involve specific stretching exercises or other training methods related to the waist. It not only serves as a fundamental training exercise but is also incorporated into various 'Empty Hand Forms' and 'Weapon Routines.'

Preparation Posture:

Stand with your feet shoulder-width apart. Lean forward slightly, engaging your core muscles for stability. Extend your arms to the left side of your body, with your palms facing downward. Focus your gaze on your hands (Figure 3.17).

Practice Methods:

- Use your hips as the axis. Circle your arms from the right side to the left, then return to the right as you turn your waist. Allow your upper body to spin with the motion.
- As you circle your arms and spin your waist, let your upper body follow the motion, creating a fluid and coordinated movement. This movement is known as a right-circle waist (Figure 3.18, 3.19, 3.20).

- Practice the exercise by alternately circling your arms and waist in both directions (left to right and right to left).
- Maintain a smooth and continuous motion throughout the exercise, ensuring a comfortable range of motion for your body.

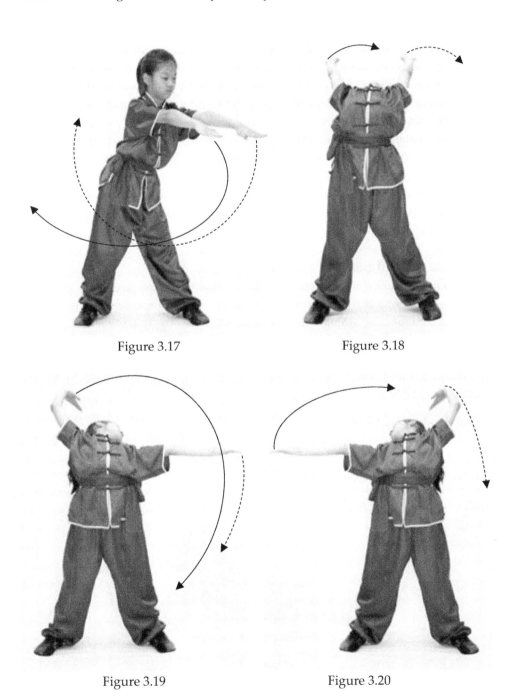

Figure 3.17

Figure 3.18

Figure 3.19

Figure 3.20

Key Points:
- Focus on performing the exercise in a smooth and flowing manner, ensuring that your arms and waist work together in a coordinated fashion. Avoid any jerky or abrupt motions that can disrupt the fluidity of the exercise.
- Keep your feet firmly planted on the ground throughout the exercise. To promote balance and stability, maintain a slight bend in your knees. This will help you stay grounded, centered, and maintain control during the movement.
- Begin the exercise with a comfortable range of motion. As you become more proficient and flexible, gradually increase the speed and range of your arm and waist movements. However, always listen to your body and avoid pushing beyond your limits to prevent injury.
- To ensure balanced training, practice the exercise by circling your arms and waist in both clockwise and counterclockwise directions. This helps develop symmetry, coordination, and control on both sides of your body.
- Incorporate the 'Circle Waist' or 'Circle Trunk with Arms Swinging' exercise into your Wushu training routine to improve your waist flexibility, coordination, and overall body control.

7. Xià Yāo or Bridge

'Xià' (下) means 'down' in English. 'Xià Yāo' (下腰) can be translated to 'bend back into a bridge' or 'bridging.' It is an excellent exercise for enhancing core stability, flexibility, and body techniques. By strengthening the waist, it effectively targets the gluteus and hamstring muscles, improving their strength. Additionally, it promotes elasticity and flexibility in the spine, waist, and surrounding muscles. This exercise is considered essential in both traditional Chinese and contemporary Wushu training. Here are the instructions for performing this exercise:

Practice Method 1: Short Bridge
- Start by lying on your back with your hands resting by your sides. Bend your knees and place your feet flat on the ground, separating them about shoulder width apart. Relax and gaze upwards (Figure 3.21).

Figure 3.21

- Press your feet firmly into the ground, engaging your glutes and abdominal muscles. Lift your hips off the ground as high as possible, creating an arched line from your knees to your shoulders. Maintain your gaze upwards (Figure 3.22). Repeat this movement.

Figure 3.22

Practice Method 2: Full Bridge

- Start by lying on your back with your knees bent and feet flat on the ground, separating them about shoulder width apart. Place your hands by your ears, with your palms touching the ground and fingers pointing towards your shoulders. Look up towards the ceiling (Figure 3.23).
- Press your hands and feet firmly into the ground as you lift your hips. Arch your back and straighten your arms and legs, creating a bridge shape with your body. Keep your head facing forward and gaze toward the ceiling (Figure 3.24).
- Once you have formed the 'Bridge,' try to move your feet closer to your hands as much as possible, gradually increasing the stretch and flexibility in your spine and waist. Hold this position for a few seconds to maintain balance and stability.
- Slowly lower your body back down to the starting position, reversing the movement in a controlled manner. Repeat the exercise by lifting your hips and arching your back into the full bridge position.

Figure 3.23   Figure 3.24

Practice Method 3: Build a Bridge

- Start by standing upright with your feet shoulder-width apart. Extend your arms forward, parallel to the ground, and keep your gaze straight ahead (Figure 3.25).
- Begin to bend backward at the waist, lifting your head, straightening your chest, and opening your shoulders (Figure 3.26, 3.27).
- Gradually lower your hands towards the ground, aiming to place your palms on it. Continue the movement by shifting your weight onto your hands and feet, lifting your hips and torso. Simultaneously, extend your arms fully, maintaining a straight line from your hands to your feet, forming a complete bridge position. Keep your gaze upward and concentrate on preserving stability (Figure 3.28).
- Hold the bridge position for a few seconds, focusing on breathing and maintaining proper alignment. Feel the stretch in your back, shoulders, and legs.
- To return to the starting position, slowly lower your hips and torso towards the ground, bending your arms and allowing your back to relax (Figure 3.29). If possible, gently roll your spine back up to a standing position.
- Repeat the exercise, gradually working on increasing your flexibility and range of motion as you become more comfortable with the movement.

Note: Building a bridge requires a good level of flexibility and strength. If you're a beginner, it's important to progress gradually and avoid overstraining.

Figure 3.25

Figure 3.26

Figure 3.27   Figure 3.28

Figure 3.29

Key Points:
(1) Maintain alignment by keeping your fingers and toes aligned with your body. Avoid turning them outward and ensure that your knees are facing forward.
(2) Focus on stretching your chest and hips as you lift your waist with your shoulders. Strive to create a significant arch in your back, emphasizing the extension.
(3) Keep your heels on the ground throughout the movement to maintain stability and proper weight distribution. If you experience any pain, reduce the intensity or duration of the exercise. Never force yourself into a position that causes pain.
(4) Progress gradually and be patient with your practice. It may take time to build up to a full bridge, so listen to your body and avoid pushing yourself too hard.

Once you have formed the 'bridge,' fully extend your arms and legs, pushing your shoulders over your head. You can ask someone to gently push your knees to help deepen the stretch, but always prioritize safety and avoid applying excessive force (Figure 3.30). Alternatively, have someone beside you to assist (Figure 3.31).

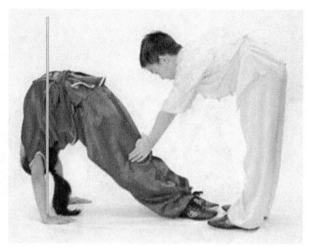

Figure 3.30

Figure 3.31

The axial rotation of the waist plays a crucial role in Wushu training, offering several significant effects:

(1) Power Generation:

The axial rotation of the waist enables power transfer from the lower body to the upper body and extremities. By utilizing the rotational force generated through the waist, practitioners can increase power in their strikes, kicks, and other techniques. This

78

rotational power adds speed, strength, and effectiveness to their movements, allowing for a more significant impact and potential for success.

(2) Core Strength and Stability:

The axial rotation of the waist engages and strengthens the core muscles, including the abdominal, oblique, and lower back muscles. These muscles provide stability and support to the body during dynamic movements and help maintain balance and control. Developing a strong and stable core through waist rotation enhances overall body control, balance, and coordination in Wushu practice.

(3) Range of Motion:

The waist's axial rotation increases the range of motion in movements, especially in techniques involving twisting, turning, and spinning. By actively engaging the waist's rotational capabilities, practitioners can execute more dynamic and visually impressive techniques with fluidity and ease. The increased range of motion also allows smoother transitions between different techniques, adding grace and aesthetics to Wushu performances.

(4) Flexibility and Agility:

The axial rotation of the waist requires a certain degree of flexibility in the waist and lower back muscles. Regular waist rotation exercises improve flexibility in these areas, allowing for greater freedom of movement and preventing stiffness or limitations in executing various techniques. Enhanced flexibility also improves agility, as practitioners can move quickly and efficiently while maintaining control and balance.

(5) Expressiveness and Artistry:

The axial rotation of the waist adds expressiveness and artistry to Wushu performances. By incorporating waist rotations into techniques, practitioners can convey a sense of fluidity, grace, and dynamic motion. The ability to skillfully control and coordinate waist movements enhances the aesthetic quality of the performance, captivating the audience and showcasing the beauty and artistry of Wushu.

In summary, the axial rotation of the waist in Wushu training has several important effects. It enables power generation, enhances core strength and stability, increases range of motion, improves flexibility and agility, and adds expressiveness and artistry to performances. By developing and refining waist rotation techniques, practitioners can elevate their overall performance and excel in the practice of Wushu.

Chapter 4
Zhàn - Zhuāng Gōng Fū
站椿功夫
Standing Post Kung Fu

The primary distinction between Chinese and Western martial arts largely hinges on their approach to footwork, which in turn profoundly shapes their techniques and overall stylistic characteristics.

Plum Blossom Posts

   Chinese Wushu strongly emphasizes static techniques, prioritizing stable legs and firmly planted feet. Foundational practices like 'Zhàn Zhuāng' (站椿) are commonly recommended for beginners. The philosophy of Chinese Wushu revolves around maintaining balance and a grounded center of gravity in all movements, encapsulated in the famous saying, 'The form does not break, and the power does not leak.' Consequently, Chinese footwork of martial arts typically involves alternating single-foot movements. One foot maintains contact with the ground while the other moves, whether attacking, retreating, or kicking. The concept of kicking with both feet off the ground simultaneously, as often seen in Kung Fu movies, is essentially an art form or a fictional story.

Western Wushu, in contrast, is characterized by dynamic martial arts that prioritize continuous movement to maintain balance. Techniques such as leaning forward or delivering piercing punches indicate this dynamic nature. In Western martial arts, including boxing, footwork typically involves both feet moving simultaneously, whether it's during an attack, retreat, or lateral movement. The emphasis here is on agility and flexibility, with frequent shifts between dynamic and static stances resulting in constant motion. For example, during attacks, retreats, or lateral changes, a single leg moves only half a step instead of alternating.

The dynamic nature of Western Wushu often makes techniques like flying kicks attractive and popular among Western practitioners. Dr. Yuan, in his book 'Wushu – The Way of Chinese Exists,' explains that traditional Chinese Wushu, rooted in the culture of the yellow race, emphasizes 'five short body statures,' which encompass four limbs and the neck. This creates an isosceles triangle physique (with the tip pointing upward), formed by the waistline and legs, resulting in a lower center of gravity. This physical form embodies a national agricultural mentality that values the land and emphasizes returning to one's roots.

In contrast, competitive boxing, originating from Western cultures encompassing whites and blacks, features taller and stronger individuals with chests and arms forming an opposite isosceles triangle physique (with the tip pointing downward). This physique results in a higher center of gravity, reflecting a national mentality characterized by industrial and commercial progress beyond the agricultural focus.

These differing approaches to footwork and physique are fundamental to the distinct styles and philosophies of Chinese and Western martial arts.

The Western way of life and work is often characterized as enterprising, adventurous, and progressive, marked by positive attributes. In contrast, the Chinese way of life and work is described as self-sufficient, stable, and internally focused, with regular features.

From both national psychological and physiological perspectives, the fundamental Wushu techniques in the East and West are well-suited and consistent. A psychological pursuit characterized by enterprising traits leads to positive action, while a self-protective mentality results in more stable action. In an inverted isosceles triangle physique, with its high weight and broad shoulders, achieving physical stability by solely lowering the center of gravity can be challenging. However, quickly adjusting the center of gravity by moving the feet can yield better results. On the other hand, in an upright isosceles triangle physique, with its low weight and wide buttocks, relying solely on footwork to adjust the center of gravity may be cumbersome, making the lower stances an effective way to enhance stability.

This is why Chinese Wushu greatly emphasizes 'Zhàn Zhuāng,' as reflected in the proverb: 'Practice 'Zhàn Zhuāng' before practicing martial art.' The rationale behind this emphasis lies in the fundamental principle that one's feet must be firmly rooted in the ground to prevent opponents from disrupting the stability of their actions, a crucial element for manifesting practical fighting skills.

'Zhàn Zhuāng,' often translated as 'standing exercise' or 'standing post' in English, constitutes a fundamental aspect of traditional Chinese Wushu.

'Zhàn' signifies standing, while 'Zhuāng' refers to pile or post. 'Zhàn Zhuāng' is a foundational training method that utilizes the art of remaining still to nurture and refine the practitioner's internal Qi, enhance physical strength, and fortify their fundamental forms of practice.

The 'Zhàn Zhuāng' practice encompasses diverse methodologies, typically categorized into two principal attributes: static and dynamic.

Static 'Zhàn Zhuāng': This form entails assuming and maintaining specific postures for extended periods, emphasizing a relaxed yet alert stance. It aims to cultivate inner strength, facilitate energy flow, and promote balance and coordination.

Dynamic 'Zhàn Zhuāng': This approach integrates subtle movements and shifts within static postures, allowing for a continuous flow of energy and the engagement of various muscle groups. Dynamic 'Zhàn Zhuāng' fosters physical and mental flexibility, endurance, and responsiveness.

These two attributes of 'Zhàn Zhuāng' provide practitioners with distinct pathways for harnessing their internal energy and physical strength. They serve as essential components of Chinese Wushu training, contributing to the development of martial skills and holistic physical and mental well-being.

What is meant by 'Dynamic Standing Post'?

The term 'Dynamic Standing Post' in the context of Chinese Wushu refers to a practice where practitioners maintain a standing posture while actively engaging the entire body with internal force. Despite the appearance of stillness, this practice involves utilizing power throughout the body and maintaining a consistent expansion of the chest. The primary goal is to facilitate the flow of Qi (energy) within the body. However, due to the emphasis on stretching the chest and using the entire body to exert force, directing Qi downward to the Lower Dantian (an energy center in the body) can be challenging, often requiring additional practice to effectively release any stagnant Qi.

In contrast, the 'Still Standing Post' focuses on achieving a state of movement within stillness. This approach aims to ensure the smooth circulation of Qi and blood throughout the body. The key method involves clearing the mind of distractions, maintaining an upright, comfortable, centered, and stable posture, and gradually attaining a tranquil state through relaxation and controlled breathing. The practice of the 'Still Standing Post' employs several common postures, each serving specific purposes in cultivating inner strength and promoting holistic well-being.

Wuji Stance: In this posture, the practitioner stands with feet shoulder-width apart, arms hanging naturally at the sides, or palms facing downward. The focus is on keeping the spine straight, relaxing the shoulders, and maintaining deep and even breathing. This posture is often a starting point for other standing postures (Figure 4.1).

Horse Stance: Horse Stance is a fundamental posture in various martial arts disciplines, including Kung Fu and Taichi Quan. It entails standing with the feet positioned wider than shoulder-width apart, with the toes pointing forward. The practitioner bends the knees and lowers the hips while maintaining a straight spine. The arms can be held out in front of the body or extended forward. This stance is highly beneficial for enhancing leg strength and promoting stability (Figure 4.2).

Golden Rooster Standing on One Leg: In this posture, the practitioner stands on one leg with the other leg lifted and bent at the knee, with the foot resting against the inner thigh of the standing leg. The arms are held to the sides to maintain balance. The focus is on steady, even breathing while holding the posture (Figure 4.3).

Figure 4.1　　　　　　　　Figure 4.2　　　　　　　　Figure 4.3

Overall, the 'Zhàn Zhuāng' practice is fundamental to Chinese Wushu training. It helps practitioners develop internal strength, enhance balance and stability, and cultivate a calm and focused mind.

Sì-Píng-Mǎ-Bù-Zhuāng
四平马步桩
Four-Level Horse Stance Standing Post

When translated, 'Sì-Píng-Mǎ-Bù-Zhuāng' is often rendered as 'Four-Level Horse Stance Standing Post.' However, this translation may not fully clarify the term's original meaning. In this translation, 'Sì' (四) represents four, 'Píng' (平) signifies level or flat, 'Mǎ' (馬) denotes horse, 'Bù' (步) represents stance, and 'Zhuāng' (椿) translates to standing post. In Chinese lexicons, 'Ping' typically conveys 'level or flat,' while also carrying connotations of serenity. As such, the term 'Four-Level Horse Stance Standing Post' encapsulates several essential aspects:

(1) Keep the **head** consistent with the ground (one Ping).
(2) Maintain level **shoulders**, ensuring they are parallel to the ground (two Ping).
(3) Sustain a flat position in the **thighs** (three Ping).
(4) Foster mental calmness to cultivate a tranquil **mind** (four Ping).

'Sì-Píng-Mǎ-Bù-Zhuāng' commonly referred to as 'Mǎ-Bù' or the 'Horse Stance,' serves as a foundational posture prevalent across various styles of Chinese Wushu. In combat scenarios, 'Mǎ-Bù' is a transitional stance, facilitating swift shifts to other stances. The stance commences with the feet positioned slightly wider than shoulder-width apart, parallel to each other, and pointing forward. The knees are flexed at a 90-degree angle, and the torso descends in alignment with a plumb line. The sacrum curves gently forward and inward, distributing weight evenly (50-50) between both feet, resulting in a highly stable stance. 'Mǎ-Bù' is frequently employed for conditioning and enhancing knee strength. Many Kung Fu instructors require students to sustain the 'Mǎ-Bù' position for at least five minutes before advancing to forms or routines (Figure 4.4). The detailed practice of this stance involves:

Horse Stance Post
Figure 4.4

Begin by assuming a straight standing position, your feet spaced wider than shoulder-width apart, approximately three times the width of your foot, with your toes pointing forward. Bend your knees and descend into a half-squat position, ensuring that your knees do not extend beyond your toes and that your thighs align almost parallel to the ground. Maintain both feet firmly planted on the floor while keeping your center of gravity between your legs. You can hold your fists at your waist or extend your left fist to the left.

This stance constitutes a fundamental component of any Chinese Wushu practitioner's training regimen. Failing to master the standard 'Four Levels Horse Stance Pile' could leave one vulnerable to an opponent's initial strike. As a venerable Wushu proverb advises, 'Practice Wushu without honing all the essential conditioning and skills (Gong), and you will end up with nothing' (練武不練功到老一場空). Crucial aspects to bear in mind when practicing the 'Four Levels Horse Stance Pile' encompass:

- Chest Expansion: Maintain an expanded chest.
- Upright Waist Posture: Keep an upright waist position.
- Hip Lowering: Lower the hips.
- Slight Forward Tilt: Incline slightly forward.
- Heel Alignment: Gently push the heels outward and keep them in contact with the ground.
- Knee Alignment: Ensure the knees don't turn inward.
- Breathing: Practice abdominal breathing throughout the exercise.

For beginners, it is advisable to start with practice sessions lasting 1 to 2 minutes and gradually increase the duration as proficiency develops.

Gōng-Bù-Zhuāng
弓步椿
Bow Stance Post

The 'Gōng-Bù,' also known as the 'Bow Stance,' is alternatively referred to as 'Dēng Shān Bù' (Mountain-Climbing Stance) or 'Gong Jian Bu' (Bow and Arrow Stance). In this posture, the front foot is directed straight ahead, forming a 90-degree bend in the front leg. The trailing foot is positioned at an outward angle of approximately 45 degrees, aligning the heel with that of the leading foot. While the trailing leg may be slightly bent in traditional practice, it must be fully extended in Contemporary Wushu, resulting in a 'Lunging' pose.

In the Long Fist category, the front toe is pointed forward, and weight distribution typically favors the front foot at around 70%, with 30% on the rear foot. Key focal points to remember during 'Gong Bu' practice include maintaining an upright torso, lowering the hips, ensuring stance stability, and ensuring that the knee of the leading leg remains positioned above the ankle (Figure 4.5).

In the context of martial arts applications, 'Gōng-Bù' is frequently employed for offensive maneuvers. The stance configuration offers partial protection to the groin while enabling martial artists to deliver powerful punches by driving the rear leg into the ground. Moreover, the back leg can be swiftly repositioned for kicking attacks. The detailed practice of this stance is as follows:

- Begin by stepping to the left with your left foot, maintaining a distance between your feet four to five times the length of your foot. Slightly angle your left toes inward, not exceeding 15 degrees, and bend your left knee until left thigh is nearly parallel to the ground. Ensure your left knee and toes align almost perpendicular to a straight line.
- Straighten your right knee and pivot your right toes inward, angling them towards the front at approximately 45 to 60 degrees. Confirm that both feet are firmly anchored to the ground.
- Gently lean your upper body slightly forward. When the left leg is bent, it forms the left bow stance, while bending the right leg creates the right bow stance. Alternate between these stances during your practice sessions.

Left Bow Stance   Right Bow Stance

Figure 4.5

Key Points:
(1) Maintain an extended chest, an erect waist, and lowered hips. Bend the front leg while keeping the back leg stretched, ensuring both feet align in a straight line. Ensure the back foot and heel remain firmly grounded.
(2) Maintain abdominal breathing consistently throughout your practice. For beginners, begin with 2 to 3-minute sessions and gradually extend the duration.
(3) Practice alternately with both the left and right legs to achieve balanced development and proficiency.

Xū - Bù-Zhuāng
虚步椿
Empty Stance Post

'Xū-Bù,' also known as the 'Empty Stance,' is a term commonly used in English to describe a stance in which all the weight is on the rear leg, used mainly in the category of 'Long Fist,' except for internal Kung Fu styles such as Taichi Quan, Xingyi Quan, and

Bagua Zhang. There should be little to no pressure on the front leg, allowing for quick kicking or attacking. This stance is often considered the most challenging and, therefore, the most valuable for building leg strength.

A common mistake when practicing the 'Empty Stance' is leaning forward at the hips to shift some weight onto the front leg. While the front foot should touch the ground with the heel up, lifting it should not affect the stance. The detailed practice method is:

- Stand straight with your feet shoulder-width apart. Step out with your right foot at a 45-degree angle and bend your right knee, lowering it into a half squat. Lift your left heel off the ground and pivot it inward slightly while keeping your toes on the ground.
- Shift your weight onto your back leg, keeping your front leg relaxed with minimal weight on it. Hold your fists at your waist or in a position depicted in the accompanying image (Figure 4.6).
- When you perform this stance on your right leg, it is called the left empty stance; when you perform it on your left leg, it is called the right empty stance. Practice alternating between the left and right empty stance.

| Left Empty Stance | Right Empty Stance |

Figure 4.6

Key Points:
(1) Keep your chest extended, waist straight, and your hips lowered.
(2) Distinguish between the real leg and empty leg.
(3) The practice time should depend on your physical condition.
(4) Ensure that there is no weight on your front foot when your toes touch the ground.

In conclusion, practicing the critical points of 'Zhàn - Zhuāng Gōng Fu' in Chinese Wushu involves focusing on the following aspects:

(1) Posture and Alignment: Maintain an upright and balanced posture. Ensure that your head is held high, your back is straight, and your shoulders are relaxed. Keep your chin slightly tucked in and your gaze forward. Your feet should be shoulder-width apart, and your weight should be evenly distributed between them.

(2) Foot Placement: Pay attention to the positioning of your feet. In many stances, the toes of one foot should align with the heel of the other, creating a stable base. Keep your feet flat on the ground and avoid lifting your heels.

(3) Knee Position: Bend your knees appropriately based on the specific stance you are practicing. Some stances require deep knee bends, while others involve shallower knee flexion. Ensure that your knees are aligned with your toes, and do not go beyond them. Be mindful of where your weight is distributed within the stance. In some stances, more weight may be on one leg than the other. Maintain a sense of balance and stability.

(4) Center of Gravity: Keep your center of gravity low and centered. This helps with balance and agility. Avoid leaning too far forward or backward.

(5) Hand and Arm Position: Depending on the stance, your hands and arms may have specific positions. They could be held in a guarding position, extended for balance, or placed on the waist. Pay attention to these details.

(6) Breathing: Practice controlled and steady breathing. Inhale and exhale smoothly, coordinating your breath with your movements. Proper breathing enhances your focus and energy.

(7) Muscle Engagement: Engage your core muscles to support your posture and stability. This also helps with power generation when transitioning from stances to movements.

(8) Transitions: Pay attention to how you transition between stances. Movements should be fluid and controlled. Avoid abrupt or jerky transitions.

(9) Practice and Repetition: Stance training in Chinese Wushu often involves holding positions for extended periods. Gradually increase the duration of your stance practice to build strength, endurance, and muscle memory.

(10) Balance and Flexibility: Work on improving your balance and flexibility, as these are crucial for maintaining stances and executing techniques precisely.

(11) Mental Focus: Maintain mental focus and concentration during stance practice. Visualize the correct alignment and posture, and use mindfulness to refine your technique.

Remember that mastering 'Zhàn - Zhuāng Gōng Fu' in Chinese Wushu requires patience and consistent practice. It's essential to start with a strong foundation in stances as they form the basis for more advanced movements and techniques in Wushu.

Part 2
Wushu Basic Technique
武術基本技術

Chinese Wushu exudes a captivating charm, captivating both native Chinese and foreigners, often shrouded in an air of mystique. If you aspire to learn Chinese Wushu, embarking on regular training in its fundamental skills and techniques is essential.

The practice of Chinese Wushu may initially seem intricate due to its demands for flexibility, speed, strength, stamina, and the execution of complex, combined movements. However, achieving these requirements hinges upon establishing a robust foundation in the basic techniques. Only with a solid grasp of these fundamentals can you advance and refine your skills, embodying the essence of the proverb 'sharpening the ax will not hinder the cutting of firewood' (磨刀不誤砍柴工). This proverb suggests that preparing and improving one's tools or skills is not a waste of time but rather an essential part of being effective and efficient in one's work. In other words, investing in preparation can lead to better results in the long run.

The repertoire of 'Basic Techniques' in Wushu encompasses training in both individual 'Basic Movements' and their seamless integration into 'Combined Movements.'

Chapter 5
Basic Movements (1)
Shǒu - Xíng - Shǒu - Fǎ
手型 手法
Hand Form and Hand Technique

'Basic Movements' are essential in various forms of Chinese Wushu, as they serve as the foundation of training. These movements are simple yet indispensable, acting as the building blocks for mastering more intricate techniques. In the Long Fist category, which includes 'Empty Hand Forms' and 'Weapons,' these components encompass hand forms, hand techniques, stances, footwork, leg techniques, balance, jumps, and tumbling. Subsequent sections will comprehensively introduce these fundamental movements, offering a detailed understanding of their significance and execution.

Shǒu Xíng or Hand Form

'Shǒu Xíng' translated as 'Hand Form,' also recognized as 'Hand Shape,' embodies a fundamental and intricate element within the realm of Chinese Wushu. It pertains to the various configurations achieved through the flexion and extension of the fingers, encompassing forms such as the fist, palm, hook, claw, and finger. Each 'Hand Form' has a distinct structure, functional attributes, and applications in offensive and defensive techniques.

Taoism, Buddhism, and classical philosophical thought have significantly influenced Chinese Wushu's 'Hand Form' development. Given the diversity of Wushu schools across China, the 'Hand Forms' associated with each school exhibit commonalities and distinctions. Consequently, the 'Hand Forms' terminology can vary from school to school.

Within the pages of this book, readers will be introduced to select 'Hand Form' belonging to the Chang Quan (Long Fist) tradition, offering insights into the rich and multifaceted world of Chinese Wushu.

1. Quán or Fist

'Quán' (拳), translated as the 'Fist,' is a fundamental element in Chinese Wushu and other martial arts. However, precision in 'Fist Techniques' is paramount in Chinese Wushu. The fist has multiple components, each with unique functions, including the fist eye, fist heart, fist face, fist back, and fist wheel. While Chinese Wushu offers numerous fist variations, this book will primarily use Chang Quan or Long Fist in English as an illustrative model.

Movements: To form a Long Fist's fist, begin with your palm extended, curl your four fingers inward, and fold your thumb over the second knuckle, positioning it between the index and middle fingers. Ensure that both the face and back of the fist remain flat.

The Long Fist tradition distinguishes various parts of the 'Fist,' including the fist-back, fist-face, fist-eye, fist-heart, and fist-wheel, as depicted in Figure 5.1.

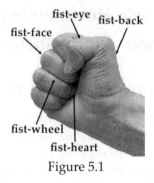

Figure 5.1

Furthermore, the orientation of the fist heart or center can be either upward or downward, which is referred to as a 'Horizontal Fist' (Figures 5.2 and 5.3). When the fist eye is directed upward or downward, it is termed a 'Vertical Fist' (Figures 5.4 and 5.5).

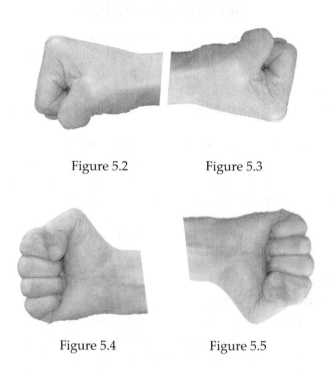

Figure 5.2   Figure 5.3

Figure 5.4   Figure 5.5

The diverse forms of 'Fist' formation serve as an asset, enriching the range of techniques and applications within the realm of Chinese Wushu. This style of 'Fist,' renowned for its capacity to harness and channel force throughout the entire body, resulting in substantial impact, undoubtedly offers distinct advantages. However, it has inherent limitations, particularly concerning its precision and efficiency in penetrating a target.

Key Points:

(1) Form your fist by clenching it with the thumb pressed firmly against the second knuckle between the index and middle fingers.

(2) Flatten the front of the fist to create a 'Square Fist,' ensuring a secure grip.

(3) Maintain a straight wrist to optimize the form and function of the fist.

Square Fist

Common Errors:

(1) Failing to flatten the front of the fist or holding it too loosely.

(2) Overextending or not extending the wrist enough.

(3) Neglecting to press the thumb against the second knuckle between the index and middle fingers.

In Competitive Wushu Competitions, deduction points may be applied for:

(1) Uneven formation of the fist.

(2) Failure to ensure that the thumb is pressing against the second knuckle of the middle finger.

2. Zhǎng or Palm

'Zhǎng' (掌), translated as the 'Palm,' holds a significant place in Chinese Wushu, distinguishing it from Western Martial Arts, where palm techniques are seldom utilized. This contrast underscores one of the fundamental disparities between Chinese Wushu and Western boxing. In Chinese Wushu, diverse palm shapes are employed, each designed for specific functions, along with inherent limitations. The crucial element lies in the practitioner's adeptness at applying these shapes with flexibility. Examples include the 'four flats palm' (四平掌), 'willow-leaf palm' (柳葉掌), 'five flowers palm' (五花掌), 'eight-character palm' (八字掌), 'dragon-shape palm' (龍形掌), 'tiger claw,' 'eagle claw,' 'mantis claw,' monkey claw,' and many more. This discussion in the book will exclusively delve into the 'Willow-Leaf Palm' within the Long Fist style.

The 'Willow-Leaf Palm' is one of Chinese Wushu's most frequently employed palm-form techniques. It derives its name from its shape, resembling a willow leaf, and is recognized for its fluid and adaptable movements. In the traditional style, the palm has a slight curvature, and the fingers maintain a little distance from each other. However, in Contemporary Competition Wushu routines, the palm should be fully extended, with all fingers together. This technique mainly targets the opponent's ribs, chest, and abdomen.

Movement 1: Begin by extending and aligning all four fingers, then inwardly bend the knuckle of your thumb. Subsequently, rotate your wrist inward and point your fingers upwards; this position is called the 'Vertical' or 'Stand Palm' (Figure 5.6).

Movement 2: Transition by straightening your wrist, ensuring the thumb side and arm form a straight line. This posture is known as the 'Straight Palm' (Figure 5.7).

To execute the 'Horizontal Palm,' tilt your wrist inward, guiding the thumb toward your body, with the palm facing downward. At the same time, position the side of your little finger forward, ensuring that your fingertips point to the left side (or right side if using the left palm as an example) (Figure 5.8).

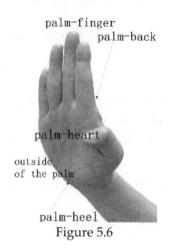

Figure 5.6

Figure 5.7   Figure 5.8

The palm comprises several distinct parts, including the palm-tip, palm-finger, palm-back, palm-heart, palm-heel, and outer palm. Each element plays a crucial role in the execution and versatility of 'Palm Techniques' in Chinese Wushu.

Key Points:
(1) Ensure that the palm and fingers are extended backward, resembling the shape of a willow leaf.
(2) Maintain flexibility in the wrist throughout the movement.

Common Errors:
(1) Failing to keep the index finger, middle finger, ring finger, and little finger held together.
(2) Allowing the index finger, middle finger, ring finger, and little finger to remain not completely straight.

In Competitive Wushu' Competitions, deductions may be applied to the 'Willow-Leaf Palm' for:

(1) Fingers not being entirely straight and held together.
(2) The thumb is not being bent and held securely.

3. Gōu or Hook

'Gōu' (勾) translated as the 'Hook,' often called the 'Hook Hand,' is one of the three fundamentals 'Hand Forms' in Chinese Wushu. It encompasses variations such as the five-finger hook, three-finger hook, two-finger hook, and crane-mouth hand. In practical combat scenarios, the 'Hook' primarily serves for blocking, striking with the hook tip, rotation, and wrist manipulation to facilitate offensive and defensive maneuvers. In this book, we will focus on the 'five-finger hook' within the framework of the Long Fist style.

Movements: To execute the 'five-finger hook,' bend your wrist downward while tightly combining all five fingers. The hook-tip should be directed downward, consisting of both a hook-top and a hook-tip (Figure 5.9).

hook-top

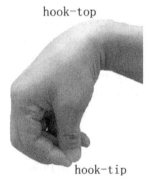

hook-tip

Figure 5.9

Common Errors:

(1) Failing to securely combine the fingers, resulting in a weak hook shape.
(2) Maintaining excessive stiffness in the wrist, which can adversely affect the flexibility and power of the hook hand.

In Competitive Wushu Competitions, deduction points may be applied for:

(1) The five fingers are not held tightly together.
(2) The wrist is not completely hooked.

These are just a few examples of Chinese Wushu's many 'Hand Forms' and variations. Each 'Hand Form' is carefully designed to serve specific purposes and techniques within the martial arts, emphasizing precision, control, and effectiveness in combat or performance.

Shǒu Fǎ or Hand Technique

'Shǒu Fǎ' (手法), translated as 'Hand Technique' in English, constitutes a fundamental element of Chinese Wushu. It encompasses an array of striking methods, such as punches, pushes, chops, and finger strikes, representing indispensable skills for every Wushu practitioner. 'Hand Technique' is broadly classified into four main groups: 'Fist Technique,' 'Palm Technique,' 'Hook Technique,' and 'Claw Technique,' each possessing distinct characteristics and applications.

The proper execution of the 'Hand Technique' relies on sound body mechanics. This includes maintaining the correct posture, distributing weight effectively, positioning the hands accurately, generating power efficiently, and ensuring precise targeting. For example, when performing a basic punch, the fist should be clenched securely with the thumb on top. The punch should be executed with explosive power generated from the legs and hips, transmitted through the torso and arm. It should travel straight, with the arm fully extended and the elbow locked. Ideally, the point of impact should be the fist's first two knuckles, often referred to as the fist face.

In addition to precise technique execution, 'Hand Techniques' in Chinese Wushu demand focus, speed, and accuracy. Practitioners must concentrate on their target, mentally visualizing the strike passing through it while executing the technique swiftly and precisely. As a result, dedicated practice and a keen focus on the technical nuances are essential for achieving mastery of 'Hand Technique' in Chinese Wushu. In the following sections, the author will introduce readers to fundamental 'Hand Technique' in Chang Quan or Long Fist.

1. Chòng Quán or Punch

'Chòng Quán' (衝拳), translated as 'Punch' or 'Punch the Fist,' represents a fundamental striking technique within Chinese Wushu. It involves a rotational strike initiated from the waist, emphasizing the use of the knuckles. This technique is primarily employed for offensive purposes and can be executed in various orientations, such as a 'Horizontal Punch' with the fist-heart facing downward (Figure 5.10) or a 'Vertical Punch' with the fist-eye pointing upward (Figure 5.11).

Figure 5.10   Figure 5.11

Practice Methods (using the right fist as an example):

Preparation Posture: Begin by standing straight with your feet spaced shoulder-width apart. Position your fists at your waists, orienting the hearts of your fists upward, and have your elbows directed backward. Maintain your gaze forward (Figure 5.12).

Movements: Utilize the fist-face as the force point. Initiate the action by inwardly rotating your right arm from the waist. Execute a straight punch directly forward, impacting with your knuckles. Ensure your right arm is fully extended at shoulder height and slightly pull back your left elbow (Figure 5.13, 5.14 for the horizontal punch with right fist and left).

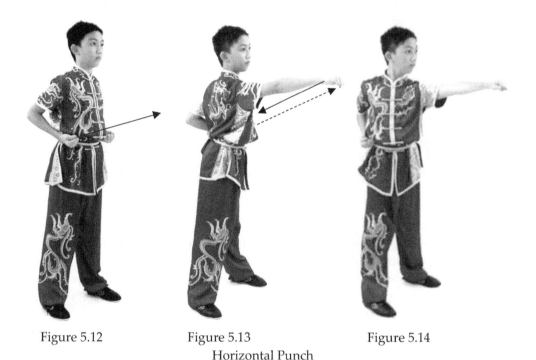

| Figure 5.12 | Figure 5.13 | Figure 5.14 |

Horizontal Punch

- **Force Point:** The point of force is situated at the initial two knuckles of the fist, delivering the strike with the fist face.
- **Action Orbit:** The punch traces a force direct and unobstructed path from its starting position to the intended target.
- **Direction:** The direction of the punch can vary, whether it's aimed forward, upward, downward, left, or right, depending on the specific target or objective.
- **Starting and Ending Point:** The punch commences its motion from the waist and culminates at the moment of impact with the target.

During practice, focus on your fist used for punching or keep your gaze straight ahead. Alternate between performing 'Horizontal and Vertical Punches' (Figure 5.15, 5.16).

Figure 5.15   Figure 5.16

Vertical Punch

Key Points:

(1) Maintain proper posture with a straight chest, an upright waist, and engage your abdomen by tucking it in to establish a stable foundation.

(2) Generate explosive and spiraling power starting from your legs and hips, and then transmit it through your torso and arm to execute the punch swiftly and effectively.

(3) Tightly grasp your fists and ensure the first two knuckles align with the wrist to avoid injury. Twist your waist, push your right (or left) shoulder slightly forward, and rotate your right (or left) forearm inward while punching. Avoid swinging your lower limbs or shaking your body.

(4) Ensure that the horizontal and vertical fists form a square shape with a flat face, back, and wheel of the fist.

(5) Throw the punch in a straight line. Fully extend the arm. Lock the elbow to maximize power and accuracy.

(6) Inhale during the preparation phase and exhale forcefully during the punch to increase power and maintain focus.

(7) Concentrate on the target and maintain eye contact throughout the punch to improve accuracy and effectiveness.

(8) Repeat the punch to enhance accuracy, speed, and power. Incorporate it into various combinations and techniques but prioritize proper form and technique over speed. Avoid rushing through the movements.

Common Errors and Corrections:
(1) Incorrect Fist Position: The fist should be aligned with the wrist and forearm, and the first two knuckles should be slightly protruding. Avoid shrugging the shoulders and lifting the elbow, as this can cause strain and reduce power.
(2) Insufficient Rotation: The punch should originate from the waist and incorporate a swift rotation at the end. A common mistake is punching in a straight line without proper rotation, which can diminish both power and accuracy.
(3) Over-Extension: Avoid over-extending the arm at the end of the punch, which involves pushing your shoulder too far forward. Be cautious not to hyperextend, as this can strain the elbow joint, reduce power, and lose balance.
(4) Lack of Power Generation: The power for the straight punch should come from the body's rotation and the weight transfer from the back foot to the front foot. Avoid relying solely on arm strength, resulting in a weak punch. Also, avoid punching too slowly, which can cause the force point to be suboptimal on the fist.
(5) Lack of Focus: The practitioner should focus on the target and visualize punching through it. Avoid losing focus or looking away before the punch is completed, as this can result in a weak or inaccurate punch.

2. Tuī Zhǎng or Push with the Palm

'Tuī Zhǎng' (推掌) translated as 'Push Palm' or 'Pushing with the Palm,' typically entails using the heel of the hand with the wrist settled down, fingers vertical, and the palm facing diagonally forward. This action is primarily employed for offensive purposes.

Practice Methods (using the right palm as an example):

Preparation Posture: Begin by standing upright with your feet positioned shoulder-width apart. Place your palms on your waists with your palms facing upward. Your elbows should point backward and maintain a straight gaze ahead (Figure 5.17).

Movements: Begin by bending your right elbow, using the outside of your right little finger as the force point. Simultaneously, initiate an inward rotation of your right arm from your waist. Push your right hand forward in a straight line, directing it in front of your nose. After pushing, ensure that your right arm reaches shoulder height, with your fingers pointing upwards and the wrist kept stable. While executing the push, gently draw your left elbow backward and slightly advance your right shoulder to generate the opposite power for the push (Figure 5.18).

Maintain a forward gaze or concentrate your mental focus on the palm you are pushing with, alternating between hands during practice (Figure 5.19).

Important Notes: When executing the push, utilize your waist as the central axis. The power originates from your feet, flows through your legs, engages your waist, transfers to your right (or left) shoulder, continues down to your right (or left) elbow, wrist, and ultimately manifests in your palm. Avoid loosening your knees or swaying your body in the movement. Keep your body aligned and unified, maintaining a sense of oneness.

| Figure 5.17 | Figure 5.18 | Figure 5.19 |

- **Force Point**: The force point is situated at the heel of the right palm, emphasizing a short and explosive inch-force (寸勁) technique.
- **Action Orbit:** The action orbit adheres to a direct, linear path directed towards the designated target.
- **Direction:** The direction of the push may vary depending on the circumstances, encompassing forward, downward, left, or right, as dictated by the situation.
- **Starting and Ending Point:** This technique should be initiated from the waist, with the movement culminating at the precise point of impact with the intended target.

Key Points:

(1) Maintain a proper posture with a straight back and eyes looking forward. Keep your chest straight, tuck in your abdomen, and settle your waist. The palm should be straight, and the fingers vertical.

(2) Push with spiral power and maintain a fast pace. Tighten your palm, rotate your waist, push your shoulder slightly forward, and extend your elbow.

(3) Use your waist as an axis to generate power from your feet through your legs to your waist and finally to your palm. Keep your knees steady and do not swing your body while pushing.

(4) Aim for the heel of your palm with an inch force, a short explosive force, when hitting the target.

(5) Proper breathing is essential for generating power and maintaining focus. Inhale deeply before the push and exhale forcefully during the execution.

(6) The body should be relaxed, with tension only in the arms and waist in the execution.

(7) Consistent practice is essential for developing proper technique, power, and accuracy in push palm.

Common Errors and Corrections:

(1) Improper posture by failing to keep the chest straight, abdomen tucked in, and waist settled.

(2) Failure to use the waist as the axis for generating power when pushing with spiral force at a fast pace.

(3) Not tightening the palm, rotating the waist, pushing the shoulder slightly forward, and bending the elbow during the push.

(4) Swinging lower limbs or shaking the body while pushing, which can lead to a loss of power and balance.

(5) Not aiming for the inch force at the heel of the palm, which is essential for delivering a short explosive force and hitting the target accurately.

(6) Not hitting at the same point (in front of the nose) with both left and right pushes, which can impact the consistency and effectiveness of the technique.

(7) Failing to keep the palm straight and the fingers vertical, including forming the vertical side palm when applicable (Figure 5.20).

Vertical Side Plam	Palm Faces Fully Forward	Side Palm
Correct Shape	Incorrect Shape	Incorrect Shape
	Figure 5.20	

3. Pī Quán or Split with a Fist

'Pī Quán' (劈拳), translated as 'Split Fist,' also known as 'Split with a Fist' or 'Split with a Hammer' in English, is an offensive technique where you extend your arm and utilize the fist heel or 'fist wheel' as the point of force to execute a top-to-bottom split swiftly.

Practice Methods (using the right fist as an example):

Preparation Posture: Begin by standing upright with your feet positioned shoulder-width apart. Raise your right fist above your head with the fist face pointing upwards. Straighten your right arm and maintain a forward gaze (Figure 5.21).

Movements: Utilize the fist wheel on the right wrist's side as the focal point for force. Execute a rapid vertical split motion from top to bottom with your arm held straight. Ensure your gaze remains fixed on the target (Figure 5.22). Practice by alternating between left and right fists.

Figure 5.21   Figure 5.22

- **Force Point:** Concentrate on delivering a brief, explosive force precisely at the fist wheel on the side of your wrist.
- **Action Orbit:** The motion follows a circular path.
- **Direction:** The direction of the Pi Fist can be directed downward, to the left, or the right, contingent upon the intended target.
- **Starting and Ending Point:** Initiate the strike from an elevated position above and conclude it at the target.

Key Points:

(1) Ensure your arm remains straight and your body maintains stability throughout the execution of the 'Split Fist.'

(2) The power is from your feet, through your legs, into your waist, and ultimately into your fist. This sequential power transfer is vital for an effective strike.

(3) Target the fist wheel as your focal point for force and aim to deliver a short, explosive burst of power at this location.

(4) Maintain unwavering focus on your intended target throughout the entire execution of the 'Split Fist.' This is essential for accuracy and effectiveness.

Common Errors and Corrections:

(1) Elbow Bend and Shoulder Shrugging: A common mistake is bending the elbow and elevating the shoulders while executing the fist split. This can significantly diminish the effectiveness of the technique, as it disrupts the power and accuracy of the strike.

(2) Insufficient Power Generation: Failing to generate power from the feet, through the legs, into the waist, and ultimately to the fist results in a weak and ineffective strike. Proper power generation is critical for the technique's success.

(3) Neglecting the Fist Wheel Force Point: Not utilizing the fist wheel as the focal point for force or neglecting to target the short, explosive force at the fist wheel can lead to reduced impact and accuracy in the strike.

(4) Body or Arm Swinging: Swinging the body or arm while executing the Pi Fist can result in a loss of balance and power, making the technique less effective. It's crucial to maintain stability during the strike.

(5) Incorrect Fist and Arm Position: Failing to keep the fist facing upwards and the arm fully extended and straight can weaken the strike and compromise accuracy. Proper positioning of the fist and arm is essential for delivering a powerful and precise Pi Fist.

When practicing the 'Swing Split with the Fist' technique, it's important to perform a full vertical circle motion with your arm, mimicking the rotation of a wheel before executing the splitting action.

Movements:

Begin by positioning your right fist on the left side, with the fist-eye facing upwards. Straighten your right arm and focus your gaze on your right fist (Figure 5.23).

Then, inwardly rotate your right arm and initiate a swinging motion of your right fist from the left, moving it upwards, passing through the head region, and eventually splitting towards the right side of your body. Maintain your fist at shoulder height and keep the fist-eye facing upwards throughout this motion. Direct your gaze towards the right (Figure 5.24, 5.25).

This movement is known as a 'Swing Split on the right.' Practice by alternating between the left and right sides to develop your proficiency in this technique.

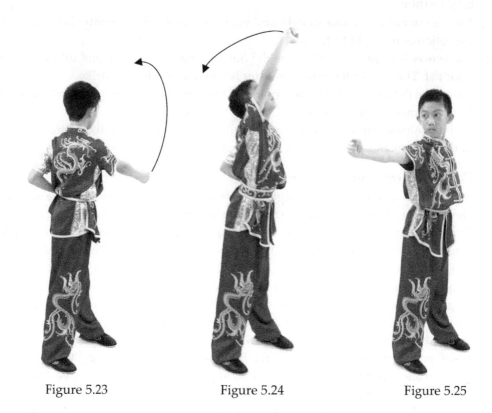

| Figure 5.23 | Figure 5.24 | Figure 5.25 |

Key Points:

(1) Maintain a straight arm and ensure the fist-eye faces upwards before commencing the swing.
(2) Initiate the swing and split motion by inwardly rotating the arm.
(3) Throughout the technique, perform a full vertical circle with the arm.
(4) After the split, keep the fist at shoulder height.
(5) Look in the direction of the split to ensure proper execution.

Common Errors:

(1) Arm Misalignment: Failing to keep the arm straight or the fist-eye facing upwards before initiating the swing.
(2) Lack of Arm Rotation: Not rotating the arm inward before commencing the swing and split motion.
(3) Incomplete Circle: Failing to complete a vertical circle with the arm before splitting or bending the splitting elbow.
(4) Incorrect Splitting Height: Splitting at a height different from shoulder height can affect the technique's effectiveness.
(5) Wrong Gaze Direction: Looking in the wrong direction during the split can lead to inaccuracies in the execution of the technique.

4. Pī Zhǎng or Split with the Palm (劈掌)

Movements: The movement for 'Pī Zhǎng' (劈掌) is identical to 'Pi Quan.' Simply transition from a fist to an open palm (Figure 5.26 and 5.27).

Figure 5.26   Figure 5.27

'Swinging Arm and Split with the Palm' is a technique similar to the 'Swing Split with the Fist,' with the main distinction being the use of an open palm instead of a closed fist (Figure 5.28, 5.29, 5.30). Here are the key points and common errors for practicing this technique:

Key Points:
(1) Keep your back straight and your shoulders relaxed throughout the movement.
(2) Employ your waist as a pivotal axis to generate power, transmitting it from your feet through your legs, controlled by your waist, and ultimately expressed to your palm.
(3) Maintain the correct hand form and ensure yourfive fingers are tightly combined.
(4) Execute a circular arm motion, aiming for a rapid and explosive split with your open palm.

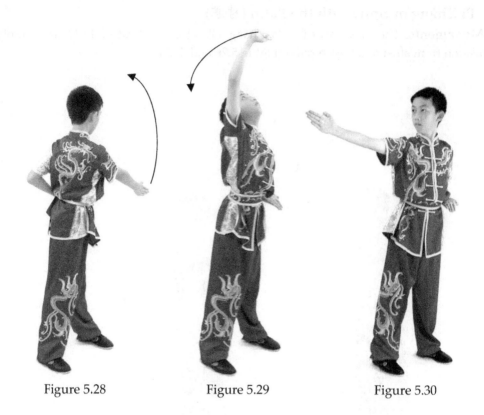

Figure 5.28   Figure 5.29   Figure 5.30

Common Errors and Corrections:
(1) Poor Posture or Neglecting Waist Engagement: Avoid the error of failing to maintain proper posture or neglecting to use your waist as the central axis for power generation.
(2) Slow or Weak Split: Steer clear of performing the split with your palm at a slow or feeble pace. Focus on making it fast and explosive.
(3) Lax Palm Grip or Incorrect Hand Form: Ensure that your palm remains tightly gripped and that you maintain proper hand form. Avoid any relaxation of the palm during the technique.
(4) Lack of Circular Arm Motion: Do not skip the circular arm motion; ensure your arm moves in a circular path. Additionally, aim for a swift and forceful split with your open palm.

5. Zāi Quán or Planting the Fist

'Zāi Quán' (栽拳) also known as 'Planting the Fist' in English, involves a downward punch with the knuckles of the fist striking low. In contrast to conventional punches, which typically involve bending the arm and inward rotation, the 'Zāi Quán,' employs the fist-face as the focal point for force. It generates power through a spiraling strike from top to bottom, primarily serving as an offensive technique.

Practice Methods (using the left fist as an example):

Preparation Posture: Start by standing upright with your feet slightly wider than your shoulders. Elevate your left palm over your head, positioning the palm to face right, while placing your right fist alongside your body. Maintain a forward gaze (Figure 5.31).

Movements: Hold your left fist and inwardly rotate your left forearm, orienting your fist with the face turned downwards. Punch downward in a straight line toward your left knee with the knuckles of your fist, ensuring that your fist remains tightly clenched. Keep the fist-eye inward in the punch (this is left 'Zāi Quán). Concurrently, raise your right fist above your head, bend your right elbow, and hold the fist-heart up diagonally. Direct your gaze to the left (Figure 5.32). Practice by alternating between left and right fists.

- **Force Point:** The force point for the planting fist punch is at the face of the left fist.
- **Action Orbit:** The movement follows an arch shape.
- **Direction:** The punch is executed in a downward direction.
- **Starting and Ending Point:** The punch begins from the top and ends at the bottom.

Figure 5.31	Figure 5.32

Key Points:

(1) 'Zāi Quán,' employs a downward punch, with the knuckles of the fist striking low. It utilizes a spiral strike from top to bottom, with the fist-face serving as the force point.

(2) Execute the punch along an inner circular path, incorporating a downward drilling force. Maintain a slight bend in the elbow after delivering the punch.

(3) Ensure that your posture remains correct and stable throughout the entire movement.

Common Errors and Corrections

(1) Missing Downward Drilling Force: Ensure that you generate the necessary downward drilling force in the punch to maintain its effectiveness.

(2) Lack of Arm Rotation and Incorrect Force Point: Avoid the error of not inwardly rotating the arm and neglecting to utilize the fist-face as the force point. These are crucial elements of the Zai Fist technique.

(3) Overextension of the Elbow: Be cautious not to overextend the elbow during the punch, as this can compromise both power and technique.

6. Liāo Quán or Uppercut the Fist

The 'Liāo Quán' (撩拳), also referred to as the 'Uppercut the Fist' in English, is a martial arts technique characterized by the straightening of the arm and the utilization of the fist-eye as the primary force point. This technique entails a swinging motion either directly forward or diagonally upwards from a lower position. In the case of a reverse 'Liāo Quán' the force point can be the fist-heel, fist-back, or fist-heart. The term 'Liāo' originally denotes the action of lifting something hanging, such as curtains or the hem of a skirt. The 'Liāo Quán' technique imitates this action by employing an arm motion that resembles slicing upward with the arm held relatively straight. This technique is typically employed as an offensive maneuver in Chinese Wushu.

Practice Methods (using the right fist as an example):

Preparation Posture: Assume a high left bow stance with your right fist positioned behind your body. Place your left fist on your left waist. Direct your gaze towards your right fist (Figure 5.33).

Movements: Straighten your right arm, employing the side of your right thumb as the focal point for force. Engage in a circular motion, swinging either directly forward or diagonally upward from a lower position. Maintain your gaze on your right fist or keep it fixed straight ahead (Figure 5.34). Practice alternately between left and right.

Besides utilizing the fist-eye as the primary force point, the 'Liāo Quán' technique can also be performed using alternative force points, including the fist-heart and fist-back, or by inwardly rotating the right fist and employing the fist wheel as the focal point for force.

- **Force Point:** Positioned at the right palm-eye.
- **Action Orbit:** Progresses along an arched trajectory.
- **Direction:** Advances forward.
- **Starting and Ending Point:** Commences at the rearward position and culminates at the forward position.

108

Figure 5.33   Figure 5.34

Key Points:

(1) The Liao Quan involves a swinging motion of the arm, directed either directly forward or diagonally from a lower position. The primary force point is the fist-eye. For the reverse Liao Quan, alternative force points such as the fist-heel, fist-back, or fist-heart can be used.

(2) Engage your waist to generate power and facilitate the forward motion of your arm.

(3) Employ both your fist and forearm in the execution of the uppercut. Maintain proper form and posture throughout the entire movement.

Common Errors and Corrections:

(1) Elbow Bend and Wrong Force Point: Avoid the error of bending the elbow and using an incorrect force point. Proper technique relies on keeping the arm relatively straight and using the designated force point.

(2) Lack of Muscle Engagement: Ensure that you engage your muscles and not rely solely on the arm or fist to execute the technique. The power generated should involve the whole body, with the waist playing a crucial role.

(3) Incorrect Arm Motion: Practice the correct arm motion and direction, as incorrect arm movement can lead to inaccuracies in the technique.

(4) Improper Form and Posture: Maintain proper form and posture throughout the entire duration of the movement. Neglecting this aspect can affect the effectiveness of the technique.

7. Liāo Zhǎng or Uppercut the Palm

The 'Liāo Zhǎng' (撩掌), employs the same motion as the 'Liāo Quán,' However, instead of using a closed fist, employ an open palm and execute the same swinging motion, either directly forward or diagonally from a lower position. The force point must be precise, and the power should be generated from your waist to propel your arm forward. This technique is also primarily employed for offensive purposes.

Key Points:

(1) Ensure that you do not bend your arm during the execution of the 'Liāo Zhǎng' and focus on achieving precision with the force point.
(2) Utilize your waist to propel your arm forward, transferring power from the core to the extremity.
(3) Avoid relying solely on the palm or forearm to execute the 'Liāo Zhǎng.' The entire arm should be engaged in the movement.

Common Errors and Corrections:

(1) Arm Bending and Inaccurate Force Point: One common error is bending the arm, leading to an inaccurate force point. Ensure that your arm remains straight.
(2) Overreliance on Palm or Forearm: Do not solely rely on the palm or forearm to execute the movement, as this can reduce power and effectiveness. Engage the entire arm for maximum impact.

8. Tiǎo Quán or Pick the Fist Up

In the Long Fist, the 'Tiǎo Quán' (挑拳), also recognized as the 'Pick Up Fist' or 'Flick Up Fist' in English, is a Wushu technique performed by slightly bending your right (left) arm and utilizing the right fist-eye (left fist-eye) as the force point. The motion involves a circular movement where you swing forward or upward from a lower position to the top. The term ' Tiǎo' originates from lifting something with a stick, such as hanging a lantern from the end of a pole or pushing a bale of hay up to a hayrack using the end of a pitchfork. In the Long Fist, this technique mimics the action of a lifting arm flicking the wrist at the culmination of the movement. The 'Tiǎo Quán,' is predominantly employed as an offensive maneuver in martial arts.

Practice Methods (using the right fist as an example):

Preparation Posture: Start by assuming a high left bow stance, with your arms extended forward and backward. Ensure that your thumbs point upward, and your gaze is directed at your left hand in preparation (Figure 5.35).

Movements: Initiate the movement by pivoting your left toes outward at a 45-degree angle. Shift your body weight forward and step with your right foot, forming a right empty stance. Simultaneously, execute a circular motion with your right arm and fist, directing it downward towards the front. As your right fist approaches your right hip and the front of your body, flick your wrist upward and bend your elbow. Deliver a precise strike with your right fist, targeting your opponent's chin or groin, with your fist-eye as the force point. Maintain a forward gaze throughout the execution of the technique (Figure 5.36). Repeat the sequence alternately to enhance proficiency and effectiveness in executing the Tiao Fist technique.

Figure 5.35   Figure 5.36

- **Force Point:** The focal point for the Tiao Quan is situated at the right fist-eye.
- **Action Orbit:** Execution of the strike should adhere to a circular trajectory.
- **Direction:** The strike is directed forward, targeting the intended opponent or target.
- **Starting and Ending Point:** Commencing either from the rear or a lower position, the strike progresses forward toward the designated target.

Key Points:
(1) Enhance the power of your strike by flipping your fist upward and slightly bending your elbow during execution.
(2) Maintain an angle of at least 90 degrees between your upper arm and forearm to generate maximum tension and power.

Common Errors:
(1) Incorrect Wrist Movement: Avoid the mistake of flicking your wrist inward from bottom to top during the technique.
(2) Force Point Accuracy: Ensure that the force point remains precisely on the fist-eye to achieve effective results.
(3) Angle Neglect: Be attentive to the angle between your arm and forearm, ensuring it is not less than 90 degrees to optimize the technique's power and efficiency.

9. Gài Quán or Covering the Fist

In Chinese Wushu, 'Gài Quán' (蓋拳), translated as 'Covering the Fist' or 'Lid Fist,' is a close-range hand technique. It involves employing one hand to cover or shield against an opponent's attack while simultaneously using the other to deliver a strike. This technique can be executed in various ways, including using the forearm, hand, or elbow as a shield while the fist is utilized for striking. Depending on the specific circumstances, the striking hand can target various areas of the opponent's body, such as the head, chest, or lower body. 'Gài Quán' is often seamlessly integrated with other techniques to create a continuous flow of attacks and defenses. It necessitates practical hand and body coordination and is commonly employed in close-range combat scenarios.

Practice Methods (using the right fist as an example):

Preparation Posture: Begin by standing upright with your feet shoulder-width apart. Hold your right fist closer your abdomen or chest while placing your left palm in front of your chest. Ensure that your left fingers are pointing towards the right side with your palm facing downwards. Imagine covering your opponent's attack with your left palm or the inner side of your left forearm, with your right fist hidden behind your left arm, ready to retaliate. Keep your gaze straight ahead (Figure 5.37).

Movements: To execute the technique, employ your right fist-back as the force point. Move it from your abdomen, extending it through your face, and then strike forward or downward in front of you (Figure 5.38). Simultaneously, slightly press your left palm down, mimicking the act of neutralizing your opponent's attack, before delivering your strike. Repeat the sequence alternately while practicing.

Figure 5.37   Figure 5.38

- **Force Point:** The focal point for the Gai Fist technique is positioned at the right fist-back.
- **Action Orbit:** Execution of the Gai Fist technique follows a circular trajectory.
- **Direction:** The strike should move from the inside towards the outside.
- **Starting and Ending Point:** The initiation of the strike begins at the chest region, and its culmination is the intended target area.

Key Points:

(1) The accuracy of the force point is of utmost importance when executing the 'Gài Quán' technique. Utilize your elbow as an axis and ensure a flip action during the strike for maximum effectiveness.

(2) 'Gài Quán' is typically employed in conjunction with another hand technique. Ensure that both hands are harmoniously coordinated with each other to achieve the highest level of effectiveness.

Common Errors and Corrections:

(1) Incorrect Hand Positioning: One common mistake involves placing the covering hand too high or too low, leaving vulnerable areas of the body exposed to potential attacks. Proper positioning of the covering hand is crucial to effectively shield against an opponent's attack.

(2) Lack of Coordination: 'Gài Quán' demands coordination between both hands and the body. A common error is overemphasizing one hand over the other, resulting in an unbalanced or less effective technique. Achieving balance and coordination between the hands and body is essential for success.

10. Lǒu Shǒu or Brush the Hand

The 'Lǒu Shǒu' (搂手) translated as the 'Brush the Hand,' is a Wushu movement involving a circular brushing motion with one hand to deflect an opponent's arm from inside to outside. The technique's name is derived from the traditional method of harvesting wheat or rice, where one hand holds the bundle of grain while the other uses a sickle to cut it from the root. This technique can be used both defensively and offensively in Wushu practice.

Practice Methods (using the left hand as an example):

Preparation Posture: Begin by making a right bow stance and placing your left palm in front of your right shoulder with your palm facing outward. Hold your right fist at your right waist and look at your left hand (Figure 5.39).

Movements: Squat down completely to form a left 'Crouch Stance,' ensuring you have a firmly stable root. Simultaneously, turn your upper body to the left. Slightly move your left palm close to your right shoulder (Figure 5.40). Then, use the outside of your left forearm and palm as the force point and circle it outside diagonally towards your left foot, creating a semicircular motion (Figures 5.41).

Figure 5.39

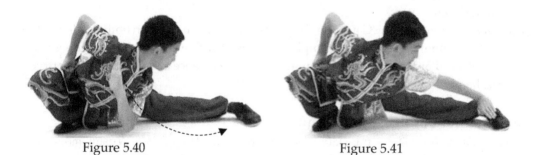

Figure 5.40   Figure 5.41

Keep your gaze fixed on your left palm as you turn. Utilize internal force as you brush your hand. Repeat the movement on the opposite side and alternate between both sides. This technique encompasses both defensive and evasive aspects, allowing you to redirect an opponent's attack while simultaneously preparing for a counterattack.

- **Force Point:** The force point for this technique is located at the outside of your left forearm and left palm. This is where you generate the force to deflect your opponent's arm.
- **Action Orbit:** The movement follows a semicircular line, which means it's a half-circle motion.
- **Direction:** The technique involves moving from right to left or from the inside to the outside. This movement is used to deflect the opponent's arm.
- **Starting and Ending Point:** The motion starts from the front of your shoulder and ends at your left foot.

Key Points:

(1) Utilize the outside of your left forearm and palm as the force point while brushing your hand.

(2) Execute a precise semicircular motion with your arm like hold the wheat before sickling it.

(3) Maintain your focus on your left palm throughout the movement.

Common Errors and Corrections:

(1) Using the Incorrect Force Point: One common error is not using the correct force point. It's essential to use the outside of your left forearm and palm as the force point to effectively deflect the opponent's attack.

(2) Creating a Circular Motion: Another mistake to avoid is creating a circular motion instead of a semicircular one. The technique should follow a half-circle path for optimal effectiveness.

(3) Losing Focus on the **Left Palm**: It's crucial to maintain your gaze on your left palm throughout the technique. Losing focus on your palm can lead to errors in execution.

11. Chuān Zhǎng or Threading Palm or Penetrating Palm

'Chuān Zhǎng' (穿掌) translated as 'Threading Palm' or 'Penetrating Palm' in English, is a technique that involves extending the arm to deliver a strike using the fingers, either passing over or under the leading arm. The palm can be positioned in various ways, including upwards, downwards, angled, or sideways. A proverb aptly describes this technique: 'penetrating palm strikes like a meteor.' It is primarily employed as an offensive maneuver in martial arts.

Practice Methods:

Preparation Posture: To begin practicing the 'Penetrating Palm' technique, start in a standing position with your right foot positioned in front. Place your right palm on your right waist, with the palm facing upward. Simultaneously, hold your left hand in front of your body, with a slight bend in the elbow. Orient your left fingers to point diagonally to the right, with the palm facing outward (Figure 5.42). You are now ready to proceed.

Movement 1 (Upward Thrust the Right Palm - 'Swallow Passes Through the Forest'):

Begin by utilizing your right finger as the point of force. Extend your right hand forward, passing it either over or under your left wrist. Simultaneously, raise your left knee in front of your body to protect your groin area. This dynamic motion imitates an upward movement, resembling the execution of a penetrating palm thrust aimed at your opponent's throat. The left hand serves a defensive purpose, pressing or covering against your opponent's attack while concealing your right hand behind it (Figure 5.43).

This technique is often referred to as 'Swallow Passes through the Forest.' After completing this movement, shift your focus to your right palm.

115

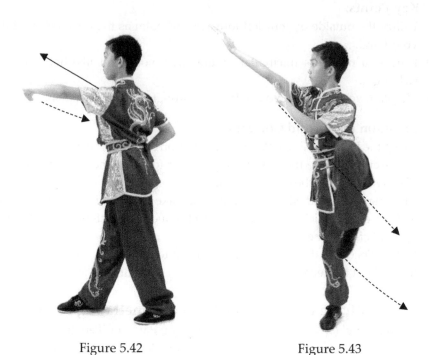

Figure 5.42   Figure 5.43

Movements 2: (Lower Thrust with the Left Palm - 'Swallow Scoops the Water'):
Connect the previous 'Penetrating Palm' movement seamlessly. Then transition into a complete left 'Crouch Stance,' keeping your right palm in position. Thrust your left palm along the inside of your left leg, extending it toward your left foot. This movement simulates evading an opponent's high kick while using your left palm to target your opponent's groin area. This technique is known as 'Swallow Scoops the Water.' Once more, focus your attention on your left palm (See Figure 5.44). Practice these movements alternately, switching sides.

Figure 5.44

- **Force Point:** The force point for the Penetrating Palm technique is situated on the fingertips.
- **Action Orbit:** Execution of the technique follows a diagonal straight line.
- **Direction:** Perform the Penetrating Palm strike from the inside to the outside.
- **Starting and Ending Point:** Initiate the technique from the waist, and it moves diagonally either upward or downward, depending on the specific execution.

Key Points:
(1) Ensure that your right arm extends forward in a straight diagonal line from the bend and lean slightly to the right during the execution.
(2) To generate more force during the palm thrust, twist your upper body in the opposite direction, meaning thrust your right palm while turning to the left.
(3) When executing the forward thrust, cross the back of your left wrist with your right hand. Visualize this as a defensive action where your left hand blocks your opponent's attack while your right palm thrusts toward their throat.

Common Errors:
(1) Failing to maintain a straight body throughout the movement.
(2) Neglecting to stretch your thrust-palm, resulting in the force point not being on the fingers.
(3) Not covering your left palm downward, and not crossing the back of the left wrist with your right hand during the thrust.

12. Zá Quán or Pounding Fist

'Zá Quán' (砸拳), translated as 'Pound the Fist,' also known as a 'Smashing Punch,' is a technique involving a downward hammer fist followed by using a fist back to strike. This technique is primarily used for offensive purposes.

Practice Methods (using the right hammer as an example):

Preparation Posture: Begin by balancing on your left leg while raising your right knee in front of your body. Simultaneously, lift your right arm and position your right fist over your head. Place your left hand on the left side at shoulder height. Keep your gaze fixed straight ahead (Figure 5.45).

Movements: Utilize the back of your right fist or fist wheel as the point of force. Execute a sweeping motion with your right arm, forcefully driving your right fist from the top to the bottom. As you vigorously pound your right fist downward, position your left palm on your abdomen and slap your left palm with the back of your right fist. Simultaneously, swiftly stamp your right foot close to your left foot, adding to the punching effect and creating a 'Half Squat with Feet Together Stance.' Focus on your right fist throughout the movement and maintain your gaze directed toward it (Figure 5.46). Practice these alternating movements to refine your technique.

| Figure 5.45 | Figure 5.46 |

- **Force Point:** Positioned at the back of your right fist.
- **Action Orbit:** Follows a linear trajectory.
- **Direction:** Moves from the top to the bottom.
- **Starting and Ending Point:** Begins at the top of your head and concludes at your abdomen.

Key Points:
(1) Utilize the back of your right fist or fist-wheel as the force point.
(2) Coordinate the movement by stamping your right foot close to your left foot simultaneously with the pounding fist.
(3) Before executing the pounding motion, focus on condensing Qi, holding your breath, sinking Qi while stamping, and exhale without making any sound from your mouth or nose.
(4) Maintain constant attention to your right fist throughout the entire movement.

Common Errors:
(1) Incorrect stance or posture, characterized by improper extension or bending of the arm when pounding the fist downward.
(2) Neglecting to use the back of the fist or fist-wheel as the designated force point.

118

13. Kǎn Zhǎng or Chopping Palm

'Kǎn Zhǎng' (砍掌), translated as 'Chop Palm,' is a potent and efficient offensive technique. It utilizes the outer edge of the palm as the force point, with the palm either upward or downward, and employs a horizontal sweeping motion to the left or right.

Practice Methods (using the right hand as an example):

Preparation Posture: Stand upright with your feet shoulder-width apart. Place your right palm on the right side, at shoulder height, with the palm facing up. Look at your right palm (Figure 5.47).

Movement 1: Palm Up

Utilize your waist as an axis. Perform a horizontal chopping motion with your right palm from the right side to the front. Ensure that you maintain a straight arm without bending it. Your right palm should be oriented with the palm facing up during this movement (Figure 5.48). Practice this movement alternately.

| Figure 5.47 | Figure 5.48 |

Movement 2: Palm Down

Start with your right palm in front of your left shoulder, oriented with the palm facing downward (Figure 5.49). Initiate the technique by chopping with your right palm, transitioning it from a bent position to a straight one towards the front. The force point for this movement is located on the edge of your right palm. Following the chop, allow your right fingers to tilt towards the left, forming a horizontal palm position. Throughout this motion, maintain your focus by keeping your gaze fixed straight ahead (Figure 5.50).

These variations provide different approaches to the 'Chopping Palm' technique. Practicing both options enhances your versatility and proficiency in executing this powerful offensive move in Chinese Wushu.

Figure 5.49   Figure 5.50

- **Force Point:** The force point should be located on the outside of the palm, not the fingers.
- **Action Orbit:** The technique can follow both a straight and circular line, offering versatility in its execution.
- **Direction** (Palm Up): When the palm is facing up, the direction of the Chopping Palm movement is from right to left.
- **Direction** (Palm Down): When the palm is facing down, the direction of the Chopping Palm movement is from left to right.
- **Starting and Ending Point** (Palm Up): The movement initiates from the right side and concludes on the left when the palm faces up.
- **Starting and Ending Point** (Palm Down): The motion begins on the left side and concludes on the right side when the palm faces down.

Key Points:
(1) Ensure the force point is on the outer part of the palm, not on the fingers.
(2) Maintain a straight wrist when you are chopping with the palm facing up, and when the palm is facing down, keep the wrist bending inward.
(3) Employ your waist to generate power and achieve a fluid, synchronized movement.
(4) Keep your body upright and centered throughout the entire motion.

Common Errors:

(1) Bending the elbow and relying solely on the forearm to execute the chopping action.
(2) Shrugging the shoulders and elevating the elbow during the chopping motion.
(3) Leaning to either side, causing the body to lose its upright posture.

14. Chā Zhǎng or Thrusting Palm

'Chā Zhǎng' (插掌), also known as 'Thrusting the Palm,' or 'Stab the Palm' in English, is an offensive action that involves extending the arm and applying power to the fingertips while keeping the wrist straight. Follow the practice methods below to execute this technique effectively and avoid common errors.

Practice Methods (using the right hand as an example):

Preparation Posture: Start by standing upright with your feet shoulder-width apart. Place your palms on your waist, palms facing upward, with your elbows pointing backward. Maintain a forward gaze (Figure 5.51).

Movements: Use your fingertips as the force point and thrust forward from your waist with a straight wrist. There are two methods of execution:

(1) **Horizontal Thrust:** In this variation, the palm can face either up or down to do the thrusting (Figure 5.52).
(2) **Vertical Thrust:** In this version, the palm faces inward, and the thumb points upward (Figure 5.53). Ensure that the thrust is fast and powerful, resembling the speed and precision of a needle. Practice alternately between the different variations.

Figure 5.51   Figure 5.52   Figure 5.53

- **Force Point:** Located on the fingertips.
- **Action Orbit:** Follows a straight-line trajectory.
- **Direction:** The thrusting palm technique can be executed in various directions, including forward, upward, downward, left, and right.
- **Starting and Ending Point:** The movement initiates from the waist and concludes at the point where the strike makes contact with the target.

Key Points:
(1) The force point should be on the fingertips, and the wrist must remain straight.
(2) Perform the movement with speed and power.
(3) Extend your arm forward from the elbow, maintaining a straight line of motion.
(4) Ensure that your palm is stretched, facilitating the quick transmission of power from your body to your fingertips.

Common Errors:
(1) Avoid incomplete arm extension during the thrust.
(2) Keep the wrist and fingers straight; do not bend them.
(3) Prioritize speed and accuracy over excessive strength.

15. An Zhǎng or Press Palm

'An Zhǎng' (按掌), translated as the 'Press Palm,' is a hand technique in Chinese Wushu that entails striking with the palm in a downward pressing motion. This technique is commonly employed both offensively, targeting an opponent's vital points like the chest, abdomen, or joints, and defensively, as a means to block the opponent's attacks.

Practice Methods (using the left hand as an example):

Preparation Posture: To perform 'Press Palm,' you typically start from a standing position with your feet shoulder-width apart or feet together and raise your left hand in front of your forehead with fingers pointing to the right. Hold your right palm on your right waist. Look at your left hand (Figure 5.54).

Movements: Start by slightly bending your left elbow and using your left palm as the force point. Execute a downward pressing motion in front of your body with a horizontal palm while simultaneously raising your right knee toward your chest. Imagine this action as deflecting your opponent's attack with your left palm and keeping your focus on your left hand. Additionally, raise your right knee to protect your groin area (See Figure 5.55). Practice these movements alternately.

- **Force Point:** Located at the palm.
- **Action Orbit:** Follows a circular trajectory.
- **Direction:** Executed in an up-down motion.
- **Starting and Ending Point:** Begins from a high position and ends at the point of contact with the target, moving downward.

Figure 5.54   Figure 5.55

Key Points:
(1) Make sure the force point is located at the heel or the center of the palm.
(2) When practicing the 'Press Palm,' keep in mind that it's not merely a hand movement; it should involve your entire body. Specifically, slightly lean your upper body forward during the downward pressing motion to amplify the power behind your attacking or defensive palm.
(3) Integrate the pressing power with your whole body, ensuring unity. Simultaneously, concentrate on sinking Qi to your Dantian.

Common Errors:
(1) Incorrect Force Point: It is crucial to ensure that the force point is located at the palm's heel or center to prevent hand and finger injuries.
(2) Lack of Integration: Avoid the mistake of pressing your palm downward without bending your elbow, as this can hinder the effective transmission of power to your palm.
(3) Lack of Coordination: Be sure to establish proper coordination between your upper body and palm to integrate your body and palm into your motion seamlessly. This coordination is essential for effectively applying power against your opponent.

16. Liàng Zhǎng or Flash the Palm
'Liàng Zhǎng' (亮掌), also known as 'Flash the Palm' in English, is a Chinese Wushu Long Fist technique that involves extending one arm above the shoulder and quickly

snapping the wrist inward like a flash. Although this technique has no actual attack or defense meaning, it is an expressive form in Chinese martial arts. It is a challenging technique to master and requires a lot of practice and training to perfect, including snapping the flashing wrist, quickly turning your head, and supporting the palm upward and outward. However, with proper training and dedication, it can be a powerful and effective technique for performance and expressing the spirit in the Long Fist Style.

Practice Methods (using the right hand as an example):

Preparation Posture: Stand straight with your feet shoulder-width apart. Raise your right arm to shoulder height with the thumb side pointing up. Hold your left palm on your left waist and look at your right hand (Figure 5.56).

Movements: Swing your right arm to the same side of your head or overhead, then bend your arm slightly and snap your right wrist inward, with the palm facing up. Quickly turn your head to the left (Figure 5.57). Practice alternately.

Figure 5.56   Figure 5.57

- **Force Point:** Located at the wrist.
- **Action Orbit:** Follows a circular trajectory.
- **Direction:** Moves from the outside to the inside.
- **Starting and Ending Point:** Begins from the upper right and concludes at the wrist.

Key Points:

(1) Snap the wrist inward rapidly, as quick as lightning. The crucial aspect of this movement is to fully open the shoulder, particularly on the same side as the striking hand, while avoiding any shrugging.

(2) Keep your arm slightly curved above your head, with the right palm facing upward as if supporting the sky.

(3) Ensure that the slap of the hand and the turn of the head are perfectly synchronized. After snapping your hand, align your shoulders parallel without leaning.

(4) Coordinate the slap of the right hand and the turn of the head to the left with a quick twist or engage the power of the waist.

Common Errors:

(1) Less Insufficient Wrist Snap: Avoid merely moving the arm inward without a proper wrist snap and turning the palm inward. This diminishes the effectiveness of the technique.

(2) Improper Elbow Position: Ensure that the arm forms a proper arch; it should neither be excessively straight nor too bent. An incorrect elbow position can result in a loss of power.

(3) Lack of Coordination: Make sure the snap of the wrist and the turn of the head are coordinated and executed simultaneously. Avoid leaning the upper body to the left, as it disrupts balance and technique.

17. Jià Quán or Upholds Fist

'Jià Quán' (架拳) translated as 'Uphold Fist' or 'Framing Fist,' is a fundamental technique in Chinese Wushu that entails punching with a closed fist while the other hand is held up in a defensive position to protect the head. The term 'Uphold Fist' derives from the positioning of the defensive hand, which appears to support the weight of the fist. This technique is frequently employed for defensive and counteroffensive purposes, enabling the practitioner to block and counter the opponent's attacks effectively.

Practice Methods (using the left fist as an example):

Preparation Posture: Start from a punch with a horse stance (Figure 5.58).

Movements: Bend your left arm slightly, rotate your left forearm inward, and move it down in a circular motion. When your left arm reaches your right chest, rotate your left forearm outward, circle upward, and use the outside of your little finger as the force point to raise it horizontally over your head. Keep the fist-heart pointing up. While doing this, turn left to form a left bow stance and punch your right fist, tilting downward in front of your body. Look at your right fist (Figure 5.59). Practice alternately.

The key point for practicing 'Uphold Fist' is to employ a spiral block technique to neutralize an opponent's attack, rather than simply raising your forearm and making direct contact with your opponent's body, which may result in pain or injury. In Chinese

Wushu, this is referred to as 'Spiral Force.' By mastering the spiral block, you can adeptly nullify an attack and position yourself for an effective counterattack.

- **Force Point:** on the outside of your left forearm and left fist-wheel.
- **Action Orbit:** follows a circular path.
- **Direction:** moves from the left side, downward, and then upward.
- **Starting and Ending Point:** initiates from the left side and ends at the top of your head.

Figure 5.58   Figure 5.59

'Shǒu Fǎ,' or 'Hand Technique,' stands as a foundational cornerstone within Chinese Wushu, exerting profound influence over the outward expression of Wushu movements and assuming a pivotal role in showcasing Wushu combat proficiency.

The concept of 'Hand Form' represents a specific embodiment of 'Hand Technique,' the seamless transitions between these various 'Hand Forms' underscore the adaptability inherent to Hand Technique. These fluid transitions are common in diverse Wushu routines, including Long Fist, Nan Quan, and Taichi Quan, involving shifts from 'Fist Technique' to 'Palm Technique' or from 'Palm Technique' to 'Hooking Technique.' Notably, while these routines may not engage in actual combat, they are expected to encapsulate the very essence of combat. This distinction is why it is referred to as 'Wǔ Shù' (武術 martial art) rather than 'Wǔ Shù' (舞術 dancing art). Despite the shared pronunciation, the distinct spelling carries a markedly different inner meaning. Consequently, the transitions between hand forms must harmonize with the demands of Wushu combat.

From a strictly competitive sports perspective, the rapid and fluid transitions between 'Hand Forms' are pivotal in enhancing wrist and finger flexibility, elevating one's performance in a competitive arena. Moreover, from an aesthetic vantage point, these graceful transitions between 'Hand Forms' are equally indispensable, contributing significantly to heightened effectiveness in competitive training.

Wushu places fundamental demands on all 'Hand Techniques,' emphasizing four key aspects: 'speed, accuracy, power, and stability.' These requirements are intrinsic to the functional elements of martial arts. As the saying goes, 'Among all martial arts, speed is the key to victory.' Therefore, swift execution remains the foremost prerequisite for 'Hand Techniques.' Precision in targeting is the second critical factor, followed by the imperative of formidable striking power. Finally, maintaining stability during execution remains of utmost importance.

From a Wushu combat perspective, 'Hand Techniques' primarily facilitate effective striking against opponents. It is crucial to differentiate between 'Hand Techniques' and 'Hand Forms' – while closely related, they are not synonymous. 'Hand Forms' are static representations, whereas 'Hand Techniques' are dynamic applications. For example, Fist, Palm, and Hook are categorized as 'Hand Forms,' whereas the 'Fist Technique,' 'Palm Technique,' and 'Hook Technique' are practical implementations of these forms. In essence, 'Hand Technique' represents the functional utilization of 'Hand Form.' It's worth noting that a single 'Hand Form' can yield multiple 'Hand Techniques.' For example, the 'Palm Form' can be employed for executing techniques like pushing palm, chopping palm, or scooping palm, while the 'Fist Form' can serve as a basis for techniques such as straight punching, hammering punch, or poking punch.

The distinct 'Hand Technique' exhibits variations in striking directions, force points, and movement trajectories. For instance, the 'Palm Technique' emphasizes a forward exceptional direction, focusing on the palm's base for force application, whereas the 'Chopping Technique' involves a downward particular motion, emphasizing the palm's outer edge for force generation. 'Hand Technique' encompasses essential aspects, including movement trajectories, force application points, and force points, each with unique martial art implications. The author has elaborated upon these aspects.

One of the primary challenges in mastering Long Fist techniques often lies in the deficiency of movement structure and power execution within the 'Hand Technique.' In other words, the 'Hand Technique' frequently lacks the necessary force, fails to create the desired forms, and does not convey the essence of spirit, energy, and focus. While many practitioners prioritize training in 'Body Technique,' concentrate on generating power through the waist and hips, they frequently overlook fundamental 'Hand Technique' training. Unfortunately, qualities like hand endurance, explosive strength, and flexibility are often neglected.

It is common among Wushu athletes and coaches to either remain unaware of the significance of 'Hand Technique' training or not dedicate themselves to specialized 'Hand Technique' training, even if they acknowledge its importance. Consequently, the 'Hand Technique' skills of most athletes suffer, thus hindering the effectiveness of their techniques. Effective power generation from the waist, hips, shoulders, and elbows can be transmitted to the hands, enabling the execution of the 'Hand Technique' with force.

However, suppose hand endurance, flexibility, and explosive power haven't been developed. In that case, they cannot maximize power transmission from the entire body to the hands, ultimately affecting the effectiveness of the techniques. Therefore, fundamental 'Hand Technique' training prepares the whole body, with the hands being the most versatile and agile striking tools. The author strongly recommends that Wushu students dedicate ample practice time to the 'Hand Technique' in each class under the guidance of coaches or instructors, ensuring this fundamental aspect is never overlooked.

Chapter 6
Basic Movements (2)
Bù - Xíng - Bù - Fǎ
步型 步法
Stances and Footwork
Bù Xíng or Stances

In Chinese Wushu, 'Bù – Xíng,' translated as 'Stances,' refers to specific postures adopted during training, involving the coordinated positioning of the legs and feet, along with the knees, ankles, and other joints, to create distinct static shapes. These stances serve as the foundational building blocks for practitioners and are essential for maintaining proper form. The primary goal of practicing 'Stances' is to enhance the lower body's speed, strength, agility, and stability during movement.

Chinese Wushu encompasses various 'Stances,' some of which share similar names but have differing technical requirements. Within the Long Fist category, the five most commonly used stances are the bow stance, horse stance, empty stance, rest stance, and crouch stance.

Famous Chinese Wushu athlete Sun Peiyuan has captured various competition 'Stances' in his pictures, showcasing their standard diversity.

1. Gōng Bù or Bow Stance

'Bow Stance' (弓步) holds a fundamental place in Chinese Wushu, and its movements and key points are identical to those of the 'Pile Stance' discussed in Chapter 4.

To execute a left 'Bow Stance,' bend your left leg while keeping your right leg straight (Figure 6.1). Conversely, to perform a right 'Bow Stance,' bend your right leg while maintaining your left leg straight (Figure 6.2).

Figure 6.1   Figure 6.2

Key Points:

(1) In the 'Bow Stance,' the front leg should be bent to create a bow-like shape, while the back leg should remain fully extended.

(2) Maintain an extended chest, an upright waist, and lower the buttocks. In the Long Fist Competitions, ensure the front thigh is parallel to the ground.

Common Errors:

(1) The vertical line of the front knee extends beyond the front toe or does not reach the back foot. The front thigh in the 'Bow Stance ' is not parallel to the ground, and the rear leg is not correctly bent and extended.

(2) The back toe is not pointing inward, and the buttocks protrude. The back heel is lifted off the ground, and both legs are extended too high, almost as if standing up.

In a Competitive Wushu Competition, judges take into account specific deduction points, which encompass:

(1) The knee of the front leg is not aligning above the instep.

(2) The thigh of the front leg does not maintain parallel alignment to the ground.

(3) Any portion of the sole of the rear leg conspicuously lifted off the ground.

(4) The rear foot is not angled inward, with the toes pointing obliquely forward.

2. Mǎ Bù or Horse Stance

The 'Horse Stance' (馬步) shares the same movements and key points as previously described in Chapter 4 (Figure 6.3). Consistent practice of this stance is crucial to enhance your stability and leg strength.

Figure 6.3

Key Points:

(1) Maintain proper posture with your chest out, waist straight, and head lifted.
(2) Push the heels outward, turn the toes inward, and ensure the knees are pointing outward.
(3) Focus on sinking your Qi to the Dantian. In the Long Fist Competition, make sure the thighs are parallel to the ground.

Common Errors:

(1) Avoid turning the toes of both feet outward and ensure the thighs remain horizontal.
(2) Do not adopt a stance that is either too wide or too narrow.
(3) Prevent the knees from turning inward or extending beyond the toes of the feet.
(4) Keep both legs at an appropriate height without standing up or protruding the buttocks.

In a 'Competitive Wushu' Competition, the following are considered deduction points:

(1) Thighs not parallel to the ground.
(2) Distance between the feet narrower than the performer's shoulder width.
(3) Knees buckling inward.
(4) Heels raised off the ground.
(5) Toes of the foot/feet pointing outward at an angle of 45 degrees or more.

3. Xū Bù or Empty Stance

The movements and key points for the 'Empty Stance' (虚步) remain consistent with the description provided in Chapter 4. When the left leg is positioned in front, it is referred to as a left 'Empty Stance' (Figure 6.4), while when the right leg is placed in front, it is termed a right 'Empty Stance' (Figure 6.5). Repetition is crucial in practice, and the recommended practice duration is equivalent to that of the 'Bow Stance.'

Figure 6.4   Figure 6.5

Key Points:

(1) Maintain a protruding chest, an upright waist, and an elevated head.
(2) Differentiate between the rear leg and the virtual leg, which entails placing your total body weight on the back leg with the entire foot in contact with the ground while the other foot only lightly touches the ground with the front toes, bearing no weight.
(3) In the Long Fist competitions, ensure the back thigh remains parallel to the ground.

Common Errors:

(1) The back thigh does not reach the horizontal level.
(2) Leaning the upper body forward too much or throwing out the hip.
(3) Making the back knee extend beyond the toes of the back foot.
(4) Lifting the rear heel or placing too much weight on the front foot. The weight distribution is no more than 70% on the back leg and less than 30% on the front foot.

In Competitive Wushu competitions, deductions are made by the following criteria:

(1) Failure to align the knee of the front leg above the toe.
(2) Inability to maintain parallel alignment of the thigh of the front leg with the ground.
(3) The back heel not being lowered to the ground.

(4) An unequal distribution of weight between the legs.
(5) The gaze not being level or looking downwards.

4. Pū Bù or Crouch Stance

'Pū Bù' (仆步), translated as the 'Crouch Stance,' is indeed one of the fundamental 'Stances' in Chinese Wushu, involving squatting entirely on one leg while extending the other straight out to the side, both feet remaining flat on the ground. This 'Stance' allows for an extended 'Horse Stance' with the body's weight focused on one leg, squatting as low as possible. It is commonly employed for defensive purposes, especially in deflecting attacks targeting the upper body and groin, while also enabling the utilization of sweep-kicking techniques to target an opponent's knees and ankles, often followed by a strategic counterattack.

Movements (using the left 'crouch stance' as an example):
- Begin by turning your right toes outward at approximately 45 degrees, fully squatting down on your right leg, and bringing the back of your right thigh close to your right calf. Simultaneously, straighten your left leg to the left, with the left toes turned inward at a 90-degree angle.
- Position your right fist at your right waist and extend your left palm toward your left foot, pointing your fingers to the right. Keep your focus on the left palm (Figure 6.6).
- Straighten your left leg to assume the left 'Crouch Stance' and straighten the right leg to assume the right 'Crouch Stance' (Figure 6.7).
- Practice these movements repeatedly, dedicating the same amount of practice time as you would for the 'Bow Stance. '

Figure 6.6   Figure 6.7

Key Points:
(1) Keep a straight chest, waist, and left leg. Stretch your neck and relax your shoulders.
(2) Sink your hips and pivot your right foot outward at a 45-degree angle while turning your left foot inward at a 90-degree angle. Ensure that the outside of your left foot and the heel of your right foot remain in contact with the ground.
(3) Ensure that your right knee and toes align in a vertical straight line.

133

Common Errors:

(1) Bending the left knee or lifting the outside of the right foot and heel off the ground. Not bringing the back of the right thigh and calf together.
(2) Lifting the outside of the left foot off the ground.
(3) Allowing the right knee to collapse inward or not moving the left foot inward enough.

In a 'Competitive Wushu' Competition, the following deduction points apply:

(1) Not ensuring that the back of the thigh of the squatting leg meets the calf.
(2) The extended leg is not fully extended.
(3) Not turning the extended foot inward, keeping the sole flat on the ground.

5. Xiē Bù or Rest Stance

'Xiē Bù' (歇步), translated as 'Rest Stance,' legs crossed and sitting, the rear knee tucked into the hollow of the front knee. This 'Stance' is tricky, especially for those with poor flexibility, because you must put one leg behind and twist it until you can sit on your back heel. The 'Rest Stance' is crucial because it provides a stable and balanced foundation for other movements and 'Stances' in Chinese Wushu. It also helps develop proper posture, balance, and alignment, essential for effectively and safely executing techniques.

Movements (using the left leg as an example):

• Begin by crossing your legs and squatting down entirely. Turn your left toes outward at a 45-degree and place your left foot on the ground. Allow the front sole of your right foot to touch the ground, keeping your right knee close to the inside of your left knee. Sit on your right heel with your hips while keeping your legs tightly together.
• Place your fists on your waist or in a position shown in the pictures below. Your gaze should be on your right fist (Figure 6.8). This 'Stance' is called the left 'Rest Stance' when the left foot is in front, and it's called the right 'Rest Stance ' when the right foot is in front (Figure 6.9).
• Practice repeatedly, and the practice time is the same as the bow stance.

Figure 6.8   Figure 6.9

Key Points:

(1) Maintain an upright chest, a straight waist, and a lifted head.

(2) Ensure the legs are tightly together, with no gap between them.

Common Errors:

(1) Failure to rest the hip on the rear calf.

(2) Creating excessive distance between the feet, leading to a gap between the legs.

(3) The rear leg not making contact with the front leg.

(4) Failing to cross the legs.

In Competitive Wushu Competitions, deductions are applied for the following reasons:

(1) Failure to cross the two legs.

(2) The buttocks not making contact with the calf of the supporting leg.

6. Zuò <u>Pán</u> or Cross-Legged Sitting Stance

'Zuò Pán' (坐盤), translated as the 'Cross-Legged Sitting Stance' in English, refers to a seated position on the ground with the legs curled and crossed. This 'Stance' can exhibit various variations and styles, which the specific Wushu school and techniques influence. It often serves as the foundational posture for particular movements and techniques within martial arts. The following is the standard form in the Long Fist of Chinese wushu.

Movements (using the left leg as an example):

• Begin by sitting on the ground and crossing your legs. Bend your right leg so that the outer side of your entire right leg touches the ground and bring your right heel close to your hip. Cross your left leg in front of your right leg and bring your left thigh close to your chest. Extend your arms out to the sides of your body with your palms facing down. Focus your gaze on your left hand (Figure 6.10).

• If the left leg is in front, it's called a left 'Cross-Legged Stance.' If the right leg is in front, it's called a right 'Cross-Legged Stance' (Figure 6.11).

• Repeat the 'Stance' practice, gradually increasing the practice time.

Figure 6.10   Figure 6.11

Key Points:
(1) Cross your legs tightly, making sure the outside of your left foot remains in contact with the ground.
(2) If you're not flexible enough, stretch your legs more before attempting this 'Stance.' Alternatively, you can hold your legs with your hands to stretch them at the beginning.
(3) Keep your waist straight and your left heel as close to your hips as possible.

Common Errors:
(1) The upper leg doesn't touch the chest.
(2) The legs aren't crossed tightly enough.

In Competitive Wushu Competitions, deductions are applied for the following reasons:

(1) Neither buttock is in contact with the floor.
(2) Neither foot is in contact with the floor.

7. Dīng Zì Bù or T-Stance

'Dīng Zì Bù,' (丁字步), also known as 'T-Stance' in English. In Wushu's Long Fist, the T-stance involves bending both knees. One foot fully touches the ground, while the other foot's toe lightly touches close to the inside of your supporting foot. This 'Stance' resembles the shape of the letter 'T,' hence its name. The weight distribution is approximately 70% on the supporting foot and 30% on the non-supporting foot.

Movements (using the left leg as an example):
• Begin by standing upright with your feet together. Then, bend your knees to form a half-squat. Root your right foot entirely on the ground and lift your left heel. Move your left toes inward and touch the ground to form a T-stance. Finally, close your left foot to the inside of your right foot while keeping your weight on your right leg (Figure 6.12).
• If your left toes touch the ground, it is called a left 'T-stance.' If your right toes touch the ground, it is called a right 'T-stance' (Figure 6.13).
• Practice this stance repeatedly, for the same duration as the bow stance.

Key Points:
(1) Keep your upper body straight and your shoulders relaxed.
(2) Your supporting foot should point straight ahead, and your non-supporting toes or sole of the foot touch the ground.
(3) Bend both knees but keep your weight slightly back on your supporting foot to maintain stability.

Common Errors:
(1) Not bending both knees enough, which affects balance and stability.
(2) The non-supporting foot's toe pointing in the wrong direction.

(3) The weight distribution is not correct, causing instability.
(4) Upper body leaning forward or backward, affecting posture and balance.

In a competitive Wushu Competition, deductions may occur if the above errors are present, resulting in a lower score.

Figure 6.12   Figure 6.13

Requirements for 'Stance' Practice

(1) The first goal for beginners is to make and maintain the practice for each 'Stance,' then gradually increase the practice time.
(2) 'Stance' training is not as simple as it may seem; it requires perseverance and patience. You may initially experience discomfort or pain but remember this is normal. So, be sure to persist in your practice.
(3) While practicing, you must remain completely immobile in every 'Stance.' One effective way to achieve this is by practicing in front of a mirror or checking your movements with your mind.
(4) Try to lower your 'Stance,' but do not push yourself too hard to avoid damaging your body, especially your knees.
(5) 'Stance' training is the best way to help you master the correct routine movement and lay a solid foundation for further advanced learning.
(6) Try to understand each 'Stance' detailed requirements, key points, and error-prone places. Learn how to maintain balance and stability.
(7) Building your standing stamina step by step is crucial to increase practice time. Once you have developed the sufficient ability, the 'Stances' should become 'comfortable,' 'solid,' and ready to express explosive power.

Bù Fǎ or Footwork

'Bù Fǎ,' translated as 'Footwork,' is also one of the most fundamental components of Chinese Wushu, with the primary objective of enhancing leg speed and flexibility. It differs from the 'Bu Xing' or 'Stance' discussed above in this Chapter.

'Bù Xíng' or 'Stance' refers to the static state of the lower limbs after both feet have landed, such as the 'Horse Stance,' 'Bow Stance,' etc. On the other hand, 'Bù Fǎ,' or 'Footwork' is a dynamic structure that refers to the principles or guidelines for the direction, size, speed, and other aspects of foot movement in Wushu routines or combat activities, for example, advancing steps, retreating steps, and front or back cross-steps, etc. In the Chinese Wushu community, there has always been a saying, 'In teaching, the master mostly only teaches the Wushu routines but does not teach the Wushu 'Footwork.' This is because if the master teaches the 'Footwork' to their students, masters worry that someday their students will defeat them.' This illustrates the importance of 'Footwork' in practical combat. In practice, even if one's punching and kicking or other martial techniques are excellent, it is difficult to approach the opponent and achieve effective strikes without agile footwork. As the saying goes, 'Practice routine a hundred times cannot compare to just practicing 'Footwork' only one time.' This fully expresses that agile and versatile 'Footwork' can not only render the opponent's fierce attack ineffective but also enable one to achieve unexpected victories, turning danger into safety.

In the Long Fist of the Wushu routine, 'Footwork' is characterized by its need for rapid, agile, and effortless transitions, enabling practitioners to swiftly change direction and position while maintaining optimal balance and stability while executing diverse techniques. Additionally, sound 'Footwork' plays a significant role in conserving energy and elevating the overall performance level.

1. Gài Bù or Front Cross-Step

'Gài Bù' (蓋步), translated as the 'Front Cross-Step,' is also known as the 'Cross-Over Step.' In the Chinese dictionary, 'Gai' means 'cover' and 'over.' The 'Front Cross-Step' involves bringing the rear foot through to cross in front of the other foot while stepping forward.

Movements (using the right leg as an example):
- Start in a natural stance with your feet shoulder-width apart (Figure 6.14). Shift your weight onto your left foot and step your right foot to the left, crossing it over in front of your left foot. Bend your right knee and turn your right toe outward, putting the weight mainly on your right leg (Figure 6.15).
- Usually, the back heel should leave the ground, and the front heel should touch the ground when crossing your foot forward.
- Practice alternately by switching legs. The left leg is in front, called the left 'Front Cross-Step,' and when the right leg is in front, it is called the right 'Front Cross-Step.'

Figure 6.14   Figure 6.15

Key Points:
(1) Maintain stability and an upright upper body throughout the movement.
(2) Step using the balls of your feet and ensure a soft landing.
(3) Execute the steps with quickness, lightness, and precision.

Common Errors:
(1) Bringing the feet too close together during the cross-step, potentially impacting balance and stability.
(2) Leaning the upper body forward or to the side while stepping, which can compromise both balance and power.

2. Jiāo Chā Bù or Back Cross-Step

In Chinese, 'Jiāo Chā' (交叉) refers to cross, intersect, and overlap, while 'Jiāo Chā Bù' (交叉步) can be translated as the 'Back Cross-Step' in English. It closely resembles the 'Front Cross-Step,' with the primary distinction being that it involves stepping one foot behind the other and crossing the legs while touching the toes down.

Movements (using the right leg as an example):
• Begin from a natural stance with your feet shoulder-width apart (Figure 6.16). Transfer your weight onto your left leg. Move your right foot behind your left foot, crossing it over, and lightly touch your right toes.

139

- Subsequently, bend your left knee and rotate your left toe outward, with most of your weight supported by your left leg (as depicted in Figure 6.17). Generally, ensure that the back heel is slightly elevated off the ground.
- Practice alternately. When the left leg is positioned in front, it is called the left back cross-step, whereas when the right leg is in front, it is called the right back cross-step.

Figure 6.16   Figure 6.17

Comparison each other between the 'Front Cross-Step' and 'Back Cross-Step':
(1) Front Cross-Step: Involves stepping over the front foot, with the heel touching the ground first.
(2) Back Cross-Step: Involves stepping behind the front foot, with the sole touching the ground.
(3) Both steps necessitate twisting your waist in the same direction. For instance, when executing a right 'front cross-step,' you should twist to the right. Similarly, when performing a left 'back cross-step,' you should twist to the left.

3. Jī Bù or Kick Heel Step

'Jī ' (擊) means strike, beat, or hit in Chinese. Therefore, 'Jī Bù' (擊步) can be translated as the 'Kick Heel Step,' also known as the 'Hitting Step.' It involves pushing off the lead foot and jumping forward, tapping the rear foot against the lead foot in the air, and then landing with the back foot first. This footwork is commonly used to generate momentum for jump kicks, particularly in conjunction with the 'Jumping Front Straight Kick.'

Movements:
- Stand upright, with your feet together. Place your fists on your waists and maintain a forward gaze (Figure 6.18).
- Lean your entire body forward and exert force against the ground with your feet. Step your left foot forward, lift your back foot off the ground (Figure 6.19), and propel yourself with a leap. While in the air, bring your back foot to hit the heel of your front foot (Figure 6.20).
- Upon landing, allow your back foot to touch the ground first (Figure 6.21), followed by your front foot (Figure 6.22). Maintain a forward gaze throughout the movement.

Key Points:
(1) Maintain an upright posture with your upper body straight and keep your left shoulder forward while jumping in the air.
(2) Shift your center of gravity onto your left leg when initiating the 'kick heel step,' and transfer it to your right leg when jumping in the air.
(3) The point of contact for the kick is between the inside of your right foot and the heel of your left foot. Fully extend your legs and ankles when hitting the heel.
(4) The movement of your right foot should resemble a quick slide forward, emphasizing speed rather than excessive height.

Figure 6.18   Figure 6.19   Figure 6.20

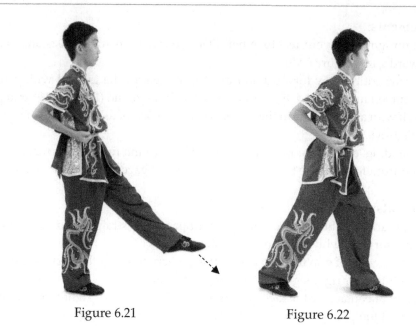

Figure 6.21   Figure 6.22

This movement is often accompanied by swinging the arms and is particularly connected to the 'Jump Front Straight Kick' (Figure 6.23 A ,B, C, D, E, F, G, H, I).

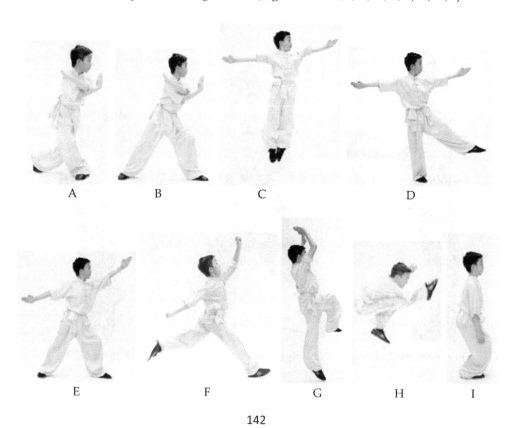

A   B   C   D

E   F   G   H   I

A: Front cross-legged step with the right foot; B: Step forward with the left foot;
C: Jump and kick heel step; D: Land the right foot; E: Land the left foot;
F: Stride the right foot forward; G: Ready to jump; H: Jump, front straight kick;
I: Land with the left foot or both feet.

Common Errors:
(1) Failure to make contact between the back foot and the heel of the front foot; remember to lean your body forward.
(2) Avoid lowering your head or arching your back during the movement.
(3) Ensure that your knees are fully extended, and your legs are close together when hitting the heel.

4. Diàn Bù or Skip Step

Since there is no direct corresponding word for 'Diàn Bù' (墊步) in English, it is commonly translated as 'the skip step,' also known as the 'hop step.' This technique involves bringing the rear foot forward and lifting the front foot off the ground, allowing the back foot to take its place, thus advancing while maintaining the same stance.

In Chinese Wushu, 'Dian Bu' is a specific footwork technique commonly used to approach an opponent or change the angle of attack quickly. Dian Bu emphasizes using light and agile steps for swift movement while maintaining balance and stability. This footwork technique finds wide application across various martial arts styles and combat techniques, helping to cultivate agile body control and quick responsiveness.

Movements:
- Stand with your feet together. Place your fists on your waist, maintaining an upright posture (Figure 6.24). Begin by stepping forward with your left foot and shifting your weight onto it (Figure 6.25).
- Lift your right foot off the ground and position it to land in the same spot where your left foot was previously placed. Simultaneously, push off with your left foot and propel yourself forward by jumping (Figure 6.26).
- As you land, bend your left knee and lift your left foot (Figure 6.27), landing your left foot in front of you (Figure 6.28). Maintain a forward gaze throughout the movement.
- Practice the skip step repeatedly, ensuring smooth transitions and maintaining balance and stability throughout the movement. It is important to coordinate the timing of the footwork and maintain control over your body positioning.

Key Points:
(1) Ensure that when performing the skipped step forward, your right foot lands on the ground with the entire foot, followed by the left foot.
(2) When landing with the right foot, imagine it is sliding forward smoothly. It should be a quick movement without excessive jumping.
(3) Maintain stability and avoid leaning your body excessively, which can lead to instability during the movement.

| Figure 6.24. | Figure 6.25 | Figure 6.26 |

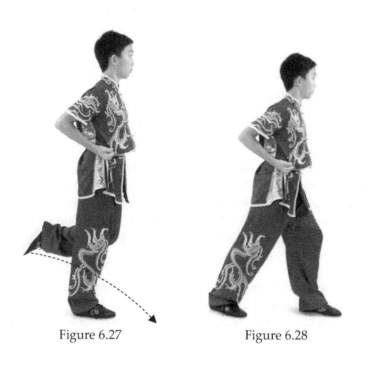

| Figure 6.27 | Figure 6.28 |

Common Errors:

(1) Avoid jumping too high with the right foot during the skip step. Maintain control and focus on the quickness and efficiency of the movement.

(2) Be mindful not to slow down the push-off with the right foot. Maintain a dynamic and swift transition between steps.

(3) Ensure that your body remains balanced and stable throughout the movement, avoiding excessive leaning that can disrupt your control in the air.

5. Hú Xíng Bù or Circular Walking Step

'Hú Xíng' (弧形) in Chinese means curve, arc, or arch. 'Hú Xíng Bù' (弧形步) mainly means that the walk line in motion should form a curve or a circular motion. Thus, it is commonly translated as the 'Circular Walking Step.' This dynamic footwork technique is widely utilized in the Long Fist category routines and swordplay disciplines. The circular walking step serves multiple purposes, including preserving distance from opponents, creating advantageous attack angles, enhancing overall footwork skills, and more.

Proper weight distribution and precise foot placement are crucial for maintaining stability and fluidity throughout the circular movement. This footwork also provides more flexibility and balance, adding an aesthetic element to combat or performance.

In practice, the size and speed of the 'Circular Walk Step' are usually adjusted according to specific movements and technical requirements. Practitioners must maintain a continuous flow of movement, transitioning seamlessly between different steps and directions. Pay attention to coordination between the upper and lower body, along with a strong sense of balance and control.

Through consistent practice of circular walking, practitioners can develop improved coordination, agility, and spatial awareness, ultimately enhancing their performance in Long Fist and swordplay disciplines.

Movements (using the left-side walking as an example):

- Stand tall with your feet together, maintaining proper posture. Place your fists on your waist and direct your gaze straight ahead, focusing on a fixed point (Figure 6.29).
- Begin by slightly bending your knees, creating a stable and balanced base. Step forward with your right foot towards the left corner slightly, allowing your toes to point slightly outward (Figure 6.30).
- Next, bring your left foot forward, moving it through the inside of your right foot (Figure 6.31) while positioning your toes slightly inward (Figure 6.32).

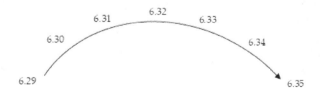

The Movement Trajectory of the Rightward Movement

145

Figure 6.29   Figure 6.30   Figure 6.31   Figure 6.32

- Continuing with the circular walking method, maintain a fluid and continuous motion by alternately stepping with both feet along the circular path (Figure 6.33, 6.34, 6.35).

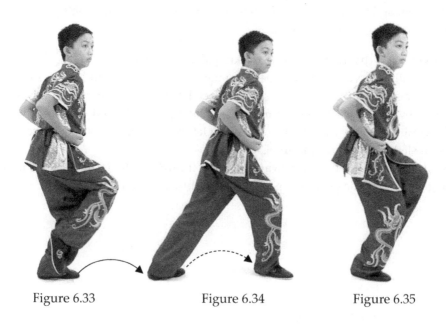

Figure 6.33   Figure 6.34   Figure 6.35

The width of each step should be approximately shoulder-width apart. When performing circular walking to the right, ensure that your right toe is slightly pointed outward, while your left foot should be angled slightly inward. Conversely, the foot positions will be reversed when walking in the opposite direction.

By adhering to these walking techniques, you can smoothly and confidently move forward along the circular line. It is important to practice maintaining the appropriate foot positions and maintaining a consistent and controlled pace throughout the movement.

Key Points:
(1) Maintain an upright posture, keeping your chest and waist straight while maintaining a squat position.
(2) Ensure your weight distribution is smooth and stable during the walking motion, avoiding excessive up and down movement of your body.
(3) When taking each step, focus on swiftly moving your heel forward and engaging your waist in a twisting motion.

Common Errors:
(1) Be mindful of maintaining a consistent center of gravity without excessive fluctuations. Avoid uneven steps that resemble a small running motion.
(2) Do not lean your upper body forward or protrude your buttocks, as it can disrupt your balance and stability.
(3) Be cautious not to overstretch your legs, as it can raise your center of gravity too high and compromise your stability.

In the 2017 China National Wushu Taolu Championship, the first-place winner, Kan Wen Cong, showcased exceptional skill in practicing Jianshu, incorporating the 'Circular Walking Step' into the Sword routine.

Chapter 7
Basic Movements (3)
Zhǒu Fǎ
肘法
Elbow Techniques

'Zhǒu Fǎ,' translated as 'Elbow Techniques' in English, is a fundamental technique of Chinese Wushu, involving the skilled utilization of the bent arm and the protruding tip of the elbow for offensive and defensive purposes. These techniques excel in close quarters combat due to their unique characteristics of sharpness, difficulty, and significant attacking power. The movements associated with elbow techniques are known for their stability, speed, brevity, and inherent danger, constantly adapting and changing to the situation. In close combat scenarios, elbow techniques are highly effective for attacking and defending.

Chinese Wushu schools have developed various elbow fighting routines, such as the 'Six Elbow Heads,' 'Elbow Mother,' 'Eighteen Elbow Methods,' and 'Shaolin Thirty-Six Elbows,' which have gained widespread recognition and popularity. These routines offer a diverse range of attack and defense strategies, providing practitioners with an extensive repertoire of techniques to enhance their combat abilities. In practical application, elbow techniques offer several key advantages:

(1) Offensive Strikes: Elbow strikes are formidable weapons for close-range combat. They can target vital areas such as the chin, temple, jaw, ribs, or solar plexus, delivering significant impact and potentially incapacitating opponents.
(2) Counterattacks: Elbow techniques excel at countering incoming attacks. Swiftly retracting or raising the arm can intercept and redirect opponents' strikes, acting as a defensive barrier while simultaneously launching a powerful counterstrike.
(3) Joint Manipulation: The elbow can target an opponent's joints, including the elbow joint itself, the wrist, or the collarbone. Applying pressure or leveraging the elbow joint against these vulnerable areas can cause pain, immobilization, or joint locks, granting control over the opponent.
(4) Close-Quarters Combat: Elbow techniques are particularly effective in confined spaces with a limited range of motion. Their short and compact nature allows for quick and forceful strikes, making them valuable in self-defense situations and grappling and clinching scenarios.
(5) Combination Techniques: Elbow strikes can be seamlessly combined with other strikes, kicks, or grappling techniques, maximizing their effectiveness. For instance, following a punch with an elbow strike or combining a knee strike with an elbow strike can create devastating combinations, overwhelming opponents.

148

1. Dǐng Zhǒu or Elbow Strike

'Dǐng Zhǒu' (頂肘), also known as 'Elbow Strike' in English, involves striking with the point of the elbow. It is a prominent straight-line technique commonly utilized in Chinese Wushu.

During the execution of the elbow strike, the practitioner directs the forceful strike toward the target using the point of the elbow. The technique emphasizes a linear and direct path of attack, delivering a powerful impact to the opponent.

Practice Methods:

Preparation Posture: Start by standing on your right leg. Bend your left elbow inward and hold a fist, with the fist-heart facing downward, in front of your body. Place your right palm close to the face of your left fist. Direct your gaze to the right (Figure 7.1). Prepare yourself for the strike.

Movements (using the left elbow as an example):

- Use the tip of your left elbow as the primary force point and strike to the left. Maintain a horizontal position with the left elbow, bending the tip of the elbow forward. At the same time, push the face of your left fist with your right palm. While executing the strike, step to the left with your left foot, assuming a left bow stance (Figure 7.2).
- Engage your hips, legs, and right hand to generate a supportive force during the strike. Synchronize these three forces to achieve a complete and adequate elbow strike. Keep your gaze forward. Practice in an alternating manner.

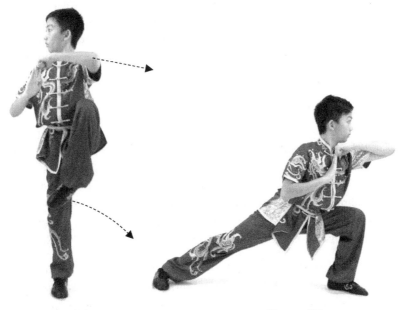

Figure 7.1   Figure 7.2

- **Force Point:** The primary force is applied at the tip of your left elbow (Figure 7.3).
- **Action Orbit:** The motion follows a horizontal straight line.
- **Direction:** The movement advances from the rear to the forward direction.
- **Starting and Ending Point:** Commence the action from the right side and conclude it on the left side.

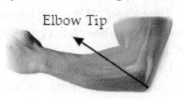

Figure 7.3

Key Points:

(1) Maintain proper alignment of your body, ensuring that your elbow is in line with the target and that your striking arm is fully extended. This alignment enhances the impact and effectiveness of the elbow strike.

(2) Maintain stability and balance throughout the movement by positioning your body's center of gravity appropriately. This stability allows for greater control and power in executing the elbow strike.

(3) Focus on striking vulnerable areas of your opponent's body, such as the ribs, abdomen, chin, or temple, to maximize the effectiveness of the technique. Precise targeting increases the chances of successful execution.

(4) Generate power by engaging the muscles of your entire body, utilizing rotational force from your waist and hips to add momentum to the strike. Proper utilization of body mechanics amplifies the impact of the elbow strike.

(5) Maintain a high level of focus and control during the execution of the elbow strike. This ensures precision and accuracy in targeting the intended area, increasing the effectiveness of the technique.

(6) Elbow strikes are versatile techniques that can be seamlessly integrated into various combinations, making them valuable in both offensive and defensive strategies. However, developing the necessary skills, timing, and accuracy required for effective elbow strikes necessitates proper training and consistent practice.

2. Pán Zhǒu or Hook Elbow, Winding Elbow

The 'Pán Zhǒu' (盤肘), or the 'Hook Elbow,' also known as the 'Winding Elbow' or 'Pan Elbow,' in English, is a circular-line elbow attack technique. It involves executing a horizontal strike with the forearm, directed inward. This technique was widely used in traditional Wushu forms such as 'Cha Quan, Hua Quan, and Shao Lin Quan,' it is also employed in contemporary competition routines. For example, the 'Elbow Strike in a Horse Stance' in the third Duan of the Elementary Long Fist or the 'Elbow Strike with a Bow Stance' in the First Set Long Fist of the International Competition Routine.

Preparation Posture: Begin in a right bow stance, with your right foot forward and your left foot slightly angled to the side. Place your right hand in a hook position behind your body and position your left hand on your right shoulder. Direct your gaze towards your left hand (Figure 7.4).

Movements (using the right elbow as an example):

- Initiate the movement by brushing your left arm from your right shoulder to the left side of your body.
- As you do this, raise your left arm and elbow, bringing your left fist to your left waist. Simultaneously, transition your right hand from a hook position into a fist. The focus of the technique is on the right elbow, which serves as the force point. Execute a circular motion, forcefully moving your right elbow from the outside to the inside. The striking point of the technique should be at the tip or close to the end of your right elbow (Figure 7.5).
- Practice the technique alternately, repeating the movements on both sides.

Figure 7.4   Figure 7.5

- **Force Point:** The force point of the technique is at the tip or close to the end of your right elbow.
- **Action Orbit:** The movement follows a circular line, tracing the path of the right elbow as it moves from the outside to the inside.
- **Direction:** The movement is primarily horizontal, with the circular motion directed towards the front of your body.
- **Starting and Ending Point:** The movement begins on the right side of your body and ends at the front, where the striking point of the technique is directed.

Key Points:

(1) Generating Power: The effectiveness of the 'Hook Elbow' technique relies on two forces. First, driving force from the leg by pushing off the ground with your foot. The second rotational force is generated by your body's rotation from the waist. These two forces combine to deliver significant power in the strike.

(2) Horizontal Elbow Strike: The 'Hook Elbow' technique is designed to strike the opponent's face, neck, and chest with the elbow tip or the outside of the forearm. It is an effective technique for targeting vulnerable areas.

(3) Comprehensive Force Generation: To maximize the technique's power, it is important to generate force collectively from the waist, legs, shoulders, and elbow. Proper coordination and synchronization of these body parts will enhance the overall effectiveness of the strike.

Common Errors:
(1) Excessive Elbow Angle: One common error is bending the elbow at an angle greater than 90 degrees. It is important to maintain the proper angle to ensure effective execution of the technique.
(2) Incorrect Forearm Movement: Another error is swinging the forearm instead of bending it from the outside to the inside. The movement should follow a circular path, maintaining control and precision.
(3) Inaccurate Force Point and Attack Route: It is crucial to accurately identify the force point and direct the strike along a horizontal path. Striking with the correct angle and trajectory will enhance the power and effectiveness of the technique.

3. Yā Zhǒu or Press Elbow

'Yā Zhǒu' (壓肘), or the 'Press Elbow' technique, involves lifting the bent elbow (left) and pressing it down towards the opposite side. One application of this technique is to control an opponent's arm by bringing it across your shoulder. For instance, if your opponent grabs your left shoulder with their right hand, you can use your right hand to grab their right hand, preventing them from escaping your shoulder (Figure 7.6). Then, roll your left arm over their arm and press down on their trapped elbow (Figure 7.7). This move represents another common circular-line elbow attack technique in Chinese Wushu.

Figure 7.6 Figure 7.7
Grab the Shoulder and Press the Elbow Down

152

Practice Methods:

Preparation Posture: Stand upright with your feet slightly wider than shoulder-width apart. Place your left fist on your left waist. Lift your right arm and fist to the right side at shoulder height. Direct your gaze towards your right fist (Figure 7.8).

Movements (using the right elbow as an example):
- Begin by bending your right elbow. Rotate your right forearm outward, positioning the outside of your right forearm and elbow as the force point. From this position, initiate a circular motion with your right arm. Press from the outside towards the inside and then downward. Simultaneously, lower your body into a horse stance while maintaining stability and balance (as shown in Figure 7.9).
- Throughout the movement, keep your focus on your right forearm. Practice the technique alternatingly, likely switching between your left and right arms.

This exercise combines martial arts elements, such as circular motion and balance in a horse stance, with arm strength and coordination training. It's essential to perform these movements mindfully and correctly to avoid injury and derive the intended benefits from the exercise.

Figure 7.8   Figure 7.9

- **Force Point:** The force point is located on the outside of your right elbow. This is the part of your arm that will be applying pressure during the exercise.
- **Action Orbit:** During the execution of the technique, your arm should follow a circular path or orbit.

- **Direction:** The movement direction is from the right side to the front. This means you start the exercise on your right side, and as you perform the circular motion, your arm moves toward the front of your body.
- **Starting and Ending Point:** You begin the movement from the right side of your body with your arm at shoulder height, and you conclude the movement at the front of your body, likely at a lower position as you lower your body into the horse stance.

Key Points:

(1) Spiral Force and Power: When executing the press elbow technique, focus on generating a spiral force from the outside to the inside. Simultaneously, apply power from top to bottom despite the limited range of the strike.

(2) Utilize Body Mechanics: Engage your waist to mobilize your arm, ensuring your feet are firmly rooted into the ground. Keep your head lifted, creating a solid tensile force by elongating both directions.

(3) Stability and Balance: Maintain a stable and balanced position throughout the movement. Securely hold your right fist and stabilize your right arm. Avoid leaning in any direction while pressing your elbow and performing the squat.

Common Errors:

(1) Incorrect Force Point: Ensure that the force point is on the outside of your right forearm, not on the back of the fist. Focusing the force on the correct area optimizes the effectiveness of the technique.

(2) Insufficient Spiral Force: Remember to rotate your arm outward to generate the spiral force required for the press elbow. Neglecting this rotation can diminish the power and efficiency of the technique.

(3) Lack of Stability: Pay attention to maintaining stability in your entire body. Avoid any instability or imbalance during the movement, as it can weaken the overall execution of the technique.

Chapter 8
Basic Movements (4)
Tuǐ Fǎ
腿法
Leg Technique

'Tuǐ Fǎ,' which translates to 'Leg Technique' in English, holds a pivotal and versatile role in Chinese Wushu. As a martial proverb aptly states: 'The fists are like the double doors, but when fighting, all depends on the feet being used to strike.' In Chinese Wushu, whether it is Traditional or Contemporary, any technique involving the use of legs for attack or defense falls under the category of 'Leg Techniques'.

Diligent practice of 'Leg Technique' allows practitioners to enhance their flexibility, agility, strength, speed, and overall leg skills. Regardless of whether you are a seasoned Wushu practitioner or a beginner, consistent practice remains essential for mastering these techniques.

However, it is crucial to remember that properly warming up and stretching the leg tendons and muscles is an indispensable prerequisite before practicing leg techniques. This not only helps prevent injuries but also prepares the body for optimal performance. As a wise Wushu proverb reminds us, stretching accounts for only 30% of the preparation, while the execution of the kick constitutes 70% of the technique's effectiveness. Below, the author will introduce some of the renowned leg techniques to readers.

Zhí Bǎi Xìng Tuǐ Fǎ
直擺性腿法
Straight Swinging Leg Techniques

In Chinese, 'Zhí' means straight, 'Bǎi' means swing, 'Xìng' refers to attributes, and 'Tuǐ Fǎ' refers to 'Leg Technique.' Taken literally, the term 'Zhí Bǎi Xìng Tuǐ Fǎ' can be translated as the 'Straight Swing Category of Leg Techniques' in English, signifying that this category of 'Leg Techniques ' is executed by extending and swinging the legs.

This category of 'Leg Technique' represents a specialized subset within Wushu. These techniques involve the skillful execution of powerful kicks through a straight-line swinging leg motion. By harnessing the leg's swinging movement, practitioners can generate significant momentum, resulting in dynamic and impactful kicks. Straight swing 'Leg Technique' mastery relies on precise timing, impeccable coordination, and adept body control.

While executing 'Straight Swing Leg Techniques,' practitioners must meticulously time their kicks to ensure they align perfectly with the intended target. Effective coordination between the upper and lower body is paramount, as it preserves balance and maximizes the power derived from the swinging action.

155

1. Zhèng Tī Tuǐ or Front Straight Kic

'Zhèng Tī Tuǐ' (正踢腿), or 'Front Straight Kick' in English, is a direct swinging kick performed with the foot dorsiflexed, keeping both legs straight. This kick is commonly featured in the Long Fist categories routines, showcasing its prominence in Wushu.

When executing the Front Straight Kick, the practitioner aims to deliver a powerful strike using the front part of the foot, typically the ball or the base of the toes. The kicking leg remains straight throughout the motion, emphasizing speed, precision, and control. By keeping the legs straight, the kick maximizes the reach and potential impact.

The Front Straight Kick is often used in Wushu for offensive and defensive purposes. It can target an opponent's torso, head, or legs, depending on the circumstances. Its straightforward and rapid execution renders it a highly effective maneuver in various combat scenarios. Through meticulous refinement of kicking technique, timing, and precision, Wushu practitioners can unlock the potential for delivering potent and pinpoint Front Straight Kicks, thereby enhancing the depth and versatility of their skill repertoire. The practice method for the Front Straight Kick is outlined below:

Preparation Posture:
*   Stand straight with your feet together. Sink your shoulders and drop your elbows. Push your chest out and straighten your waist. Look straight ahead (Figure 8.1).
*   Place your fists at your waist with the fists facing upward. Fully express your inner strength in your eyes and throughout your whole body, encompassing the essence, Qi, and spirit of Wushu (Figure 8.2).

Figure 8.1   Figure 8.2

- Powerfully push your palms to both sides of your body, stretching your fingers upward. The force points should be on the palms. Imagine using your palms to support the power from both sides. Keep your eyes open and maintain a strong spirit while ensuring your Qi is grounded and focused (Figure 8.3).

Figure 8.3   Side

Movements (using the right leg as an example):
- After are prepared, maintain your upper body posture, take a half-step forward with your left foot to shift your weight onto it (Figure 8.4).
- Hook your right foot inward. Kick forcefully upward with your right foot, aiming for your forehead or the top of your head. Keep your gaze fixed straight ahead (Figure 8.5).
- Put your right foot down in front of your left foot (Figure 8.6) but keep the weight still on your left foot. Then take a slight step forward with your right foot to prepare for the subsequent left kick (Figure 8.7).
- Continue practicing alternating kicks, repeating the movement with the opposite leg.

During practice, pay attention to the following points:
(1) Maintain proper body alignment and posture throughout the movement.
(2) Engage your core muscles for stability and control.
(3) Keep your kicking leg straight and fully extend it for maximum reach and impact.
(4) Focus on the target and execute the kick with precision and accuracy.
(5) Practice both sides equally to develop balance and coordination.

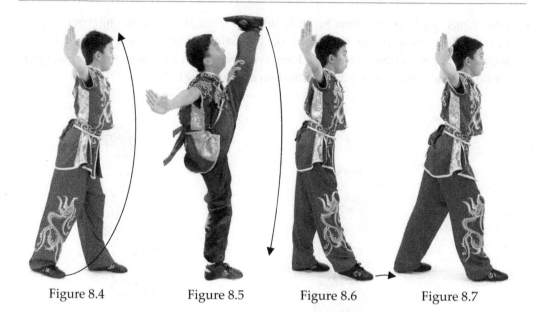

| Figure 8.4 | Figure 8.5 | Figure 8.6 | Figure 8.7 |

In a Competitive Wushu Competition, the following deduction points apply to the 'Front Straight Kick':

(1) Knee/s bent at the apex of the kick: Avoid bending your knee(s) at the highest point of your kick. To maintain a clean and precise technique, strive to keep your kicking leg fully extended throughout the kick.
(2) The heel of the supporting leg off the floor: Ensure that the heel of your supporting leg remains firmly grounded throughout the execution of the kick. Lifting the heel off the floor can lead to deductions in your competition score.

Following these guidelines during your performance will not only help you avoid point deductions but also ensure that this kick is executed with the precision and excellence expected in competitive Wushu.

Key Points:
(1) Maintain an upright posture with your chest lifted and your waist straight. Avoid leaning or tilting your upper body in any direction.
(2) Initiate the kick by hooking your foot inward. As you raise your leg, fully extend it. When lowering your leg, gradually stretch your foot and reduce its control.
(3) Keep your hips and abdomen tucked inward to maintain stability and balance throughout the kick. This will aid in generating power and maintaining control of your technique.
(4) Ensure that your arms remain straight throughout the kick. Avoid any bending or dropping of your arms during the execution of the kick.
(5) While executing the kick, avoid lifting your supporting heel off the ground. Keep the supporting leg firmly rooted to maintain balance and control.

Common Errors and Corrections:

(1) Leaning the Upper Body Forward and Bending the Knees: Focus on straightening your waist, tucking your chin in, and raising your head upward. Push your arms outward to fix your chest out. Additionally, aim to kick slightly lower and decrease the kicking speed appropriately.

(2) Lifting the Heel of the Supporting Foot Off the Ground or Sending the Hip Forward: Take smaller steps when moving your supporting foot forward. When kicking, ensure your supporting knee is stretched, and grab the ground with your toes. Consider kicking slightly lower initially to maintain stability.

(3) Slow and Weak Kicks: Practice kicking with the required speed and power by using a wall-bar or an object for support. Perform single-leg kicks at the instructed speed and alternate between left and right legs to develop speed and strength.

Practice Steps:

(1) Warm-Up and Stretching: Begin your practice session by warming up and stretching your legs. Include swinging and splitting exercises as previously learned. This helps prepare your muscles and enhances flexibility.

(2) Initial Front Straight Kick Practice: Start practicing the 'Front Straight Kick' with a lower kick height and at a comfortable speed. Your primary focus should be on maintaining proper form and technique. Gradually increase the difficulty level as you gain confidence and proficiency.

(3) Use Support: Employ a wall bar or any suitable object for support. Stand in place and practice kicking one leg at a time while emphasizing balance and control. Begin with the leg you feel more comfortable with, then switch to the other.

(4) Progress to practicing alternating kicks while walking. Follow these steps (Figure 8.8):

1) Begin with your feet together.

2) Execute a right leg kick.

3) After the kick, place your right foot down inside of your left foot, bringing your feet together. Alternatively, you can place your right foot down in front of your left foot, with only the right forefoot touching the ground.

4) Step your right foot forward and repeat the sequence, kicking your left leg up.

5) Continue alternating between the left and right legs, performing the Front Straight Kick with each leg in succession.

Indeed, maintaining proper body alignment, leg extension, and coordinated hip and body rotation are crucial for a successful 'Front Straight Kick.' Focus on executing the kicks with control, precision, and a fluid swinging motion. Regular and detailed practice will significantly aid in mastering this technique. Following these steps can gradually improve your 'Front Straight Kick.'

Remember to maintain proper form, gradually increase the difficulty, and practice both sides equally. Consistent practice and patience are key to refining your technique and achieving proficiency in the 'Front Straight Kick.'

Feet Together   Left Foot Forward   Right Kick   Right Foot Landing

Right Foot Forward   Left Kick   Left Foot Landing

Front Straight Kick

Figure 8.8

1. Shí Zì Tuǐ or Cross Straight Kick

'Shí Zì' (十字) means 'cross' in English, so 'Shí Zì Tuǐ' (十字腿) can be translated as 'Cross Straight Kick.' In Chinese Wushu, the 'Cross Straight Kick' is a striking technique where the kicking leg crosses the body midline and extends straight towards the opposite ear, forming a crossed form. It is a powerful and visually impressive kick that requires precise technique and exceptional body control. To enhance your proficiency in the 'Cross Straight Kick,' follow the practice steps outlined below:

Preparation Posture:

The preparation posture for the 'Cross Straight Kick' is identical to that of the 'Front Straight Kick.' Stand upright with your feet together, relax your shoulders, align your chest and waist, and keep your gaze fixed straight ahead (Figure 8.9).

Movements (using the right leg as an example):

- To begin the kick, take a half-step forward with your left foot, shifting your body weight onto it (Figure 8.10).
- Simultaneously, hook your right foot inward. Execute a forceful kick with your right leg, aiming towards the left side of your head or the left ear. Ensure that your leg is fully extended and perfectly straight. Maintain your focus on the target and keep your gaze straight ahead throughout the kick (Figure 8.11).
- Put your right foot in front of your left foot and prepare for the next kick (Figure 8.12).
- Practice alternating kicks, making certain to train both sides equally.

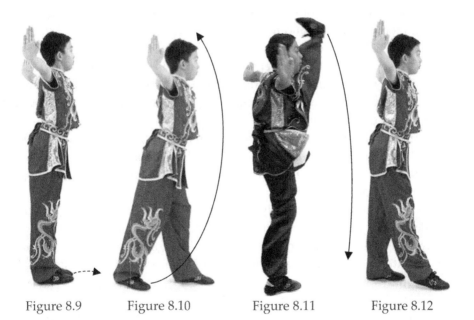

| Figure 8.9 | Figure 8.10 | Figure 8.11 | Figure 8.12 |

In 'Competitive Wushu' Competitions, it's crucial to be attentive to the following deduction points when performing the 'Cross Straight Kick':

(1) Bent knee(s) at the apex of the kick: Ensure that your kicking leg remains fully straight and extended throughout the entire kicking motion. Avoid any bending of the knee(s) during the kick.

(2) Heel of the supporting leg off the floor: Ensure stability by keeping the heel of your supporting leg firmly planted on the ground. Avoid lifting it off the floor.

Key Points:
(1) The 'Cross Straight Kick' is similar to the 'Straight Front Kick' but with the direction tilted toward the opposite side.
(2) It's important to maintain proper body alignment and avoid twisting your body while executing the kick. Keep your upper body upright throughout the movement.

Common Errors and Corrections:
(1) Common Errors, Corrective methods for the 'Cross Straight Kick' are similar to those for the 'Front Straight Kick.'
(2) Refer to the previous section on the 'Front Straight Kick' for guidance on addressing common errors and following practice steps.

Practice Steps:
The practice steps for the 'Cross Straight Kick' closely resemble those of the 'Front Straight Kick,' with the primary difference being the direction of the kick.

(1) Warm-up: Commence your practice with a thorough warm-up routine to prepare your muscles and joints for kicking exercises. Jogging, stretching, and mobility drills enhance blood circulation and flexibility.
(2) Practice the Kicking Motion: Initiate the kick by taking a half-step forward with your left foot to support your body weight. Simultaneously, hook your right foot inward and execute a forceful kick toward the opposite ear or side of your head. Maintain an upright body posture and keep your gaze straight ahead during the kick. Emphasize the importance of maintaining a straight leg throughout the movement.
(3) Alternate Kicks: After completing the kick on one side, return your right foot to the starting position and repeat the kicking motion, aiming for the other ear or the opposite side of your head. Practice alternating kicks between the left and right sides to ensure balanced development.
(4) Repeat and Refine: Continuously practice the 'Cross Straight Kick,' paying close attention to proper technique, precise body alignment, and maintaining control throughout the entire movement. Refine your execution by focusing on details such as the position of your supporting leg, the full extension of your kicking leg, and the overall fluidity of the kick.
(5) Gradually Increase Difficulty: As you become more comfortable with the fundamental execution of the Cross Straight Kick, challenge yourself progressively by increasing the kick's height and intensifying the movement's speed and power.

2. Cè Tī Tuǐ or Side Straight Kick
'Cè Tī Tuǐ' (侧踢腿), translated as the 'Side Straight Kick,' involves swinging the leg towards the same-side ear. It is a powerful and dynamic kicking technique in Wushu. The methods of practice for the Side Straight Kick are as follows:

Preparation Posture:

Assume the same starting position as the 'Front Straight Kick.'

Stand straight with your feet together, sink your shoulders, drop your elbows, extend your chest, and straighten your waist. Powerfully push your palms to both sides of your body, stretching your fingers upward. Keep your eyes open and maintain a strong spirit while ensuring your Qi is grounded and focused (Figure 8.13).

Figure 8.13

Movements (using the left leg as an example):

- Step your right foot to the left, crossing it in front of your left leg while angling your toes approximately 45 or slightly more degrees outward. Lift your left heel slightly off the ground as you turn your body to the right. Bend your right knee slightly while extending your left arm forward and your right arm backward, forming a straight line. Ensure that the fingers of your left hand point forward while the fingers of your right hand point backward. Look straight ahead (Figure 8.14). Remember to elongate both your arms in opposite directions as far as possible, making your palms straight and fingers extended. Cross your right foot in front of your left leg, ensuring that it does not obstruct your right foot's kick in the following movement.
- Hook your left foot inward and execute a powerful kick to the side of your left ear. Simultaneously, raise your right palm over your head with the palm facing upward, as if supporting the sky. Place your left palm on your right chest with the fingers pointing upward. Maintain a forward gaze (Figure 8.15).
- Lower your left foot to the ground but keep your weight on your right leg. Extend your arms forward and backward, simultaneously stretching in opposite directions. Allow your left toes to touch the ground lightly (Figure 8.16).

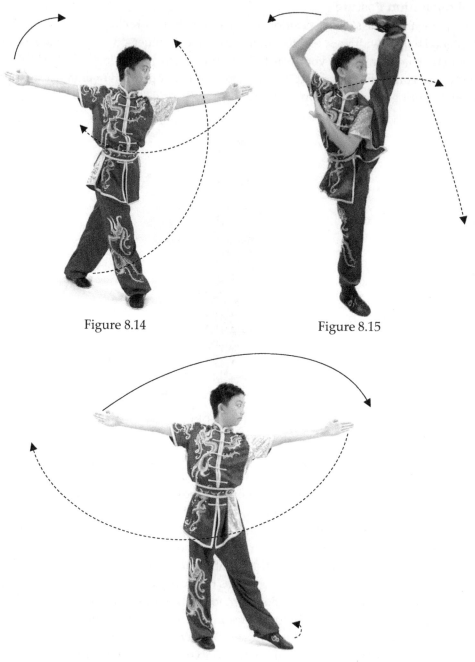

Figure 8.14

Figure 8.15

Figure 8.16

- Practice alternating kicks by repeating the same sequence on the opposite side with a dedicated focus on upholding proper form, and balance (Figure 8.17, 8.18, 8.19). Please refers to the previous descriptions.

Figure 8.17   Figure 8.18

Figure 8.19

Be meticulous about details such as the positioning of your arms, the extension of your leg, and the alignment of your body. Through regular and attentive practice, you will gradually develop the requisite strength, flexibility, and precision essential for mastering the 'Side Straight Kick' in Wushu.

165

Key Points:

(1) Maintain an upright and aligned chest and waist during the 'Side Straight Kick.' Avoid leaning forward or backward.

(2) Rotate your hips and body sideways, facing the direction of the kick, to achieve proper alignment and generate power.

(3) Engage your core muscles by pulling your abdomen inward to ensure stability and control during the kick.

Common Errors and Corrections:

(1) Insufficient Hip Rotation: Failing to rotate your hips enough can result in a weak and less impactful kick. Focus on turning your hips and upper body more toward the direction of the kick. This rotation generates power and improves the kick's effectiveness.

(2) Leaning Forward or Backward: Leaning your upper body forward or backward can disrupt your balance and reduce the kick's precision. Keep your upper body upright and aligned with your chest and waist. This ensures stability and proper form during the kick.

(3) Inadequate Core Engagement: Neglecting to engage your core muscles can lead to instability and reduced control. Pull your abdomen inward to engage your core muscles. This provides stability and better control while executing the kick.

(4) Not Targeting the Right Area: Kicking too low or too high can result in an ineffective strike. Aim to kick towards the side of your ear, which is the optimal target area for a 'Side Straight Kick' in Wushu. This ensures that your kick is both precise and impactful.

(5) Lack of Flexibility: Limited flexibility in your kicking leg can hinder the kick's range and height. Incorporate stretching exercises into your training routine to improve the flexibility of your kicking leg. This will enable you to execute higher and more extended kicks.

Practice Steps:

(1) Warm-Up: Begin with a thorough warm-up to prepare your body for kicking practice. Perform jogging, stretching, and joint rotations to increase blood flow and flexibility.

(2) Leg Swinging Motion: Lift your leg on the same side as the kicking leg, keeping it straight and extended. Swing your leg towards the same-side ear, aiming for a high and controlled kick. Focus on generating power and momentum from your hip and core muscles.

(3) Target Accuracy: Aim to kick towards the same-side ear precisely. Practice controlling the height and trajectory of your kick, gradually increasing the size as your flexibility and strength improve.

(4) Alternating Kicks: After completing the kick on one side, return your leg to the starting position and repeat the same kicking motion on the opposite side. Alternate kicks between the left and right sides, focusing on maintaining consistency in technique and power (Figure 8.20).

(5) Gradual Progression: Begin with lower kicks and gradually increase the height and power of your kicks as you gain strength, flexibility, and control. It is important to progress slowly to avoid injury and ensure proper form.

Cross Right Foot Forward   Side Left Kick   Landing

Cross Left Foot Forward   Side Right Kick   Landing

Figure 8.20

3. Wài Bǎi Tuǐ or Outer Crescent Kick

'Wài Bǎi Tuǐ' (外擺腿) can be translated as the 'Outer Crescent Kick' in English. It is one of the typical 'Leg Techniques' in Chinese Wushu that involves swinging one leg from inward to outward and sweeping across an opponent's body or legs to achieve the purpose of attacking or sweeping the opponent. In this kick, the leg swings in a smooth and controlled manner, extending to the outside of the body. The purpose is to strike the target with the outer edge of the foot or the heel, generating power and precision.

167

Preparation Posture:

Assume the same starting position as the previous movement (Figure 8.21).

Movements (using the right leg as an example):

- Step forward with your left foot and slightly turn your left toes outward (Figure 8.22). Hook your right foot inward tightly and kick upward toward the left side of your head (Figure 8.23). Swing your leg across your face from left to right (Figure 8.24), extending it outward in a smooth and controlled motion.

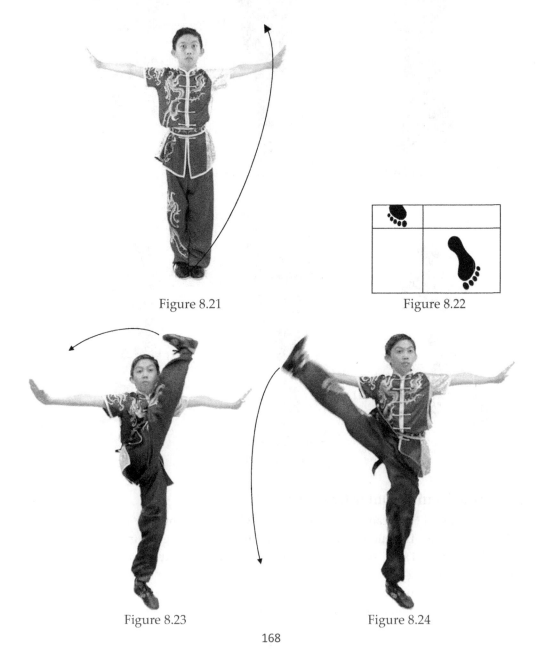

Figure 8.21

Figure 8.22

Figure 8.23

Figure 8.24

- Land on the right side of your body or return to the starting position, maintaining a balanced stance (Figure 8.25). Keep your gaze fixed straight ahead.

Figure 8.25

- As your leg swings across, you can tap the right palm on the right side of your right foot for added control and balance.
- Practice alternating kicks, repeating the same sequence with the opposite leg.

Practice Steps

(1) Warm-Up: Commence your practice session with a comprehensive stretching routine to strengthen your muscles and enhance flexibility. This will help reduce the risk of injury.

(2) Practice 'Front Straight Kick': Prioritize practicing the 'Front Straight Kick' exercise before progressing to the 'Outward Crescent Kick.' This sequential approach will assist in building a solid foundation and minimizing the risk of injury.

(3) Practice in Place: Begin by practicing the kick in a stationary position. Find a stable stance or utilize objects for support to maintain balance while performing one-legged kicks. Concentrate on proper technique and gradually increase the height and range of your kicks. Once you feel confident and meet the requirements, switch to the other leg and repeat the process.

(4) Alternating Kicks: Integrate walking into your practice routine after mastering the fundamental movements. Alternate the outward crescent kicks from left to right as you walk, maintaining a fluid and controlled motion (Figure 8.26).

(5) Foot Tapping: Incorporate foot-tapping exercises to refine your technique further. Use one hand to tap your foot's outside as you kick lightly. For instance, when

executing the outward crescent kick with your right leg, gently touch the outside of your right foot with your right hand on the right side of your body. Gradually progress to tapping your foot with both hands. For example, while kicking your right foot outward, use your left hand to touch the back of your right foot in front of your head, followed by your right hand.

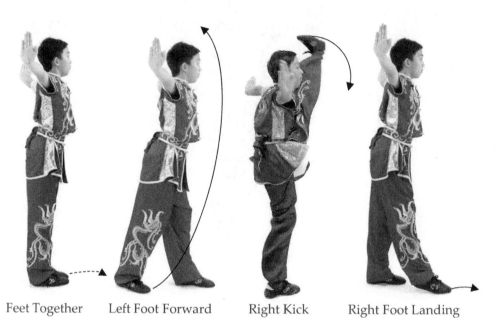

Feet Together　　　Left Foot Forward　　　Right Kick　　　Right Foot Landing

Right Foot Forward　　　Left Kick　　　Left Foot Landing

Outer Crescent Kick

Figure 8.26

In a 'Competitive Wushu' Competition, be mindful of the deduction points:

(1) Ensure the toes of the slapped foot do not go below shoulder height during the kick.

(2) Pay attention to the execution of the slap. The slap should be audible and clearly visible, without missing the target. Practice precision and consistency in delivering the slap to maximize your score.

Key Points:

(1) Maintain a straight and upright posture throughout the kick, with your chest and waist straightened and your head suspended on top. Avoid leaning in any direction or protruding your buttocks, as it can affect your balance and overall form.

(2) Keep your leg straight during the swinging motion, focusing on extending it outwards to strike the target with the outer edge of the foot or the heel. This helps with balance and accuracy.

(3) Coordinate your hip and body rotation to generate power and momentum for the kick. Ensure a smooth and controlled swinging motion, utilizing the rotation of the hip and the transfer of weight.

(4) Aim for an extensive range of motion, allowing the kick to follow a fan-shaped path. Avoid excessive bending of the knees and maintain a slight opening in your crotch.

(5) Minimize body twisting during the kick and keep your palms pushed outward.

Common Errors and Corrections:

(1) Improper Leg Alignment: Ensure your leg remains straight throughout the kick. Avoid bending the knee or allowing the leg to collapse during swinging. Practice leg extension and focus on maintaining a straight line from the hip to the foot.

(2) Lack of Power and Control: Pay attention to generating power and control through the coordinated rotation of the hip and body. Avoid relying solely on the leg movement without utilizing the full body. Practice hip and body rotation exercises, gradually increasing the power and control of the kick.

(3) Insufficient Speed: Work on increasing the speed of your kick while maintaining proper form. Focus on explosive and fast movements while keeping the legs straight.

(4) Incomplete Range of Motion: Ensure that your kicking foot reaches the intended target, such as the forehead, without being loose or hanging over the head. Practice precise and controlled kicks to develop accuracy and full range of motion.

(5) Supporting Foot Stability: Keep the heel of the supporting foot grounded throughout the kick to maintain stability and balance. Pay attention to weight distribution and grounding of the supporting foot.

(6) Correct Initiation of the Kicking Leg: Start the kick from the inside, ensuring that the leg swings outward with sufficient range. Avoid imbalance or leaning by maintaining the correct starting position and focusing on balance throughout the kick.

(7) Flexibility and Agility Exercises: Incorporate exercises that enhance flexibility and agility, such as holding the knee and extending the hip outward. These exercises can improve your overall kicking technique.

- Progressive Practice: Begin with lower kicks and gradually increase the range of the outward swing. Focus on controlled progression to develop strength and flexibility while maintaining proper technique.

4. Lǐ Hé Tuǐ or Inside Crescent Kick

'Lǐ Hé Tuǐ,' (裏合腿) translated as 'Inside Crescent Kick,' is a leg technique in Chinese Wushu. It is typically executed by kicking from outward to inward, aiming to strike the opponent with the inside of the foot. This technique involves crossing one leg to the inside of the other and utilizing internal force for offensive or defensive purposes. Executing the inside crescent kick demands a strong sense of balance, coordination, and precise leg control to ensure its practical application. It is commonly incorporated into various Chinese Wushu routines and combat techniques.

Preparation Posture:
Assume the same starting position as the previous movement (Figure 8.27).

Figure 8.27   Figure 8.28

Movements:
- Step forward with your left foot, positioning it just to the right of your body's centerline (Figure 8.28). Hook your right foot inward tightly, straighten your right leg, and kick up towards the right side (Figure 8.29). Swing the kick from the right side across your face to the left side (Figure 8.30).
- Land on the left side of your body or return to the preparation position (Figure 8.31). Keep your gaze fixed forward.

- Optionally, the left palm can pat on the sole of your right foot (Figure 8.32). Practice alternating kicks.

Figure 8.29   Figure 8.30

Figure 8.31   Figure 8.32 (Side)

In the context of 'Competitive Wushu' Competitions, deductions for the Inside Crescent Kick are assessed based on the following criteria:

(1) Toes of the swinging foot below shoulder height. Inability to maintain a controlled swinging motion.

(2) Missed or inaudible slap sound. Failure to maintain a straight leg throughout the kick.

Practice Steps:

(1) The 'Inside Crescent Kick' shares similarities with the 'Outside Crescent Kick' in terms of technique but is executed in a different direction.

(2) To enhance your practice, consider integrating striking techniques. Start by using one hand to strike your foot. For example, while executing a kick with your right leg, use your left hand to strike the sole of your right foot on the left side of your body.

(3) As you refine your 'Inside Crescent Kick,' remember to emphasize the key points mentioned earlier, which include maintaining proper body alignment and leg extension. Gradually increase your kicks' speed, height, and range of motion while prioritizing control and precision.

Key Points:

- The 'Inside Crescent Kick' is similar to the 'Outside Crescent Kick' but performed in a different direction.
- Remember to maintain proper body alignment, leg extension, and coordination of hip and body rotation.
- Focus on executing the kick with control, precision, and a smooth swinging motion.

Common Errors and Corrections:

The Common Errors and Corrections for the 'Inside Crescent Kick' are similar to those for the 'Outside Crescent Kick,' but in the opposite direction. Pay attention to the following:

(1) Improper Body Alignment: Ensure that your chest is straightened, your waist is aligned, and your head is upright. Avoid leaning in any direction or protruding your buttocks, as it can affect your balance and form. Practice maintaining a straight and upright posture throughout the kick.

(2) Insufficient Leg Extension: Keep your leg straight during the swinging motion and focus on extending it outwards. Aim to strike the target with the inner edge of the foot or the heel. Practice leg extension exercises and focus on maintaining a straight line from the hip to the foot.

(3) Lack of Coordination in Hip and Body Rotation: Coordinate the rotation of your hip and body to generate power and momentum for the kick. Ensure a smooth and controlled swinging motion by utilizing the rotation and transfer of weight. Practice hip and body rotation exercises to improve coordination and power.

(4) Inadequate Range of Motion: Aim for an extensive range of motion, allowing the kick to follow a smooth, curved path. Avoid excessive bending of the knees and maintain a slight opening in your crotch. Minimize body twisting during the kick and keep your palms pushed outward. Focus on gradually increasing your kicks' speed, height, and range of motion while maintaining control and precision.

Qū Shēn Xìng Tuǐ Fǎ
屈伸性腿法
Flexion and Extension Leg Technique

'Qū Shēn' (屈伸), translated as 'Flexion and Extension' in English, holds a fundamental place within 'Leg Technique' in Chinese Wushu. It is frequently employed in the Long Fist and external martial arts schools like Shaolin Quan, Cha Quan, and Hua Quan. This technique is the counterpart to the 'Straight and Swing' leg technique, involving dynamic movements that seamlessly transition from leg bending to extension. 'Qū Shēn' empowers practitioners to execute strikes from various angles and levels, effectively showcasing Wushu leg techniques' intricate versatility and complexity.

1. Tán Tuǐ or Front Snap Kick

'Tán Tuǐ' (彈腿), translated as the 'Front Snap Kick' in English, is a dynamic kicking technique where the leg starts from the bent before rapidly extending it forward to hit the target using the top or tip of the foot. The power generated from the rapid extension is akin to the snapping of a branch, hence the term 'snap kick,' which emphasizes speed, precision, and power.

Preparation Posture:

Begin by standing upright with your feet together. Place your fists on your waist and maintain a forward gaze (Figure 8.33).

Always prioritize the essence, Qi, and spirit within your body and mind during Wushu practice. Emphasize lifting your head upward, thrusting your chest out, pulling in your abdomen, straightening your waist, and settling your hips down. This stance prepares you to transition smoothly at any given moment.

Movements (using the right leg as an example):
Figure 8.33

- Begin by standing straight, shifting your weight onto your left leg without leaning. Bend your right knee, raising it in front of your body, ensuring that your right thigh is positioned at waist height. Consciously point your right toe downward and maintain a forward gaze (Figure 8.34).
- As your right knee approaches waist height, use it as an axis and swiftly extend your leg by straightening your knee, executing a forward snap kick. Concentrate the striking force on the top of your right toes. Ensure that the top of your right foot, thigh, and calf form a straight line at waist height. Your left leg can either stay straight or slightly bend to support your weight (Figure 8.35). Maintain a focused forward gaze and proper body alignment throughout the kick.
- Alternate kicks with both legs during practice to enhance balance and coordination.

Figure 8.34   Figure 8.35

Key Points:
(1) Maintain straightness in your chest and waist while tucking your hips in.
(2) Begin the kick by pointing your foot down before extending it forward with explosive force.
(3) Aim for accurate, crisp, and clean strikes, ensuring the force point is firm and unyielding.
(4) Maintain a solid balance by gripping the ground with your supporting foot.

Common Errors and Corrections:
(1) Insufficient Clarity in Leg Flexion and Extension: A lack of clear leg flexion and extension often results in a slower kick. Prioritize practicing the seamless transition from bending to extending the leg to improve the speed of your keel kick.
(2) Neglecting to Straighten the Knee After Leg Extension: Failing to straighten the knee after extending the leg can lead to misplaced force and improper alignment. Ensure you tuck the hip inward as you initiate the kick, followed by a powerful extension after bending the knee. Maintain proper alignment throughout the movement.
(3) Loose Kicking Knee and Toe: Allowing the kicking knee and toe to remain loose can compromise power transmission from the foot. Focus on gripping the ground firmly with your toes and consciously point your kicking toes forward while stretching. Emphasize control over the knee during practice to maintain power and precision.
(4) Elevated Supporting Heel or Leaning Body: Elevating the supporting heel or leaning the body during execution is discouraged. Initially, aim to kick from a slightly lower

position, focusing on maintaining proper form and technique. Gradually work on improving your kicking technique over time.

In 'Competitive Wushu' Competitions, deductions may occur if the kicking leg fails to transition from a visibly bent position (45° or more) to a completely straight position.

2. Dèng Tuǐ or Thrust Heel Kick

'Dèng Tuǐ' (蹬腿), also known as the 'Thrust Heel Kick,' is a type of kick in which the foot is dorsiflexed, with the toes pointing upward. This technique involves thrusting the heel forward to make contact with the target.

Preparation Posture:

Begin by standing upright with your feet together. Position your fists on your waist and maintain a forward gaze (Figure 8.36). The stance requirement is like the 'Tan Tui.'

Movements (use the right leg as an example):

- Bend and lift your right knee in front of your body, positioning the right thigh at waist height. Hook your right toes inward (Figure 8.37).
- As your right knee reaches waist height, swiftly extend your right knee and perform a forward kick using your right heel. Aim to align the thigh and calf in a straight line at waist height. Keep your left leg straight or slightly bent to maintain stability and support your body weight (Figure 8.38). Practice alternating kicks.

Figure 8.36   Figure 8.37   Figure 8.38

Key Points:
(1) The Thrust Heel Kick is similar to the Front Snap Kick, but the force point is different, with the emphasis on striking with the heel.
(2) Focus on transitioning from a bent position to fully extending the kicking leg for maximum power and effectiveness.

Common Errors and Corrections:
(1) Insufficient Height: Kicking too low can result in ineffective strikes and reduce the visual impact of the keel kick. Focus on improving your flexibility and leg strength to execute higher keel kicks, aiming for the intended target.
(2) Lack of Chambering: Neglecting to chamber your kicking leg properly before the kick can decrease its power and precision. Before executing the keel kick, bring your knee up toward your chest to create a chambered position. This enhances the kick's power and accuracy.
(3) Leaning Backward: Leaning backward while kicking can compromise your balance and reduce the kick's effectiveness. Maintain an upright posture and body alignment during the kick. Avoid leaning backward by engaging your core muscles for stability.

In a Competitive Wushu Competition, deduction points may be applied if:

The kicking leg fails to transition from an obviously bent position of 45° or more to a completely straight position.

3. Cè Chuài Tuǐ or Side Sole Kick

'Cè Chuài Tuǐ' (侧踹腿), also known as the 'Side Sole Kick' in English, is a powerful kicking technique primarily used to target various areas of the opponent's body, including the knee, waist, abdomen, chest, ribs, neck, and head. It holds significant importance in hand-to-hand combat, much like a straight punch. This kick follows a linear trajectory and is considered one of the three 'mother kicks' along with the heel, whip, and roundhouse kicks. The Side Sole Kick is renowned for its formidable attacking power, making it one of the most lethal techniques in martial arts.

Preparation Posture:
Begin in a straight and upright posture with your feet together (Figure 8.39).

Movements (using the left leg as an example):
- Cross your right foot in front of your left leg, slightly bending both knees. Turn your right toe outward slightly and lift your left heel. Cross your hands over your chest, maintaining a focused gaze to the left (Figure 8.40).
- Bend your left knee and move your left foot inward, lifting it above the ground. Simultaneously, straighten your right leg and shift your weight onto it. Keep your gaze directed to the left (Figure 8.41).
- Use your left heel as the force point and execute a horizontal kick to the left. Point your left toes inward and raise your leg to at least shoulder height. Lean your upper

body to the right while pushing your palms outward on both sides. The right arm is positioned higher than the shoulder, while the left is at shoulder height. Focus the force on both palms. Maintain your gaze to the left (Figure 8.42). Ensure you swiftly and suddenly extend your left knee when executing the kick. Open your hips and tilt the outside of your left foot upward to direct the power towards the left heel.

Figure 8.39   Figure 8.40   Figure 8.41

Figure 8.42

Key Points:

(1) Ensure that the power of the 'Sole Side Kick' originates from the feet, travels through the legs and hips, is controlled by the waist, and leverages the forward momentum generated by the center of gravity.

(2) Tilting the upper body in the opposite direction increases the striking distance and power during the kick.

(3) The kicking leg gains support from the body's strength, with the body amplifying the power of the kicking leg. Strike the opponent using the outer edge of the foot or the entire sole.

(4) Lift the knee, twist the supporting foot, inwardly rotate the raised knee, and engage the hips. The entire motion should display precise and rapid consistency.

(5) Integrate the strength into the whole body, creating a unified power. Ensure the upper body and legs remain on the same plane, preventing any distortion of the body and limbs.

Common Errors and Corrections:

(1) Insufficient Extension: A stiff and rigid kick may result from not fully extending the leg and insufficient body opening. Ensure that the kicking toe is tilted upward, forming a 'side heel kick' during practice. Focus on improving your flexibility and leg strength to execute higher 'Side Sole Kicks,' aiming for the intended target's height.

(2) Improper Execution: The execution of the 'Sole Side Kick' often involves a transition from a bent position to a straight kick, utilizing a swinging arc motion with the hips that causes the hip to protrude, forming a triangle between your upper body and kicking leg without a clear force point. Pay attention to the proper execution of the kick to avoid the swinging arc motion. Maintain a clear force point and a straighter trajectory.

(3) Misalignment of the Upper Body and Kicking Leg: Misalignment can lead to a backward shift of the center of gravity, ultimately weakening the effectiveness of the kick. Maintain an upright posture and body alignment during the kick. Avoid leaning backward by engaging your core muscles for stability.

(4) Insufficient Height: Kicking too low can result in ineffective strikes. Focus on improving your flexibility and leg strength to execute higher Side Sole Kicks, aiming for the intended target's height.

(5) Incorrect Foot Position: Placing your foot incorrectly during the kick can affect balance and accuracy. Ensure that the sole of your foot makes contact with the target and that your toes point in the intended direction of the kick.

(6) Leaning Backward: Leaning backward while kicking can compromise your balance and reduce the kick's effectiveness. Maintain an upright posture and body alignment during the kick. Avoid leaning backward by engaging your core muscles for stability.

Corrective Practice Steps:

(1) Beginners can commence slow-motion exercises and gradual progression, beginning with simpler movements before advancing to more complex ones. Breaking down

the actions into individual steps is beneficial. For instance, using a chair for support during practice can be helpful (refer to Figure 8.43).

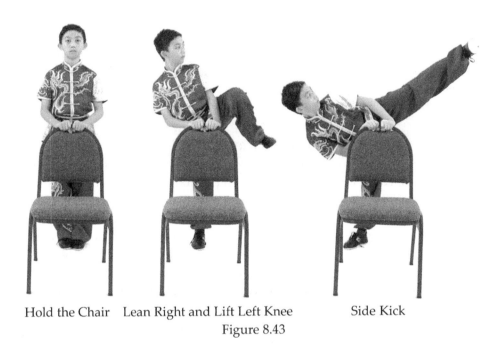

Hold the Chair   Lean Right and Lift Left Knee   Side Kick

Figure 8.43

(2) Prioritize executing the movement in the most streamlined and effortless manner while ensuring the required standards are met.
(3) After mastering the fundamental aspects of the movement, focus on building strength and increasing kicking speed.
(4) In the initial stages, the emphasis should be on practicing low kicks. Gradually refine the technique and then progress to higher kicks as proficiency improves.

In a 'Competitive Wushu' Competition, one of the deduction points for the side sole kick is when the kicking leg fails to transition from an obviously bent position (45° or more) to a fully extended and straight position. It is important to demonstrate a clear and distinct movement, showcasing the proper extension of the leg during the kick to meet the competition standards.

Săo Zhuǎn Xìng Tuǐ Fǎ
掃轉性腿法
Sweeping-Rotating Leg Techniques

'Săo Zhuǎn Xìng Tuǐ Fǎ,' also known as 'Sweeping-Rotating Leg Techniques' in English, constitute a category of rotating leg techniques within Wushu. These techniques involve the practitioner squatting on one leg while using the other to sweep close to the ground.

The primary objective of these techniques is to disrupt the opponent's balance by sweeping or tripping their ankle, thus creating a favorable position for the practitioner.

Effective execution of 'Sweeping Leg Techniques' demands precise timing, coordination, and spatial awareness. Practitioners must develop a keen sense of timing to sweep their opponent's ankle and disrupt their balance at the right moment. Precision is crucial to accurately target the opponent's ankle, while coordination between the upper body and the sweeping leg ensures proper execution. By mastering these techniques, practitioners can gain a distinct advantage in combat situations, enabling them to maintain control over the fight and potentially gain the upper hand.

1. Qián Săo Tuǐ or Sweep Leg Forward

'Qián Săo Tuǐ' (前掃腿), translated as 'Sweep Leg Forward' in English, is a technique commonly performed in both Contemporary Competition Wushu and traditional Wushu. In the Contemporary form, it is executed from a full squat position on one leg, usually the left leg, with the hands off the ground. In the traditional form, the technique involves fully squatting with both the left and the right leg, with the option of touching the ground or keeping the hands off the ground. The movement includes swiftly lowering the body's center of gravity, bending the left (or right) knee, and swinging the right leg (or left) forward. The primary goal of this technique is to disrupt the opponent's balance and stability by sweeping their ankle.

Successful execution of this move demands coordination, agility, and well-timed actions to ensure an effective sweep. Emphasize the quick drop of the body's center of gravity, the proper bending of the left (right) knee, and the controlled swing of the right leg (left) for an accurate and impactful sweep.

Preparation posture:

Begin by standing upright, with your feet together. Always emphasize the essence, Qi, and spirit within your body and mind during Wushu practice (Figure 8.44).

Movements:

- Cross your left foot behind your right leg. Raise your left heel and slightly turn your right toes outward. Simultaneously, perform a circular motion with your palms, starting from the bottom and swinging to the left, up, and right. Straighten your right arm and position your palm vertically at shoulder height. Place your left palm inside your right shoulder with your fingers pointing upward. Turn your head to the right, directing your gaze in that direction (Figure 8.45).
- Rotate your upper body to the left, completing an approximate 180-degree turn.
- Simultaneously, sweep your left arm to the left side, positioning it slightly above your shoulder. Keep your left elbow straight without bending it. Bring your right arm to the right side of your body, placing it slightly below your shoulder. Open your shoulders and extend your arms, being careful not to over-stretch.
- Maintain contact with the ground by firmly pressing your soles, facilitating your rotation and augmenting the power generated (refer to Figure 8.46).

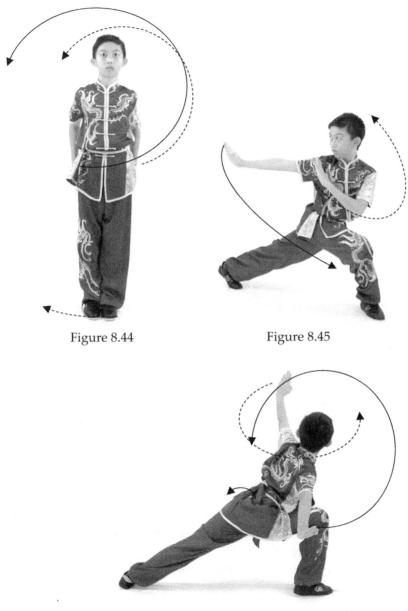

Figure 8.44   Figure 8.45

Figure 8.46

- Maintain the rotation of your upper body to the left and continue to turn your left toes outward. Simultaneously, perform a circular motion with your right palm, starting from the back, moving up, forward, and down. As you do this, bend your left arm, allowing your left palm to pass through the inside of your right arm, and place it on the upper left side of your head, with the palm facing upward. Additionally, continue the circular motion of your right palm, bringing it down and transforming it into a hook hand position, which you place behind your body with the hook tip pointing upward.

- As your left foot moves outward, bend your left knee, squat completely, and raise your left heel. Utilize your left sole as an axis, grinding against the ground. While doing this, inwardly turn your right toes and extend your right leg. Ensure that the entire sole of your right foot maintains contact with the ground. With your right leg fully extended, execute a sweeping motion to the left for one full circle (Figure 8.47).

Figure 8.47

During this action, visualize yourself using your right hand to draw a large counterclockwise half-circle from the back to the front, while simultaneously using your left hand to draw a smaller counterclockwise half-circle in front of your body.

As for 'Competitive Wushu' Competitions, there are certain deduction points to be aware of:

(1) The thigh of the supporting leg should not be positioned above the horizontal level.
(2) Ensure that the sole of the sweeping foot remains in contact with the ground after making contact for the sweeping action.
(3) The sweeping leg should not be obviously bent at an angle of 45° or more.

Key Points:
(1) Maintain an upright posture with your head up and eyes looking straight ahead while allowing your head to turn in sync with your body.
(2) Keep the correct posture of the right 'crouch stance' to ensure balance and stability. Avoid bending your right knee excessively.
(3) Coordinate the twisting of your waist with the sweeping motion of your leg. Squat completely with your left leg.
(4) Find the right balance in the speed of your sweeping leg. Avoid sweeping too fast or too slowly, as it may disrupt the flow of the movement.

(5) For beginners, it is recommended to practice sweeping the leg while in a standing position first. Bend your left knee slightly, let your right foot touch the ground, and experience maintaining balance and meeting the requirements. Once comfortable, progress to performing the entire movement. Using your hands to touch the ground while sweeping can aid in balance initially, before transitioning to performing the technique without hand support (Figure 8.48).

Figure 8.48

Common Errors and Corrections:

(1) Insufficient Bending of the Left Leg: The center of gravity is too high when sweeping the leg. The left leg is not bent enough. Pay attention to fully squatting down with your left leg before performing the sweep. Bend the left knee quickly to ensure a lower center of gravity, which provides better stability and control during the sweeping motion.

(2) Unstable Center of Gravity: The center of gravity tilts left or right, leading to instability. Maintain an upright upper body posture with your head up and eyes looking straight ahead. Support your left palm upward to improve body stability during the sweep, ensuring a balanced center of gravity.

(3) Lack of Coordination Between Leg Sweep and Waist Twist: Inappropriate force and disruptions in the sweeping action due to a lack of coordination between sweeping the leg and twisting the waist. Keep your upper body upright and coordinate the movement of twisting your waist with the sweeping motion. Avoid turning the waist too slowly or too fast. Maintain the correct angle between the left and right leg, avoiding forward leaning or excessive waist bending.

(4) Incorrect Foot Shape During Sweep and Leg Turn: Slower speed and inadequate sweeping circle due to incorrect foot placement. After assuming the right crouch stance, focus on moving your right toes inward and twisting your waist to the left. Ensure a smooth and coordinated connection between turning your head and sweeping the leg to maximize the use of inertia and generate greater speed and range in the sweeping motion.

Practice Steps:

(1) Start by practicing sweeping and turning movements in a standing position. Follow the upper limb actions as described earlier. Bend your left knee slightly and sweep your right foot in one circle. Focus on maintaining balance and coordination during the sweeping and turning motion.

(2) Once you have gained familiarity with the sweeping and turning actions, progress to practicing the technique in the crouch stance. Assume the correct crouch stance, with your right leg extended forward and your left knee bent. If necessary, use your hands to touch the ground for additional support and balance as you perform the sweeping motion.

(3) As you become more comfortable and confident in the crouch stance, gradually reduce your reliance on your hands for support. Aim to perform the sweeping leg motion without touching the ground with your hands. Focus on maintaining proper balance, posture, and coordination between the upper and lower body.

Remember to practice each step patiently and gradually progress to the next level of difficulty. It is important to develop a solid foundation in balance, coordination, and control before advancing further in the technique. Regular and consistent practice will help you master the 'Sweep Leg Forward' technique effectively.

2. Hòu Săo Tuǐ or Sweep Leg Backward

'Hòu Săo Tuǐ' (后扫腿), known as the 'Sweep Leg Backward' or 'Back Sweep Kick' in English, is a technique that entails dropping to the ground and sweeping one leg around to contact the heel. This move disrupts the opponent's balance and creates an opportunity for further attacks. Executing this technique effectively demands coordination, balance, and precise timing.

Preparation Posture:

Begin by standing upright with your feet together. Place your fists on your waist with your palms facing upward. Maintain a straight-ahead gaze (Figure 8.49).

Movements:

• Start by stepping forward with your left foot, forming a left bow stance. Simultaneously, push your palms forward from your waist, with your fingers pointing upward. Maintain a straight-ahead gaze (Figure 8.50).

• Rotate your left toes inward and lower your body into a squatting position, forming a right crouch stance. Lean forward and turn your upper body to the right. Place both palms on the ground inside your right leg, with your right hand positioned near the right foot and your left hand positioned at the back. As your hands contact the ground, initiate a twist in your upper body to the right. Utilize the sole of your left foot as the axis and generate inertial force to sweep your right foot backward in the right-rear direction. Ensure that your entire right foot contacts the ground. Direct your gaze to the right (Figure 8.51, 8.52).

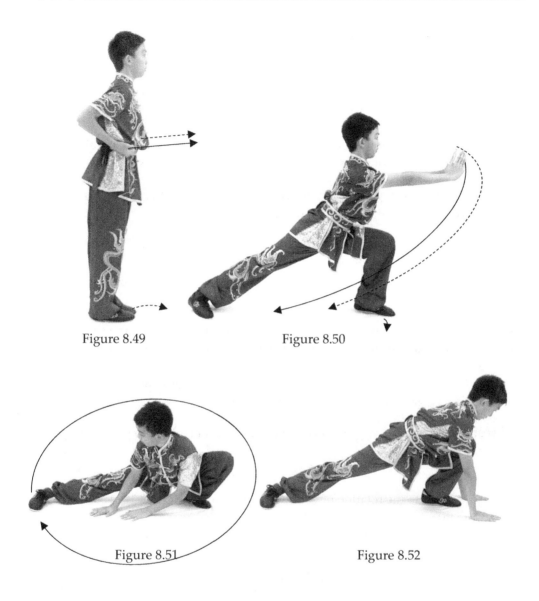

Figure 8.49   Figure 8.50

Figure 8.51   Figure 8.52

As a competitor in 'Competitive Wushu,' it is important to be aware of the following deduction points:

- Deduction: The sole of the sweeping foot leaves the ground after making contact for the sweeping action.
- Deduction: The sweeping leg is obviously bent 45° or more.

Key Points:
(1) Ensure a continuous and harmonious flow as you twist, lean, and push the ground with your hands. Avoid pausing between movements.

(2) Coordinate the movements of your upper and lower limbs, ensuring they move simultaneously without being separated.

(3) Capitalize on the inertial force generated by turning and twisting your waist, gradually increasing the speed and force of the sweep.

(4) Pay attention to the correct hand positioning on the ground. Focus on turning your body as both palms touch the ground simultaneously, with the fingers pointing in the same direction as your right foot.

(5) It is generally recommended to pass your hands under your right leg, allowing for a smooth integration of waist twisting, ground contact, and leg sweeping.

By keeping these key points in mind, you can enhance the effectiveness and precision of your sweeping leg technique in 'Competitive Wushu.'

Common Errors and Corrections in 'Competitive Wushu' Include:

Errors 1: Slow twisting of the waist: Twisting the waist too slowly results in weak twisting power and disrupts the connection between the waist and leg.

Corrections:

(1) Maintain an upright body posture and rely on your left leg for support.

(2) Practice quickly turning your head, twisting your waist, and sweeping your leg in a high posture.

(3) Focus on generating force through core rotation, leg sweeping, and coordinating your movements to achieve speed and smoothness.

Errors: 2. Incorrect hand placement on the ground and failure to place the right hand under the right knee.

Corrections:

(1) Pay attention to the rotation of your upper body to the right.

(2) Ensure that your fingers point in the direction of the sweep.

(3) Simultaneously touch the ground with both hands, with the correct hand positioning.

Jī Pāi Xìng Tuǐ Fǎ
擊拍性腿法
Slap Kick Leg Technique

'Jī' (擊) translates to 'Beat' or 'Hit,' while 'Pai' (拍) refers to 'Slap' or 'Pat' in English. The 'Jī Pāi Xìng Tuǐ Fǎ' (擊拍性腿法) signifies the 'Slap Kick,' which is a category of kicks involving the use of the palms to deliver a quick and intense strike to the sole or instep of the foot. This technique emphasizes agility, speed, and accuracy to target vulnerable areas of the body effectively. Referred to as patting foot techniques, they require consistent practice to develop the necessary skill and precision for execution with effectiveness and finesse.

1. Outside Crescent Kick Slapping

'The Outside Crescent Kick' (外擺腿擊鄉) involves contacting the hands to produce a sharp sound. The execution of this kick is like the previous technique. However, the difference lies in the timing and action. When your right leg kicks and reaches the front of your forehead, use both your left and right hands alternately to pat the top of your kicking foot.

2. Inside Slap Crescent Kick Slapping

'The Inside Slap Crescent Kick' (裏合腿) is an inward swinging kick that involves slapping the foot with the opposite side hand. The movement is similar to before. When your kicking foot is nearly complete in its motion, use the palm of the opposite hand to pat the sole of the kicking foot.

These techniques require proper coordination and timing to execute the slapping actions accurately and generate the desired sound effect. Practice is essential to develop the necessary control and precision for these kicks.

3. Pāi Jiǎo Jī Xiǎng or Pat Foot Kick Slapping

'Pāi Jiǎo Jī Xiǎng' (拍脚擊鄉) can be translated as 'Pat Foot Kick Slapping' in English. It involves extending the knee and foot, kicking straight upward while simultaneously striking the top of the foot with your palm. Usually, the palm on the same side is used to strike the foot on the corresponding side.

Preparation Posture:

Begin by standing with your feet together and extending your arms overhead as far as possible, fingers pointing upward. Maintain a straight gaze forward (Figure 8.53).

Movements:

- Begin by shifting your weight and taking a step forward with your left foot. Ensuring your upper limbs remain still. This prepares you to execute the right foot kick. Keep your gaze fixed straight ahead (Figure 8.54).
- Once your left foot is firmly planted, transfer your weight entirely onto your left leg. Simultaneously, fully extend your right leg and foot, kicking upward. At the same time, pat the top of your right foot with your right palm. Position your left arm in the upper left corner, maintaining a forward gaze (Figure 8.55).
- After the kick and pat, bring your right foot forward and land it in front of you. Shift your weight onto your right foot. Simultaneously, extend both your arms overhead with your fingers pointing upward. Maintain a straight gaze forward (Figure 8.56).
- Next, transfer your weight onto your right leg. Raise your left foot upward, fully extending it while patting the top of your left foot with your left palm. Position your right arm in the upper right corner and keep your gaze straight ahead (Figure 8.57).

In these movements, it is crucial to prioritize balance and control while executing the foot pat and maintaining proper arm positioning. Focus on achieving fluid transitions between these movements and aim for precision in both your kicks and hand strikes.

Figure 8.53   Figure 8.54   Figure 8.55

Figure 8.56   Figure 8.57

In a 'Competitive Wushu' Competition, certain deduction points are applied to leg techniques. It is important to be aware of these points and strive to avoid them:

(1) Toes of the slapped foot should not be below shoulder height: Pay attention to the height at which you perform the slap kick. Ensure that your kicking foot reaches an appropriate height, preferably above shoulder level, to demonstrate control and skill.

(2) Slap missed and/or inaudible: Accuracy and precision are essential in executing the slap kick. Make sure your hand makes clear contact with the foot, producing an audible sound. Practice the timing and coordination of the slap to ensure a distinct and noticeable effect.

Why do we always emphasize the importance of 'Leg Technique' training in the overall Wushu training system? What are the significant reasons for its importance?

(1) Foundation of Movement

The legs serve as the foundation for most movements in Wushu. Strong and well-trained legs provide a stable base, allowing practitioners to execute various techniques with power, precision, and control. In addition, emphasizing leg techniques ensures a solid foundation for all other aspects of Wushu practice.

(2) Power and Impact

Leg techniques in Wushu involve dynamic movements such as kicks, sweeps, jumps, and stomps. Training these techniques helps develop lower body strength, power, and explosiveness. Strong and well-conditioned leg muscles enable practitioners to generate greater force, enhancing the effectiveness of their strikes and movements.

(3) Flexibility and Range of Motion

Leg techniques require a wide range of motion and flexibility in the hips, knees, and ankles. Regular practice of leg techniques improves flexibility, joint mobility, and muscle elasticity in the lower body. This increased range of motion enables practitioners to execute high kicks, deep stances, and dynamic movements with fluidity and precision.

(4) Balance and Stability

Leg techniques in Wushu demand excellent balance and stability. Balancing on one leg during kicks or maintaining a low stance requires strong stabilizing muscles and body control. By emphasizing leg techniques, practitioners develop balance and stability, which are essential for executing movements accurately and maintaining control in various positions.

(5) Agility and Coordination

Leg techniques involve quick footwork, rapid kicks, and seamless transitions between movements. Practicing leg techniques improves agility, coordination, and overall body awareness. It enhances the ability to combine different techniques smoothly and perform complex sequences with speed and precision.

(6) Aesthetics and Performance

Leg techniques contribute to the visual appeal and artistry of Wushu performances. Executing dynamic and acrobatic kicks, jumps, and spins showcases the athleticism and grace of the practitioner. By emphasizing leg techniques, practitioners enhance the overall aesthetic quality of their performances and captivate audiences with their agility and control.

(7) Self-defense and Practical Applications

Leg techniques have practical applications in self-defense scenarios. Kicks can be used effectively for striking, controlling distance, and defending oneself against an opponent. By emphasizing leg techniques, practitioners develop the ability to utilize their lower body effectively in self-defense situations.

In conclusion, the emphasis on leg technique training in the overall Wushu training system is justified by its multiple benefits. It helps build a strong foundation, develop power and impact, improve flexibility and range of motion, enhance balance and stability, refine agility and coordination, showcase aesthetics and performance, and enable practical applications in self-defense. By focusing on leg techniques, practitioners can cultivate a well-rounded skill set and achieve a high level of proficiency in Wushu.

To maximize the benefits of leg technique training in Wushu, it is essential to follow a structured training program that includes exercises targeting strength, flexibility, balance, and coordination. Consistent practice, under the guidance of a qualified instructor, will enable practitioners to develop strong and versatile leg techniques, enhancing their overall performance and skill level in Wushu.

Chapter 9
Basic Movements (5)
Píng Héng
平衡
Balance

'Píng Héng,' which translates to 'Balance' in English, is a fundamental aspect of Chinese Wushu and encompasses various technical methods. It involves maintaining stability while one leg is raised, supporting the body's weight, and executing offensive or defensive movements. The objective is to remain steady without losing balance or changing foot positions, justifying its name 'Balance.' In the Chinese Contemporary Wushu Competition, 'Balance' can be categorized as 'Chí Jiǔ Xìng Píng Héng or called 'Lasting Balance' and 'Fēi'Chí Jiǔ Xìng Píng Héng' or called 'Non-Lasting Balance.'

Here, the author introduces readers to some common standard 'Balance' techniques, which serve as building blocks for mastering balance in Chinese Wushu. These techniques help practitioners develop body control, coordination, and stability, which are essential for performing advanced movements and showcasing technical proficiency.

Chí Jiǔ Xìng Píng Héng
持久性平衡
Lasting Balance

'Chí Jiǔ' (持久) refers to 'Lasting or Persistent,' while 'Chí Jiǔ Xìng Píng Héng,' (持久性平衡) commonly translated as 'Lasting Balance' in English, signifies maintaining a stable posture for a duration of two or more seconds after assuming the balanced position. This requires precise control and concentration to hold the position steadily over an extended period.

1. Yān Shì Píng Héng or Swallow Balance

'Yān Shì Píng Héng,' (燕式平衡) known as 'Swallow Balance' in English, is a 'Lasting Balance' technique commonly practiced in Wushu. It is named after a swallow's graceful and agile movements in flight. This balancing technique requires maintaining a stable posture while standing on one leg for an extended period, typically two or more seconds. To perform the Swallow Balance, follow these steps:

Preparation Posture (using the left leg as an example):
- Start upright with your feet together and your arms relaxed by your sides. Shift your weight onto your right leg, slightly bending the knee of your supporting leg, or keep it straight. Lift your left leg off the ground, bending it at the knee and bringing it toward your body. Point your left toes downward. To assist with balance, focus on sinking your Qi to Dantian and lightly gripping the ground with your right toes.

- Cross your hands on your chest, placing either hand on the outside. Palms should face outward. Maintain a forward gaze (Figure 9.1).

Movements:
- Extend your arms to the sides, parallel to the ground, with your palms facing outward. Simultaneously, tilt your upper body forward. Lift your left leg backward, forming the 'Swallow Balance' position. Maintain your balance by focusing your gaze on a fixed point before you and engaging your core muscles for stability.
- Hold this position, maintaining a steady and controlled posture for the designated duration (Figure 9.2).

Figure 9.1   Figure 9.2

Key Points:
(1) Keep both of your legs straight. The back leg should be lifted higher than your head at an angle of approximately 45 degrees upward, forming a reverse bow.
(2) Stretch your back foot, pointing the toes, and simultaneously lean your upper body forward. However, be careful not to bend lower than the waist.
(3) Maintain a straight chest and lift your head. This helps in maintaining proper posture and alignment.
(4) To enhance your balance, lightly grip the ground with your right toes, providing additional stability.

Common Errors and Corrections:
(1) Inability to Raise the Upper body and Low Lifting Leg Height: This can be attributed to poor leg flexibility and insufficient muscle control. It's important to work on

improving leg flexibility through stretching exercises and developing muscle control through targeted strength training.

(2) Bending of the Supporting Leg and Lifting Leg: The lifting leg should remain straight and elevated, while the supporting leg should maintain a slight bend at the knee. Avoid bending the lifting leg and hooking it up to the ankle, as this compromises the balance and proper execution of the technique.

(3) Unstable Stance: Instability in the stance can stem from various factors, such as an improper force point on the ground, an unbalanced center of gravity, and a lack of coordination between the upper body and the rear leg. Pay attention to your stance and ensure that you distribute your weight evenly and maintain proper alignment.

(4) Tilting of the Hips and Upper body: Excessive tilting of the hips and upper body can contribute to balance instability. Avoid significant swinging or rotation of the upper body and crotch. When leaning forward, ensure that your shoulders are at the same height, and both palms exert equal force to maintain stability. Additionally, when lifting the left leg, avoid opening or shifting the crotch.

Practice Steps:

The practice of the 'Swallow Balance' technique focuses on enhancing the flexibility of the waist and legs. There are several training methods suitable for beginners to improve their flexibility and prepare for the Swallow Balance. Here are some examples:

(1) Stretching Legs on the Wall bar: This exercise involves using a wall bar or a raised surface to stretch and lengthen the legs. By placing one leg on the bar and gradually lowering the body, you can effectively stretch the leg muscles and improve flexibility.

(2) Kicking and Holding the Leg: This exercise involves performing kicks and holding the leg at various heights. Start with low kicks and gradually increase the height to challenge your flexibility. Hold the leg in the raised position for a few seconds to improve strength and control.

(3) Practice Vibration with Split Legs: This exercise involves performing a split position and gently bouncing or vibrating the legs. This movement helps to relax and stretch the leg muscles, gradually increasing the range of motion (Figure 9.3).

Figure 9.3

195

(4) Bend the Waist Backward while Holding the Rear Foot or Ankle: This exercise targets stretching the quadriceps muscles by bending the waist backward and holding the foot or ankle. Maintain a stable posture and sustain the stretch for a few seconds, gradually increasing the intensity. For beginners, a suitable modification is to bend your torso backward step by step without allowing the range of motion to be too extensive (refer to Figure 9.4).

Figure 9.4

(5) Swing and Back kick: This exercise combines swinging the leg forward and executing a backward kick. This movement helps to improve leg control, balance, and flexibility. Here is an example, one practitioner is holding a chair for back kicking, while the other is performing a back kick in place (Figures 9.5 and 9.6).

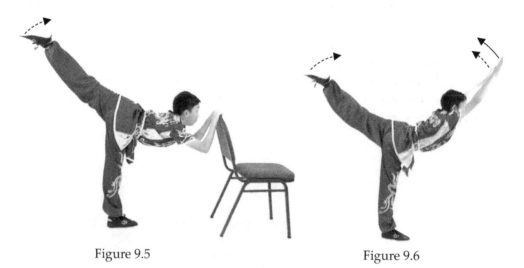

Figure 9.5   Figure 9.6

(6) Knee lift practice: This exercise involves lifting the knee toward the chest while maintaining balance and control. Alternate between legs and gradually increase the height of the knee lift for greater challenge (Figure 9.7).

Figure 9.7

In a 'Competitive Wushu' Competition, there are certain deduction points to be aware of when performing the Swallow Balance technique. Here are two common deduction points:

(1) The Torso is Below the Horizontal Level:

Maintaining proper body alignment is crucial in Swallow Balance. If the torso dips below the horizontal level, it indicates a lack of control and balance. To avoid this deduction, keep the torso upright and aligned with the supporting leg, and maintain a straight line from head to toe.

(2) Supporting Leg Bent:

The supporting leg is vital in providing stability and balance during the Swallow Balance. If the supporting leg is noticeably bent, it indicates a lack of strength and control. Keep the supporting leg straight and engaged to avoid this deduction, distributing the body weight evenly.

To prevent these deduction points, practicing proper form, alignment, and balance is essential. Work on strengthening the supporting leg and core muscles to maintain stability and control throughout the technique.

2. Wàng Yuè Píng Héng or Look at the Moon Balance

'Wàng' (望) means 'Watch' or 'Look at,' while 'Yuè' (月) means 'Moon.' So, the term 'Wàng Yuè Píng Héng' (望月平衡) can indeed be translated as 'Look at the Moon Balance' in English. It involves standing on one leg, with the other foot suspended behind and stretched while looking back over the shoulder.

Preparation Posture:
Begin in an upright position with your feet together and arms relaxed by your sides.

Movements (using the left leg lifting as an example):

- Shift your weight onto your right leg, slightly bending the knee of the supporting leg or keeping it straight. Lift your left leg off the ground and extend it or slightly bend it behind you.
- Rotate your upper body to the right, turning your head to look back over your right shoulder. Keep your chest lifted and your gaze focused on a fixed point behind you. Maintain a straight line from head to toe, aligning your lifted leg and back (refer to Figure 9.8).
- Hold this position, finding balance and stability on your supporting leg. Keep your core engaged and your body upright throughout the balance. Ensure that your lifted leg remains extended, and your gaze remains fixed over your shoulder.
- Maintain the balance for the designated duration. Slowly lower your raised leg back to the ground and return to the starting position.

In some Wushu style routines, the 'Look at the Moon Balance' may require additional variations: Lean your upper body to the left (or right), making it almost parallel to the waist height while keeping your chest out. Slightly bend your rear leg and point your toes.

Figure 9.8

In a 'Competitive Wushu' Competition, the judges may deduct points based on the following criteria:

(1) Torso Held Higher Than 45 Degrees Above Horizontal Level: The ideal execution of the 'Look at the Moon Balance' requires the torso to be parallel or close to parallel to the waist height. If the torso is held too high, exceeding the specified angle, deductions may be incurred.

(2) Waist not Twisted Toward the Rear in the Direction of the Supporting Leg: Proper execution of the balance involves twisting the waist toward the rear, aligning it with the supporting leg. If the waist is not twisted sufficiently in the required direction, deduction points may be given.

(3) The Surface of the Foot of the Raised Bent Leg is not Extended Flat: When the leg is lifted and extended or slightly bent behind, the foot should be extended flat, with the entire surface of the foot in contact with the air. If the foot is not extended flat or if only a portion of the foot makes contact, deductions may be applied.

Key Points:
(1) Keep your standing leg straight and strong, with the knee slightly bent for stability.
(2) Focus on maintaining a straight line from head to toe, aligning your lifted leg with your back leg.
(3) Rotate your upper body and turn your head to look back over your shoulder, maintaining a relaxed but focused gaze.
(4) Engage your core muscles to help stabilize your body and maintain balance.
(5) Usually, 'Look at Moon Balance' is a 'Lasting and Non-Lasting Balance.' For example, your upper body should be tilted opposite your raised leg in the front, but the latter does not need to be tilted.

Common Errors:
(1) Lack of Balance: Failing to maintain proper balance during the 'Look at Moon Balance' position, resulting in instability and difficulty holding the pose.
(2) Poor Upper Body Posture: Incorrectly tilting the upper body forward or backward, leading to an imbalanced position and potential loss of stability.
(3) Inconsistent Gaze: Not focusing on a fixed point in front can disrupt balance and concentration.
(4) Weak Core Engagement: Neglecting to engage the core muscles for stability and support during the pose.
(5) Insufficient Arm Extension: Not fully extending the arms to the sides with palms facing outward, affecting the overall posture and balance.
(6) Unsteady Leg Lift: Lifting the leg too quickly or with jerky movements makes maintaining the Swallow Balance position challenging.
(7) Shortened Duration: Inability to hold the 'Look at Moon Balance' position for the designated duration, indicating a lack of strength and control.

Correcting these 'Common Errors' involves practicing the pose, focusing on balance, posture, core engagement, and consistent form. Over time, with dedicated practice, these issues can be addressed to improve the 'Look at Moon Balance' quality in Chinese Wushu.

To execute the 'Look at the Moon Balance' movement with precision, it is crucial to give careful attention to your right foot. Begin by moving your right foot outward at an angle of approximately 25-45 degrees, ensuring that your toes firmly grip the ground. This establishes a stable foundation for balance and emphasizes a rooted connection with the floor.

Next, bend your left knee and raise your left foot behind your right shoulder. As you lean your upper body forward, maintain a straightened chest and proper alignment. Pay close attention to the positioning of your right shoulder, which should be directly opposite your left foot. Achieving this alignment requires twisting your upper body to the right, forming a graceful circular shape behind your body.

Additionally, focus on the positioning of your arms. Slightly bend your elbows, settle your wrists, and extend your fingers, creating a circular shape with your hands above your head. This adds elegance and completeness to the overall posture.

It is important to be aware of two common errors that can lead to instability in the 'Look at the Moon Balance.' Firstly, be mindful of the right foot, ensuring it does not move inward but remains properly positioned outward. This is essential for maintaining balance throughout the movement. Secondly, avoid the tendency to rush the twisting of the waist and turning of the head to the right before leaning the upper body forward. Such haste can cause the upper body to tilt towards the supporting leg (right leg), shifting the body's center of gravity away from its optimal position and compromising balance.

By attentively addressing these key points and avoiding common errors, you can achieve a harmonious and stable 'Look at the Moon Balance' in your Wushu practice.

3. Tàn Hǎi Píng Héng or Exploring the Ocean Balanc

In Chinese, 'Tàn' (探) means search and find, while 'Hǎi' (海) means the sea. 'Tàn Hǎi Píng Héng' (探海平衡) refers to 'Reach into the Sea Balance' or 'Exploring the Ocean Balance.' The movement mimics the act of searching for or exploring something from the sea by standing on the shore, extending your upper body forward. The emphasis is on achieving a straight and powerful supporting leg while assuming a prone position with the body. The front arm is extended downward, and the other leg is extended straight behind you. Let's go through the movements:

Preparation Posture: Begin in an upright position with your feet together and your arms relaxed by your sides.

Movements (use the left leg as an example):
* Shift your weight onto your right leg, keeping it straight and firm. Lean your upper body forward slightly below your waist while maintaining a straightened chest and waist.
* Extend your left leg straight backward, lifting it to at least waist height. Ensure that your leg is fully extended, and your foot is pointed with the sole facing upward.
* Simultaneously, thrust your right palm forward, extending it in front of your body, and raise your left arm backward, creating balance and harmony in your posture.

200

Ensure that both arms are aligned in a tilted straight line, stretching them in different directions to achieve a balanced and aesthetic posture.

• Ensure that your thumbs are facing upward, enhancing the aesthetic quality of the movement. Focus your gaze on the direction of your right hand, maintaining a steady and controlled posture throughout the balance (Figure 9.9).

• Practice alternating legs and repeating the sequence to develop balance and coordination (Figure 9.10).

Figure 9.9   Figure 9.10

Key Points:
(1) Ensure that the raised leg is positioned higher than your waist and maintain a straightened knee.
(2) Avoid allowing your upper body to rise above your waist level during the movement.
(3) If you feel your balance wavering, you can use your supporting foot to grab or grip the ground slightly to help regain stability.

Common Errors:
(1) Incorrect Posture: Both knees bent and the upper body rising above waist level.
(2) Dropping the Head: Drooping the head too low, which can result in an arched back.
(3) Loss of Balance: Allowing the position of the rear leg to fall below the required level.
(4) Rounded Back: Allowing the back to round or the upper body to lean forward disrupts the correct posture.

In a 'Competitive Wushu' Competition, deduction points may be incurred for the following:

(1) Bent supporting leg, deviating from the required straight position.
(2) Bent raised leg, failing to maintain the necessary straightened knee position.

4. Kòu Tuǐ Píng Héng or Tucked Leg Balance

'Kòu' (扣) in Chinese signifies 'buckle' or 'tightly hold.' 'Kòu Tuǐ' (扣腿) implies holding one foot tightly against the leg. In Contemporary Wushu Routines, 'Kòu Tuǐ Píng Héng' (扣腿平衡) refers to placing one foot behind the other knee. The supporting leg should be bent halfway. Commonly, it is translated as the 'Back Cross-Legged Balance,' also known as 'Tucked Leg Balance' or simply 'Kou Tui Ping Heng' in English. The focus is on maintaining balance while one leg is squatted with the thigh at a level position and the other foot is hooked behind the knee. This balance must often be held for at least two seconds in Long Fist Taolu competitions.

Movements (use the left leg as an example):
- Maintain a straight and upright body posture throughout the balance, ensuring no tilting or leaning.
- Bend your right knee, opting for a full or partial squat, while hooking it securely while positioning your left foot behind your right knee.
- Place your palms on either side of your body, facing outward. Alternatively, lift your palm above your head while punching your right fist to the right side.
- Focus your gaze on your right fist, maintaining concentration and stability (Figure 9.11). Practice alternating legs to achieve balance and stability on both sides.

Figure 9.11

Key Points:
(1) Squat as low as possible with your right leg, aiming for a deep and stable squat position.
(2) Hook your left foot tightly behind your right knee, ensuring a secure connection.

202

(3) Straighten your chest and waist, maintaining an upright and aligned upper body posture.
(4) Sink your shoulders and drop your hips, creating a stable and grounded stance.
(5) Focus on achieving stable and lasting balance in the posture.

Common Errors:
(1) Failure to connect the left foot tightly behind the right knee, leading to instability and a compromised balance.
(2) Inability to maintain a static state in the balance, resulting in excessive movement or wobbling.
(3) Insufficient bending of the right leg in the squat position, affecting the overall posture and stability of the balance.

In a 'Competitive Wushu' Competition, it is essential to adhere to the following guidelines to avoid deduction points:

(1) Insufficient depth in the squat or incomplete squatting position.
(2) Inadequate or insecure hooking of the foot behind the knee.

5. Pán Tuǐ Píng Héng or Basin Squat Balance

'Pán Tuǐ Píng Héng' (盤腿平衡) is similar to the 'Kòu Tuǐ Píng Héng' or 'Tucked Leg Balance' we previously discussed. The main difference lies in the former involving the hooking of one foot behind the other knee (hollow of the knee), while the latter positions the foot above on the opposite knee. It can be translated as the 'Forward Cross-Legged Balance' or 'Basin Squat Balance.' In both variations, the supporting leg should be maintained in a semi-squatted position or deeper.

The term 'Pan' suggests the image of a coil, similar to a snake coiling its body when one foot rests on the other knee. The objective is to sustain a motionless posture. During the Long Fist Taolu competition, this balance must be maintained for at least two seconds.

Movements (using the left leg as an example):
• Bend your right knee and assume a complete squat position or a half squat position, depending on your flexibility and comfort.
• Place your left ankle on your right knee, ensuring that the left sole faces upward and the left calf is nearly parallel to the ground.
• Extend your left palm above your head while simultaneously punching your right fist to the right side. Keep your focus on the right fist throughout the balance (Figure 9.12). Practice performing the balance with alternating legs.

Key Points:
(1) Maintain a deep and stable squat position with your right knee (support leg) bent.
(2) Ensure that your left ankle is securely placed on your right knee, with the left sole facing upward.
(3) Straighten your chest and maintain an upright posture throughout the balance.

(4) Extend your left palm above your head, adding a dynamic element to the posture.
(5) Focus on the right fist as you hold the balance motionless. Maintain the balance for a minimum of two seconds, with at least a half squat position.

Common Errors:
(1) Insufficient depth in the squat position, compromising stability and balance.
(2) Inaccurate placement of the left ankle on the right knee, resulting in an unstable posture. Failure to maintain a motionless state during the balance.
(3) Lack of coordination between the upper body and lower body movements.

In a 'Competitive Wushu' competition, deductions may be incurred if the thigh of the supporting leg is not maintained at a horizontal level, as specified in the requirements.

Figure 9.12

6. Cháo Tiān Dēng or Kick Sky with the Sole

'Cháo Tiān' (朝天) signifies 'Face towards the Sky.' 'Dēng' (蹬) translates to 'Kick with the heel,' denoting power transmission to the sole through the leg and foot. 'Cháo Tiān Dēng' (朝天蹬) refers explicitly to using the sole to kick upwards, with the sole of the kicking foot facing up. It can be translated into English as 'Kick Sky with the Sole.'

The essence of the movement lies in achieving balance with the supporting leg kept straight while the other foot is held on top of the head, with the opposite leg also straightforward and the sole facing directly upward. The key movements involved are as follows:

Movements (use the left foot as an example)**:**

- Begin by standing on your right leg. Bend your left knee and raise it upward.
- Typically, hold your left heel with your left hand, and you can use your right hand to grab your right toe, or alternatively, only use your left hand to lift your left heel (Figure 9.13, 9.14).
- As you lift your left foot above your head, ensure that the sole of your foot faces upward and that your foot is hooked inward. Keep your left leg as close to the left side of your body as possible. Maintain a forward gaze, looking straight ahead.
- Practice alternating legs to develop proficiency in both sides.

Figure 9.13   Figure 9.14

Key Points:

(1) Maintain a straight and aligned posture by straightening your chest, back, and waist.
(2) Slightly extend your hip to enhance stability and balance.
(3) Keep both legs straight throughout the movement. The leg that is raised should touch or be close to your ear, demonstrating flexibility and control.
(4) Focus on achieving a stable and lasting balance in the position.

In a 'Competitive Wushu' Competition, 'Ban Jiao Chao Tian Zhi Li' (Grasp the foot and bring it to head level with the leg held vertically while remaining standing) and 'Ce Ti Bao Jiao Zhi Li' (Side Kick up to catch the foot at head level with the leg held vertically while remaining standing) showcase variations of the 'Cháo Tiān Dēng' that demonstrate enduring balances requiring skill and control. To maximize your score, it is crucial to avoid the following deductions:

(1) Bending the Supporting Leg: Throughout the balance, ensure that the supporting leg remains straight and strong, providing a solid foundation for the movement. Any bending of the supporting leg will result in deductions.
(2) Allowing the Raised Leg to Bend: Maintain control and flexibility in the raised leg, keeping it straight and elevated at all times. Bending the raised leg during the balance will lead to deductions.

By focusing on maintaining a straight and strong supporting leg, and keeping the raised leg straight and elevated, you can demonstrate your technique, strength, and control in these lasting balances. Practice and refine your execution to achieve a higher score in a competitive setting.

In addition to the previously mentioned lasting balances, there are various other examples of lasting balances in Long Fist Routines. These include the 'Hou Ti Bao Jiao Zhi Li' (後踢包脚直立 back kick and holding the leg vertically balance), 'Yang Shen Ping Heng' (仰身平衡 backward leaning balance), 'Shi Zi Ping Heng,' (十字平衡 crossing balance,) and more. Each of these balances requires a combination of focus, strength, and control to maintain a stable and controlled position for an extended duration. Perfecting these balances demonstrates the practitioner's mastery of body control and adds to the overall performance quality in a competitive setting.

Non-Persistent Balance
非持久性平衡

'Non-Lasting Balance,' also known as 'Temporary or Fleeting Balance,' refers to a type of balance in Wushu and other physical disciplines that is not maintained for an extended period. Unlike 'Lasting Balances' where a stable position is held for a significant duration, 'Non-Lasting Balance' involves briefly achieving a balanced position and then transitioning to another movement or posture.

In 'Non-Lasting Balance,' the practitioner focuses on executing a controlled and balanced position for a short period of time before transitioning to the next movement or technique. These fleeting balances often require agility, coordination, and precise body control. Examples of 'Non-Lasting Balances' include quick kicks, jumps, spins, and acrobatic maneuvers where a momentary display of balance and control is essential.

While 'Non-Lasting Balances' may not be held for a long time, they contribute to the overall fluidity, dynamism, and aesthetic appeal of a Wushu routine or performance. They showcase the practitioner's ability to swiftly transition between different movements while maintaining control and stability in each momentary balance position.

In a Competitive Wushu context, 'Non-Lasting Balances' are evaluated based on factors such as precision, timing, body alignment, and smooth transitions. Deductions may occur if the balance position is not executed accurately or if there is a lack of control and stability during the transition.

The Front Knee Raised Balance, and the Side Knee Raised Balance

These balances entail maintaining a one-legged stance while elevating the opposite knee to a minimum waist height. They necessitate that the body is supported by a single leg, with the other leg bending and lifting in front of the body. The raised knee must reach a height above the waist, as this height is associated with techniques aimed at targeting the opponent's groin and chest. Furthermore, the calf can defend against lateral attacks by obstructing the opponent.

To execute these balances effectively, it's essential to maintain a solid connection with the ground through the supporting foot. Additionally, directing the gaze upward and focusing on channeling one's Qi to the Dantian are key aspects of proper execution.

1. Qián Tí Xī Píng Héng or The Front Knee Raised Balance

Using the left knee as an example, for 'Qián Tí Xī Píng Héng' (前提膝平衡), raise the left knee in front of your body, with the foot stretched downward. The toes should be slightly turned inward, and the tip of the supporting foot should point forward. Lean slightly forward and twist your upper body to the left. Direct your gaze to the left, maintaining focus (Figure 9.15).

Figure 9.15

Figure 9.16

207

2. Cè Tí Xī Píng Héng or Side Knee Raised Balance

Using the left knee as an example, for 'Cè Tí Xī Píng Héng' (侧提膝平衡), the left knee is positioned on the side of your body. The toes of the raised foot should be pointed downward, and the tip of the supporting foot should be angled diagonally outward. Lean slightly forward and maintain a straightened upper body. Look straight ahead, fixing your gaze in that direction (Figure 9.16).

These balancing techniques require meticulous attention to technique and precise body alignment. It is crucial to lift the raised knee to the appropriate height and maintain the stability and correct positioning of the supporting foot. By focusing on these key aspects, you can sustain balance and execute these movements effectively, especially in a competitive Wushu context.

How to Practice 'Balance' Movement in Wushu Routine

To practice balance movements in Wushu routines effectively, here are some key steps:

(1) Practice Body Flexibility

To effectively practice balance movements in Wushu routines, it is crucial to prioritize flexibility training and choose suitable stretching methods.

Balance movements in Wushu routines demand a wide range of motion from your limbs, making good flexibility essential to meet the required standards. Insufficient flexibility can hinder your ability to execute the movements correctly and affect their stability. To address this, give priority to ankle flexibility training when focusing on flexibility. This will help enhance your overall balance and strength.

In addition, incorporate specific stretching exercises that complement the balance movements you are practicing. For example, if you are training in the 'swallow balance' exercise, incorporate back leg stretches and vertical split exercises to target the flexibility of your back legs. Similarly, if you are working on a 'lift leg straight balance,' prioritize high leg stretching and split exercises to improve flexibility in those areas. By combining flexibility training with balance movements, you can enhance your overall performance and achieve greater stability.

Remember, flexibility is not only important for executing the movements but also for preventing injuries and maintaining proper form. Make sure to warm up properly before engaging in flexibility training and listen to your body to avoid overexertion.

(2) Practicing Balance Movements

To practice balance movements effectively in Wushu routines, it is crucial to prioritize stabilizing your center of gravity and coordinating the applied force.

To practice balance movements effectively in Wushu routines, it is crucial to prioritize stabilizing your center of gravity and coordinating the applied force.

The ultimate goal of practice is to master the standard version of each balance movement. However, when initially learning a balance movement, it is common for the force to be uncoordinated, preventing the movement from reaching a stable state. To overcome this, you must focus on stabilizing your center through repeated practice.

One effective technique is to slightly bend the supporting leg, ensuring that each part of your body works with synchronized and asymmetrical force. This approach enables all aspects of your limbs to meet the movement's requirements simultaneously. It is important to avoid slowing down one limb while accelerating the other, as it can disrupt your balance. By emphasizing coordination and applying force harmoniously, you can improve your stability and achieve the desired standard for each balance movement.

Remember to start with slower and more controlled movements, gradually increasing the speed and intensity as you gain proficiency. Practicing in front of a mirror or with a partner can provide visual feedback and help refine your technique. Additionally, focusing on maintaining proper posture and alignment throughout the movements will contribute to your overall balance and stability. With dedicated practice and attention to detail, you can enhance your balance skills and excel in Wushu routines.

(3) Using Supportive Objects for Balance Practice

To enhance your balance during training, you can incorporate the use of supportive objects.

During balance training in Wushu, utilizing an object can assist in maintaining stability. Begin by holding onto a chair or any suitable object with your hand while focusing on keeping your leg balanced. This initial step helps strengthen your muscle sense and promotes correct posture. It provides a sense of security as you work on improving your balance skills.

Once you feel comfortable and confident with the support of the object, gradually reduce the amount of support provided. Challenge yourself to rely less on the object and develop greater self-reliance. This progressive approach allows you to improve your overall balance control and develop a stronger sense of stability.

As you gradually reduce the support, focus on maintaining proper alignment, engaging your core muscles, and finding your center of gravity. This will help you maintain balance independently. It's essential to practice patience and consistency, gradually increasing the difficulty level as you progress.

By challenging yourself to maintain balance without relying heavily on supportive objects, you will enhance your balance skills in Wushu routines and develop a higher level of proficiency. Remember to always prioritize safety and listen to your body throughout the training process.

(4) Developing Individual Stillness without External Support

Challenge yourself to achieve balance independently, without relying on any external objects for support. Gradually increase the duration of your balance hold, aiming for a target time of approximately two minutes. This practice will significantly enhance your ability to maintain stability and control during balance movements.

When practicing individual stillness, it is crucial to focus on your body's alignment, core engagement, and finding your center of gravity. Start by assuming a balanced position and holding it for as long as you can. As you progress, extend the duration of your balance hold, gradually pushing your limits.

During this practice, pay close attention to your body's subtle adjustments and sensations. Maintain a calm and focused mindset, as mental stability plays a vital role in achieving physical balance. Be patient with yourself, as developing individual stillness requires time and consistent effort.

To further challenge yourself, experiment with different balance positions and transitions between them. Incorporate various Wushu techniques and footwork patterns into your balance movements, allowing for seamless transitions and fluidity.

Remember to approach this practice with mindfulness and a commitment to continuous improvement. By developing individual stillness and mastering balance without external support, you will elevate your Wushu skills and exhibit greater poise, control, and grace in your routines.

(5) Combination Exercises for Enhanced Skill Development

Integrate balance movements with footwork, jumping, and other techniques to enhance your overall skills. By incorporating balanced actions into your routine practice, you can improve your ability to swiftly transition into a stable position during quick movements. Moreover, focus on enhancing the fluidity and seamless connection between balance movements and other techniques. This integrated approach will elevate your performance and significantly improve your overall Wushu skills.

To practice combination exercises effectively, begin by selecting a series of balance movements that align with the techniques you aim to improve. For example, if you want to enhance your kicking technique, combine it with a balanced stance that requires stability and control. Work on smoothly transitioning from one balance movement to another while maintaining precise footwork and coordination.

As you progress, increase the complexity of the combinations by integrating jumps, spins, or directional changes. For instance, incorporate a jump kick followed by a landing in a balanced position, or combine a series of fast-paced strikes with quick transitions into balanced postures.

Emphasize the fluidity and connection between the different elements of the combination. Pay attention to the timing, body positioning, and weight distribution during each movement. Strive for seamless transitions and precise execution to achieve a cohesive and visually appealing routine.

Consistent practice and repetition are key to refining your skills in combination exercises. Take the time to analyze your performance, identify areas for improvement, and make necessary adjustments. Seek guidance from a qualified Wushu instructor or coach who can provide feedback and offer specific techniques to enhance your performance.

You will develop greater agility, coordination, and control by integrating balanced movements with footwork, jumping, and other techniques. This holistic approach will elevate your overall Wushu skills and enable you to execute complex routines gracefully and precisely.

Chapter 10
Basic Movements (6)
Tiào Yuè - Jump

'Jump Movements' in Chinese Wushu Routines predominantly involve using one or both legs to create propulsion off the ground, enabling the execution of various techniques, including dynamic kicks and other actions. Within the realm of Wushu, the terms 'Leaping' and 'Jumping' are commonly used to describe the unique characteristics of Wushu routines. For example, phrases such as 'rise like an ape' and 'land like a magpie' vividly depict the distinctive postures of Chinese Wushu associated with jumping techniques.

Throughout the historical development of Chinese Wushu, jumping techniques have played an enduring and essential role. Examples include the 'soaring' techniques in the Tang Dynasty, the 'rising from the ground' techniques in the Song Dynasty, the 'flying legs' techniques in the Ming Dynasty, and the 'jumping from a standing position' technique in the Qing Dynasty. These instances illustrate that jumping has consistently been a fundamental aspect of Chinese Wushu. Numerous Wushu practitioners excel in harnessing Qi and leg power for jumping.

Traditional Wushu training methods often include 'tying sandbags to the legs' or 'jumping from a deep pit upwards.' In contrast, in modern sports training systems, Wushu athletes can benefit from more advanced scientific techniques and training equipment, such as biomechanics and biochemistry, strength training, balance training, and speed training equipment and systems, guided by professionals that effectively enhance jumping abilities. With perseverance, hard work, and dedication, practitioners can achieve light and silent landings reminiscent of the graceful flight of a swallow.

The gold medal winners of the Asia Games and the World Champions Dong Xin and Sun PeiYuan have incorporated physical strength and balance training into their routines

In Modern Wushu Competitions, 'jumping' is considered a highlight of an athlete's performance. Examples of these awe-inspiring movements include the 'tornado kick connecting to a front split,' 'jump, turn, and thrust the sword,' and 'Lotus kick connecting a horse stance.' The rules of Wushu competitions outline four categories comprising a total of 16 'jumping movements.' It is mandatory for optional Long Fist routines to incorporate at least three different categories of 'jumping movements,' with failure to meet this requirement resulting in point deductions. As times change, the quantity and content of jumping movements also evolve, carrying different conceptual meanings.

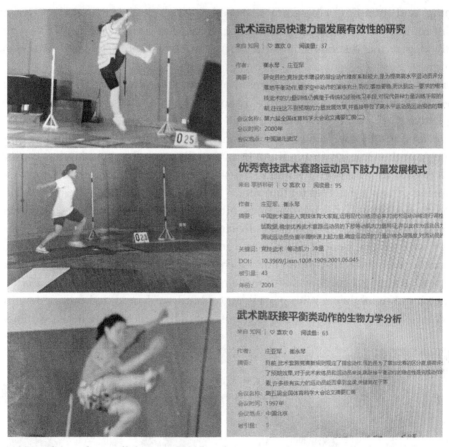

In the 1990s, the author collaborated with other researchers to study the development of jumping ability among Wushu professional athletes at Shanghai Sports University. Several research papers were written and subsequently published in various sports magazines in China.

1. Dà Yuè Bù Qián Chuān or Giant Leap Forward

In Chinese, 'Dà' (大) means 'Big and Great;' 'Yuè' (躍) means 'Leap and Jump;' 'Bù' (步) refers to 'Step;' 'Qián' (前) means 'Forward,' while 'Chuān' (穿) means 'Run and Pass Through Quickly.' Essentially, 'Dà Yuè Bù Qián Chuān'(大躍步前穿) can be translated to

'Giant Leap Forward,' also known as 'Jumping Forward with a Long Step.' It serves as a fundamental jumping movement in Wushu routines. This dynamic technique involves swinging the arms and propelling the body upwards and forward while simultaneously opening the chest. This leap aims to execute the movement with lightness and grace, emphasizing aesthetics. While it may be considered a relatively straightforward movement to learn, practitioners should focus on practicing with precision and attention to detail to establish a strong foundation for mastering more advanced jumping techniques.

Preparation Posture: Stand upright with your weight on your right leg. Bend your left knee and lift it towards your chest, extending your left foot downward. Position your right hand in front of your left shin, palm facing down, while placing your left fist on your left waist with the knuckles facing upward. Lean your upper body slightly forward. Direct your gaze towards your right palm (Figure 10.1).

Movements:
- Take a forward step with your left foot, ensuring the step is neither too small nor too large. Simultaneously, bend both knees and rotate your upper body to the left, swinging your right palm towards your left rib. Transition your left fist into an open palm, extending it downward and backward. Focus on your right palm and prepare for the upcoming jump (Figure 10.2).

Figure 10.1   Figure 10.2

- Begin by bending your right knee and propelling yourself forward, pushing forcefully off the ground with your left foot to execute a jump. Simultaneously, circle your palms forward and upward. Position your left palm above your head and extend your right palm to the right side, at shoulder height. Maintain your gaze on your right palm as it moves through the air (Figure 10.3).

- As you land, ensure your right leg touches the ground first, followed by squatting down completely. Then, bring your left foot forward and stretch it out, assuming a left crouch stance. Transition your right palm into a fist, placing it at your right waist with the knuckles facing upward.
- Continue the circular motion of your left palm, moving it from the top towards your right chest with the fingers pointing upward. Look at your left foot (Figure 10.4).

Figure 10.3   Figure 10.4

Key Points:
(1) Emphasize a long leap with a light landing. Keep your waist straight and head up.
(2) Ensure a seamless transition to the next movement immediately after landing. Coordinate the jumping action with the arms swinging while focusing on 'lift Qi.'
(3) The length of the jump stride should exceed the length of a bow stance.

Common Errors:
(1) Insufficient distance covered during the forward jump, falling short of the length of a bow stance. Lack of extension in the upper body. Inadequate pushing strength from the left foot onto the ground.
(2) Disconnection and lack of unity between the moves of the upper and lower limbs.

Imagine the 'Giant Step' as if you are crossing a small river (Figure 10.5).

Figure 10.5

Continuous Movement of 'Giant Leap Forward'

Practice Steps:

(1) Warm-Up:

Begin with a proper warm-up routine to prepare your body for the practice session. This may include light cardio, joint mobility, and dynamic stretching to increase blood flow and flexibility.

(2) Break Down the Movement:

To improve your understanding and mastery of the movements, it is essential to break down each sequence activity into smaller parts. By doing so, you can focus on specific elements such as body positioning, arm movements, leg actions, and overall coordination.

(3) Practice Each Movement Individually:

Work on mastering each movement individually before attempting to link them together. Start by focusing on the swinging movement of the upper limbs, ensuring proper technique and coordination. Then, shift your focus to the lower limbs' movements, including practicing the step forward and executing the jump with your legs. Repeat each movement multiple times, emphasizing balance, timing, and precise execution. By giving dedicated attention to each component, you can build a strong foundation and gradually progress towards seamlessly connecting the movements.

(4) Link the Movements:

Once you have gained comfort and proficiency with each individual move, it is time to start linking them together in a sequence. The key is to focus on achieving smooth transitions and maintaining a seamless flow between the movements. Pay special attention to coordinating the movements of your upper and lower limbs while also ensuring coordination with your eyes and body. Additionally, emphasize the opening of your body in the air during the jumps.

Begin by performing the sequence at a slow and controlled pace, placing emphasis on precision and technique. This allows you to solidify your understanding of the movements and ensure proper execution. As you gain more confidence and proficiency, gradually increase the speed of your execution while maintaining accuracy and fluidity. Remember to always prioritize maintaining control and grace throughout the sequence.

(5) Incorporate Breathing:

Coordinate your breathing with the movements to optimize your performance. During the preparatory postures and initial jumps, focus on inhaling deeply to gather energy and prepare your body for the movement. As you land and generate power, exhale forcefully to release tension, enhance stability, and channel your energy effectively. Syncing your breath with the movements helps promote concentration, improves oxygen intake, and enhances overall performance. It allows you to maintain a steady flow of energy throughout the sequence, contributing to your balance, power, and control.

(6) Seek Guidance and Feedback:

Engage in your practice under the guidance of a qualified instructor who can provide valuable feedback and guidance. A skilled instructor will be able to observe your movements, identify any mistakes or areas for improvement, and offer personalized corrections and insights.

Having an instructor present during your practice sessions ensures that you receive proper guidance and instruction, helping you refine your technique and enhance your overall performance. They can provide specific tips and suggestions tailored to your individual needs, allowing you to progress more effectively and efficiently.

Additionally, an experienced instructor can share their knowledge and expertise, offering insights into the nuances of Wushu practice that you may not discover on your own. They can guide you in understanding the subtleties of timing, body alignment, and energy flow, enabling you to deepen your understanding and mastery of the art.

(7) Consistency and Repetition:

Consistency and regularity in your practice are essential for reinforcing muscle memory and enhancing your overall proficiency in Wushu. Dedicate yourself to a regular training schedule, allowing sufficient time to practice and hone your skills.

Repetition plays a crucial role in developing muscle memory, which allows your body to perform the movements more naturally and efficiently over time. By consistently repeating the techniques, your muscles become familiar with the patterns and sequences, leading to smoother and more precise execution.

During your practice sessions, focus on quality rather than quantity. Pay attention to the details of each movement, striving for accuracy, proper body alignment, and fluidity. Break down complex movements into smaller components and practice them individually before integrating them into the full sequence. This approach will help you develop a strong foundation and gradually build up to more advanced techniques.

(8) Video Analysis:

Record your practice sessions and review the footage to identify areas for improvement. Compare your movements to reference videos or consult with your instructor for further guidance.

(9) Gradual Progression:

As you continue to improve your skills, it's important to gradually increase the speed, intensity, and complexity of your movements. Challenge yourself to achieve greater height and distance in your jumps while maintaining proper form and control. This progressive approach allows you to push your boundaries and continually improve your performance.

(10) Flexibility and Strength Training:

In addition to your Wushu practice, incorporate exercises that specifically target flexibility, leg strength, and overall conditioning. Devote time to stretching exercises that improve your range of motion and enhance your flexibility. Incorporate leg-strengthening exercises such as squats, lunges, and calf raise to build strength and power in your lower body. Additionally, focus on core stability exercises to improve your balance and stability during the movements.

*****All these 'Practice Steps' in 'Giant Leap Forward' are applicable to the various types of jump movement training that we will discuss next. The author will not reiterate these methods in detail in other jump practices. For specific practice techniques, please refer to these guidelines as a reference if needed.

2. Téng Kōng Jiàn Tàn or Aerial Snap Kick

The term 'Téng Kōng Jiàn Tàn' (騰空箭彈) in Chinese Wushu can be literally translated as 'Aerial Snap Kick' or 'Arrow Shooting in the Air.' This technique involves a straight jump kick resembling an arrow attack towards the opponent. It is commonly seen in Wushu routines, especially in Long Fist categories like Cha Quan, Hua Quan, and Shaolin Quan. The name is derived from the literal meanings of its components: 'Téng Kōng' means 'Soar, Rising High into the Air,' 'Jiàn' refers to an 'Arrow,' and 'Tán' relates to 'Spring, Eject,' signifying the spring-like function of the kick. The Aerial Snap Kick is significant in offensive and defensive applications, often accompanied by a forward-pushing palm strike. Its primary objectives include developing leg power, explosive force, overall coordination, and enhancing attack and defense awareness. To assist beginners in learning this technique effectively, we provide the following step-by-step guide:

Practice Methods:
(1) Step Forward, Jump with a Snap Kick, and Land

Preparation Posture: Stand straight with your feet together. Allow your arms to hang naturally at the sides of your thighs. Look straight ahead (Figure 10.6).

Movement 1: Step Forward with the Right Foot

- Take your right foot forward, ensuring your right heel touches the ground first. As you do so, swing your left arm forward, simultaneously swinging your right arm back naturally and flexibly.
- While stepping forward, lean your upper body backward, keeping your head up and maintaining a forward gaze (see Figure 10.7).

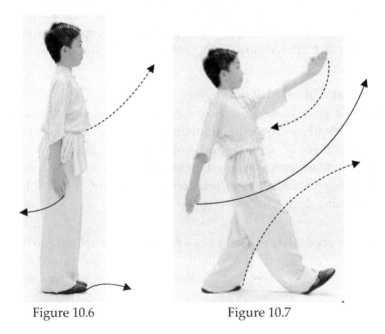

Figure 10.6   Figure 10.7

Movement 2: Swing the Right Arm and Bring the Left Leg Forward

- Building upon the previous movement, shift your body weight forward, generating a powerful push against the ground with your right foot. As you do this, swing your right arm forward from the back, with your right thumb pointing upward.
- At the same time, pull your left hand to your left waist with the palm facing inward or upward, maintaining a coordinated arm movement. Press the sole of your left foot against the ground, keeping your body straight. Bend your left knee and swing it towards the front while simultaneously extending your right leg. Maintain a forward gaze, focusing on your target, and prepare for the upcoming jump (Figure 10.8).

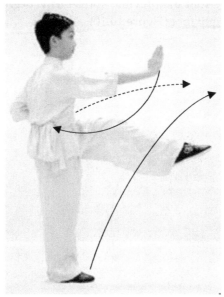

Figure 10.8

Key Points:

(1) Keep a slight bend in your legs to prepare for the upward jump. This bent position helps generate power and facilitates the explosive push off the ground using both your right and left feet. Focus on sinking your Qi (energy) to create a strong foundation for the jump.

(2) As you push off the ground, make sure your right arm swings forward rapidly, not upward. This forward motion adds momentum to your jump. Simultaneously, swing your left leg forward to increase your jumping ability and maintain balance throughout the movement.

Movement 3: Jump and Kick

- Transition seamlessly from the previous movement and generate a quick and forceful push with your right foot against the ground to initiate the leap. Start by bending your right leg, then rapidly extending it while executing a forward kick with your right tiptoe. Direct the force towards the tip of your right foot, aiming for a kick that reaches approximately waist level as your right foot stretches forward. Keep your left leg raised, with the calf bent backward for balance and stability. Circle your right hand back, forming a fist and placing it on your right waist. Also, push your left palm forward with power, extending your left arm to shoulder height. Point your left finger upward, tilting the palm to the right.

* Focus the force on the side of your left little finger and maintain a forward gaze (Figure 10.9).

Movement 4: Land

Transition seamlessly from the previous movement. Begin by landing your left foot first, followed by your right foot (Figure 10.10).

| Figure 10.9 | Figure 10.10 |

Key Points:

(1) Ensure a continuous and uninterrupted flow between the step forward, jump, and kick, maintaining a seamless connection throughout the entire sequence.

(2) Focus on maintaining a smooth, coherent, and fluid execution, emphasizing the synchronization of movements.

(3) Pay attention to maintaining balance and control during the landing, allowing for a controlled and stable descent to the ground.

(2) Running Forward, Jump and Kick

Preparation Posture: Stand straight with your feet together. Extend your arms on both sides of your body, palms facing outward, and the sides of your thumbs facing upward. Look to the left (Figure 10.11).

Movement 1: Step Forward with Your Left Foot

- Take your left foot forward, ensuring the left heel touches the ground first, keeping your head up and maintain a slight bend in your left leg to provide stability and balance. As you step forward, swing your right arm up to the left, with the thumb facing upward. Simultaneously, swing your left arm towards your right armpit from the left side in a circular motion, with the palm facing outward. Keep your gaze focused toward the left direction, maintaining a forward watch (Figure 10.12).

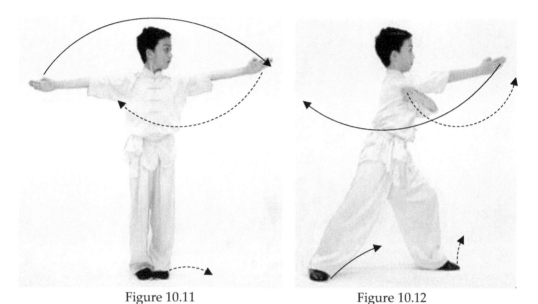

Figure 10.11   Figure 10.12

Key Points:
(1) Emphasize a robust and coordinated push from both feet to propel yourself forward during the step.
(2) Maintain proper alignment by keeping your body upright and engaging your core muscles for stability.
(3) The swinging motion of the arms adds to the overall momentum and enhances the aesthetics of the movement.
(4) Focus on maintaining a smooth and controlled execution, with a seamless transition from the preparation posture to the step forward.

Movement 2: Hitting Step

- Transition smoothly from the previous movement. As you continue the forward momentum, exert force on the ground with your left foot to propel into a leap. Swiftly extend your right leg forward and use your right foot to strike your left heel in mid-air. Simultaneously, swing your arms down to both sides of your body in a circular motion, with the thumbs side facing upward. Keep your gaze focused on your left hand, maintaining a forward gaze (Figure 10.13).

- Maintain your upper body upright and head up, emphasizing the impulsion power forward. This movement underscores the dynamic and explosive nature of the technique.

Figure 10.13

Movement 3: Landing

As the hitting step concludes, prepare for landing. Initiate the landing with your right foot, focusing on achieving a controlled and stable descent (Figure 10.14). Subsequently, place your left foot in front of your right foot, orienting the toes of your left foot slightly outward. Keep a slight bend in your knees to absorb the impact effectively and provide stability during the landing. Maintain your body's center of gravity forward and keep your arms straight on both sides. Maintain a forward gaze, directing your sight straight ahead (Figure 10.15).

Key Points:

(1) The hitting step should be executed with speed and precision, maintaining the fluidity of the overall movement.
(2) Focus on the coordination of the striking motion with your right leg and the circular motion of the arms.
(3) During the landing, prioritize stability and control, keeping a forward center of gravity to maintain balance.
(4) Maintain a steady forward gaze to enhance focus and alignment throughout the movement.

Figure 10.14   Figure 10.15

Movement 4: Step Forward with Your Right Foot

- As you transition from the previous movement, slightly rotate your body to the left and take a step forward with your right foot. Allow your right heel to touch the ground while simultaneously pushing your right hip forward. Raise your left arm while naturally lowering your right arm. Lean your upper body slightly backward, maintaining a balanced posture.
- Keep your focus straight ahead, maintaining a forward gaze (Figure 10.16). This step sets up the momentum for the subsequent jump and swing.

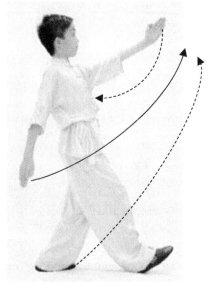

Figure 10.16

Movement 5: Jump and Kick

This movement is similar to the previous 'Jump and Kick' movement. Please refer to the instructions above for details (Figure 10.17, 10.18, 10.19).

Figure 10.17

Figure 10.18   Figure 10.19   Figure 10.20

Movement 6: Landing

This movement is similar to the previous 'Landing' movement. Please refer to the instructions above for details (Figure 10.17 (Figure 11.20).

Key Points:
(1) Maintain fluidity and control as you transition from the jump to the kick in the air.
(2) Focus on executing a quick and powerful snap kick, fully extending your right foot for maximum effect.
(3) Coordinate the movement of your arms, with the left palm pushing forward and the right palm swinging up and returning to the waist, enhancing the overall balance and aesthetic of the technique.
(4) Keep your gaze fixed straight ahead throughout the kick to maintain focus, balance, and alignment.
(5) Land smoothly by first placing your left foot on the ground, followed by your right leg, maintaining a slight knee bend to absorb the impact effectively.

Practice Steps
Step 1: Develop Fundamental Skills:
Building a solid foundation in basic skills is essential for mastering the aerial snap kick. Focus on the following key aspects:

(1) Stretching: Prioritize stretching exercises for the shoulders, waist, and legs. Adequate flexibility is crucial for performing the snap kick effectively in the air. Regularly practice leg stretches, waist rotations, and shoulder stretches to improve your overall flexibility. Remember that a higher kick and proper leg extension are only possible with sufficient flexibility.
(2) Jump Height: Emphasize developing explosive power in your legs to achieve optimal jump height. Incorporate plyometric exercises like squats, box, and vertical jumps into your training routine. These exercises enhance leg strength and help generate upward force during the jump.
(3) Flexibility and Range of Motion: Work on increasing flexibility in your hips and hamstrings, enabling higher kicks and more excellent extension during the jump. Practice a variety of kicks targeting different heights to improve leg flexibility and range of motion.
(4) Master Fundamental Kicks: Pay close attention to mastering real kicks such as front, side, and high kicks. Focus on executing these kicks with proper technique, alignment, and control. This will enhance your leg strength, coordination, and overall kicking ability.
(5) Progressive Training: Gradually increase the intensity and complexity of your training sessions. Begin with basic exercises and gradually progress to more advanced drills, explicitly targeting the aerial snap kick.

Step 2: Practice 'Snap Kick' with Step Forward
- Stand up with your feet together. Look straight ahead (Figure 10.21). Step forward with your right foot, raise your left knee and quickly perform a left 'snap kick' forward. The height of the kick should be about waist level or slightly higher (Figure

225

10.22). Simultaneously, punch your right fist forward. Usually, the height of your left arm is about shoulder level, almost parallel with your left leg.

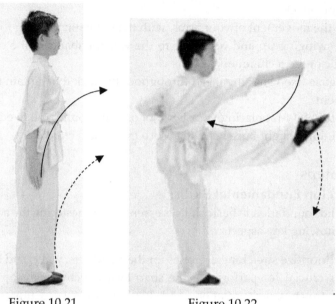

Figure 10.21	Figure 10.22

- Shift your weight forward, land your left foot (Figure 10.23), and immediately perform a right 'snap kick' like a left 'snap kick' (Figure 10.24). Straighten your knees as you kick. Practice alternating between the right and left kicks.

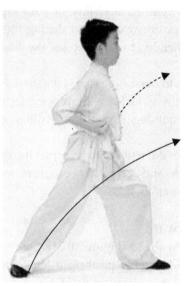 

Figure 10.23	Figure 10.24

When performing the forward kicks, pay attention to bending the knee of the kicking leg, lifting the thigh, and then quickly extending the calf to stretch the kicking foot. Emphasize a crisp, fast, and powerful kick, directing the force to your toes. Aim to raise the height of the foot appropriately, preferably not lower than waist level. Initially, you can place your fists on your core to help with the practice of the 'snap kick' (Figure 10.25).

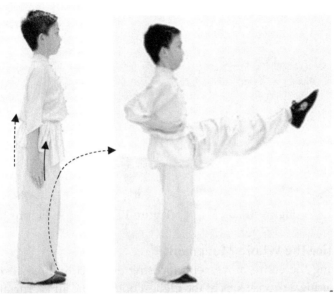

Figure 10.25

Step 3: Continue Practicing the 'Hit-Heel Step'

The 'hit-heel step' aims to improve the coordination between your steps and the alignment of your body's center of gravity. It involves gradually increasing the pace and the level of synchronization between your steps and body movements (Figure 10.26, 10.27, 10.28, 10.29).

To begin, perform three to four consecutive steps to maintain a balanced center of gravity. Gradually increase your speed as you progress, aiming for a smooth and fluid movement. The key is to find a rhythm where you can maintain relaxation and quickness while executing each step. Pay attention to the following points during the practice:

Body Alignment: Ensure your body remains upright and balanced throughout the steps. Avoid tilting your center of gravity too far forward, leading to instability and forward falls.

Speed and Acceleration: Work on gradually increasing your running speed as you perform the steps. This will help develop your explosiveness and improve your jumping height.

Repetition and Consistency: Practice repeated sets of steps, gradually increasing the number of repetitions. This will help build muscle memory and improve your overall coordination and timing.

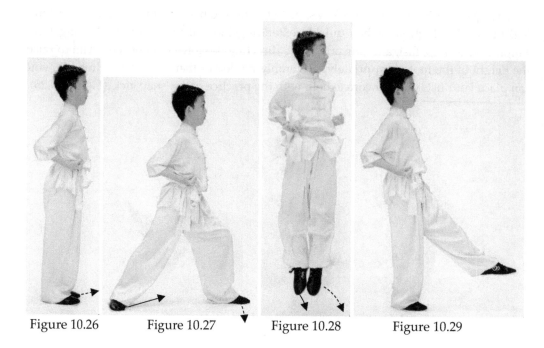

Figure 10.26   Figure 10.27   Figure 10.28   Figure 10.29

Step 4: Practice the Whole Movement

When practicing the entire movement, focusing on executing the correct movement points and delivering a precise kick at the highest point in the air is crucial. Additionally, pay close attention to the arm swing, which should follow a circular motion from bottom to top rather than moving in a straight line. Elevate your pelvis while lifting your head, maintaining a forward lean, and extending your chest. This posture generates upward momentum and contributes to the power of your movement. Ensure that your kicking point is clearly defined and precise, aiming for maximum impact and effectiveness (Figure 10.30).

Continuous Whole Movements of 'Aerial Snap Kick '

Figure 10.30

Common Errors:

(1) Running Forward Too Far: Running too far ahead before jumping can negatively impact the height of your jump. Make sure to maintain an appropriate distance to optimize your jumping height.

(2) Poor Upper Body Positioning After Jumping: After jumping, it's important to maintain proper upper body posture. Avoid excessive forward leaning, as it can affect your balance and overall control. Instead, keep your upper body upright or slightly lean back while pulling up the waist and lifting the buttocks to maintain a stable center of gravity. This will allow for better control and enable you to raise your right leg effectively.

(3) Incorrect Leg Swing: During the jump, pay attention to the swinging motion of your right leg. Remember that this is a snap kick, not a straight kick. Ensure that your right leg follows a smooth transition from bending to extending, delivering the snap kick with power and accuracy.

(4) Inaccurate Foot Positioning and Lack of Control: When executing the kick in the air, be mindful of the position of your right foot. Keep the top of your foot straight to maintain accuracy and proper force distribution. Additionally, focus on controlling the retraction of your left leg. Avoid dropping your left knee and instead strive to raise it near your chest for better form and control.

(5) Poor Coordination and Balance After Landing: After landing, maintain proper body alignment and coordination. Avoid tilting the upper body backward, as it can disrupt your balance. Aim for smooth coordination between the upper and lower limbs to ensure a fluid and controlled transition to the next movement.

In addition to practicing the technical movements, it is crucial to include 'Physical Fitness Exercises' to improve your jumping ability, enhance explosive power, and strengthen the muscles involved in these movements, including the psoas and abdominal muscles. Here are some exercises that can be beneficial:

(1) **Standing Vertical Jump:** This exercise improves vertical jump height. Start from a standing position with feet shoulder-width apart and jump as high as possible, reaching for the sky with your arms extended overhead. Land softly and repeat for multiple repetitions.

(2) **Squat Jump:** This exercise helps develop explosive power in your lower body. Begin in a squat position with your thighs parallel to the ground. Explosively jump up, extending your hips, knees, and ankles, and land back into the squat position. Repeat for multiple repetitions.

(3) **Heel Raises with Bar or Dumbbell:** This exercise targets the calf muscles and helps strengthen them for improved jumping ability. Stand with your feet hip-width apart and hold a barbell or dumbbell on your shoulders. Rise onto your toes as high as possible, then lower back down. Repeat for multiple sets.

(4) **Varying Speed Runs:** Incorporating sprints and interval training into your fitness routine can enhance speed and explosiveness. Include short sprints of varying distances and intensities to challenge your body and improve your athletic performance.

(5) **Knees Tuck Jump:** This exercise focuses on explosiveness and coordination. Start by standing with your feet hip-width apart. Jump up explosively, bringing your knees to your chest and extending your arms straight before you. Land softly and immediately repeats for multiple repetitions.

(6) **Abdomen In (Flat) with Legs Up (Leg Lift):** This exercise targets your abdominal muscles. Lie flat on your back with your legs extended upward, perpendicular to the ground. Lift your hips off the floor, contracting your abdominal muscles, and lower back down. Repeat for multiple repetitions.

When integrating these fitness exercises, scheduling them after the technical movement practice is vital to avoid excessive fatigue that may impact your form. Select 1-3 activities from the list and alternate between them to diversify your workouts. Be sure to uphold proper form and gradually raise the intensity and difficulty as your strength and conditioning progress. Towards the end of this chapter, the author will introduce specific martial arts jumping physical fitness patterns that you can reference and include in your training regimen.

****All these 'Physical fitness exercises' in 'Aerial Snap Kick' apply to the various types of jump movement training we have discussed or will discuss next. The author will not repeat these methods in detail in other jump practices. For specific practice techniques, please refer back to these guidelines as a reference if needed.

3. Téng Kōng Fēi Jiǎo or Jumping, Front Straight Kick

'Téng Kōng Fēi Jiǎo' (騰空飛腳) translated as 'Soaring Flying Kick' or Jumping, Front Straight Flying Kick' in Chinese Wushu, is a high and mighty kicking technique executed while jumping or leaping through the air. This maneuver demands strength and agility, which involves launching into the air and delivering a precise and controlled kick. Found in various martial arts styles, the execution and application of the 'Soaring Flying Kick' can vary depending on the specific martial art and its techniques.

Throughout history, this technique has been known by different names, such as 'two legs change' or 'three kick.' It is also commonly called a 'double kick' or 'flying foot.' This technique primarily focuses on kicking and is used in martial arts applications. Training for this technique typically involves three key steps:

Practice Methods:
(1) Jump From a Standing Position Without Moving

Preparation position: Begin by standing straight, keeping your feet together, and bending your knees slightly in preparation for the jump (Figure 10.31).

Movements:
- Swing your arms over your head circularly, generating upward force. Push your feet forcefully into the ground, propelling yourself into a jump (Figure 10.32). As you reach the highest point of your jump, swiftly bend your left knee, bringing it up towards your chest. Simultaneously, extend your right leg forward in a straight kick, focusing on stretching the toes of your right foot.
- Perform a striking motion with your hands. Hit your left palm on the back of your right hand, then pat the back of your right foot with your right palm. As you execute the kick, swing your left hand to the left or create a hook hand gesture (Figure 10.33). Focus on your right hand, keeping your gaze fixed upon it.

Key Points:
(1) As you kick your right leg forward in the air, aim to have your right foot above your waist level, or ideally at the waist height. In accordance with IWUF Wushu Taolu Competition Rules, the foot should be at least at shoulder level.
(2) While executing the kick, ensure that your left leg remains bent and moves to the inside of your right leg. This movement adds stability and balance to the technique.
(3) Conclude the patting motion at the highest point of your jump. The patting movement should produce a distinct sound, emphasizing control and precision.

(4) Maintain an upright position with your upper body during the jump. Tilt slightly forward, but avoid pulling your hips down, as this can disrupt your balance and overall execution of the technique.

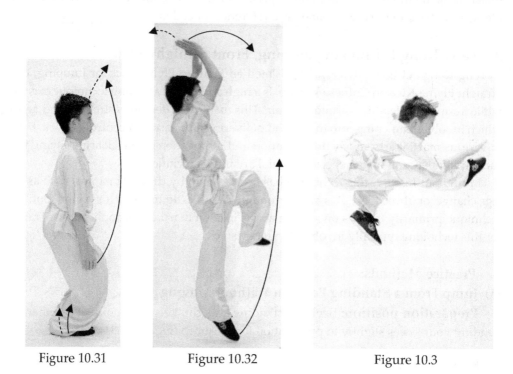

| Figure 10.31 | Figure 10.32 | Figure 10.3 |

(2) Step Forward to do the Jump, Front Straight Kick

Preparation Position: Stand straight, keep your feet together, and then bend your knees, getting ready to jump (Figure 10.34)

Movements:

- Step forward with your right foot (Figure 10.35), while swinging your left leg forward and upward. As you push off the ground with your right foot, jump into the air. Simultaneously, swing your arms forward and up from the back. Strike the back of your left hand with your right palm (Figure 10.36). Maintain your gaze straight ahead.
- While airborne, kick your right foot forward, ensuring that your right foot points straight ahead. Use your right palm to pat the back of your right foot. Additionally, bend your left knee and bring your left foot to the inside of your right leg, pointing your left foot toe downward. Simultaneously, position your left palm to the left or transition it into a hook hand. The tip of the hook hand should be down, slightly above your left shoulder. Lean your upper body forward slightly (Figure 10.37). Maintain your focus on your right hand.

232

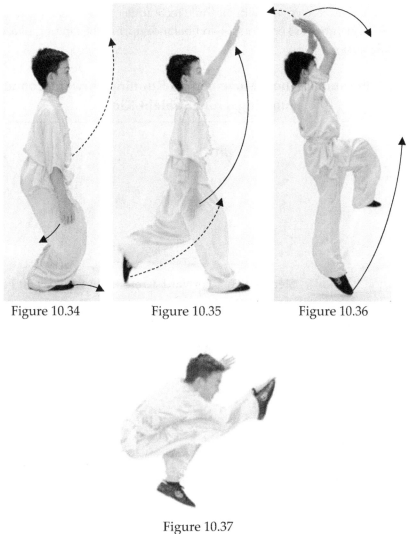

Figure 10.34   Figure 10.35   Figure 10.36

Figure 10.37

(3) Running Forward to do the jump, Front Straight Kick

To improve the execution of a 'Jump Straight Kick,' incorporating a run-up can boost speed and momentum, making the jump easier. The running technique is similar to the 'jump, snap kick.' Remember to maintain steady and controlled steps during practice. Two standard techniques that can assist in the jump are the 'hit-heel step' and the 'skip step.' Experiment with these methods to determine what works best for you. Typically, there are three landing methods after the jump:

(1) Natural landing: The left foot lands first upon descending from the jump.
(2) Both feet landing: Both feet touch the ground simultaneously upon landing.
(3) Right leg landing: The right leg makes initial contact with the ground upon landing.

Each landing method has its advantages and may be suitable for different situations. Practice and familiarize yourself with all three techniques to develop versatility in your performance. Remember to keep control and balance during the landing phase to avoid any potential injuries.

The Continuous Whole Movement of Running Forward Connects Jumping, Front Straight Kick

Preparation Position   Step Left Foot Forward Cross Right Foot   Left Foot

Hit Heel Step   Land Right Foot   Land Left Foot

Right Foot Forward   Jump   In the Air   Land

Figure 10.38

Common Errors and Corrections:

(1) Disjointed and Uncoordinated Leg Movements During the Jump:

There is a lack of coordination between the right leg pushing off the ground and the left leg swinging up. Practice specific jump exercises to improve coordination. Perform 'pushing off the ground with your right foot and jumping' while simultaneously swinging your left leg up. Coordinate the movements of your arms by swinging them up and patting your hands on the top of your head. Focus on synchronizing the leg and arm movements to achieve a smooth and coordinated jump.

(2) Excessive Forward Tilt of the Upper Body After Jumping:

The upper body tilts too much forward, compromising balance and stability. Pay attention to maintaining an upright upper body position during and after the jump. Avoid excessive forward leaning. Focus on pulling up the waist and lifting the buttocks to maintain proper alignment. This will prevent the center of gravity from shifting too far ahead. Practice exercises that involve single-foot patting or patting the foot while stepping forward to reinforce correct body posture. Start with lower jump heights and gradually increase the intensity and height as you master the accurate technique.

Practice Steps

Step 1: Single Pat Foot Practice

Depending on your flexibility and kicking ability, you have two options to choose from when practicing the 'Single Pat Foot technique ':

1) Standing Position Without Move:

- Start by positioning yourself in a standing position with your feet together. Raise both of your arms above your head. Maintain your left arm still while kicking your right leg up and extend your foot forward in a straight line.
- Aim to pat the top of your foot with your right hand while maintaining proper balance and stability. Ensure that you are familiar with the proper kicking techniques by referring to the previous chapter on 'leg techniques.'
- Practice alternating kicks between your left and right legs. Pay attention to your forms, and your kicking leg is properly extended (Figure 11.39).

2) Chair Support Practice:

- Hold a chair with your left hand to provide support while raising your right arm above your head.
- Position yourself in a standing stance with your legs separated, one leg forward and the other leg backward, similar to the 'Standing Position' (Figure 10.40).
- Practice alternating kicks between your left and right legs, gradually increasing the speed and intensity of your kicks as your confidence and proficiency improve.

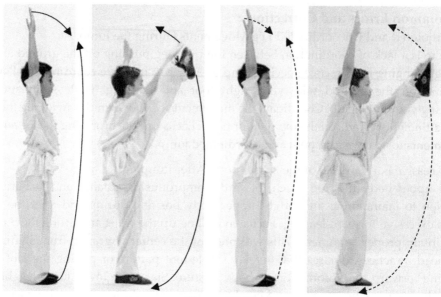

Figure 10.39

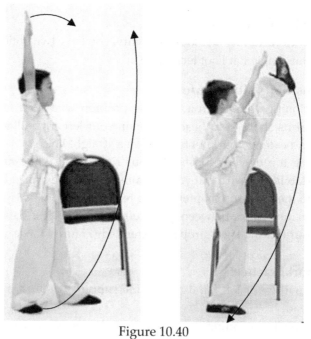

Figure 10.40

Step 2: Step Forward and Continuously Slap the Feet from Left to Right

After mastering the 'Single Pat Foot' technique, you can practice this movement while stepping forward with your feet (Figure 10.41)

- Begin standing with your feet together and your arms raised above your head.
  Take a step forward with your left foot. Keep your left arm steady while kicking your right leg and straightening your right foot. Aim to pat the top of your right foot with your right hand while maintaining balance and stability.
- After patting your right foot, place your right foot in front of you. Then, kick your left leg up, extending your left foot in a straight line. Aim to pat the top of your left foot with your left hand.
- After patting your left foot, land it in front of you. Continue this pattern of stepping forward and patting your foot as you move from left to right (Figure 10.42).

Figure 10.41

237

This movement requires coordination, balance, and flexibility. As with any physical activity, starting slowly and gradually increasing your speed and complexity is crucial as you become more comfortable with the technique.

Step 3: Leap Up Practice

- Stand straight, keep your feet together, and bend your knees, preparing to jump (Figure 10.42).
- Step forward with your right foot (Figure 10.43), simultaneously swinging your left leg forward and upward. As you push off the ground with your right foot, jump into the air. At the same time, swing your arms forward and up from the back. Strike the back of your left hand with your right palm (Figure 10.44). Maintain your gaze straight ahead.

The height of the leap up primarily depends on the correctness of the movement. Therefore, prior to learning the technique, it is important to practice leap ups repeatedly. Focus on mastering the correct method and aim to achieve the optimal 'Leap Up angle.' Develop instant coordination among all body parts and synchronize with the lead-up using your right foot.

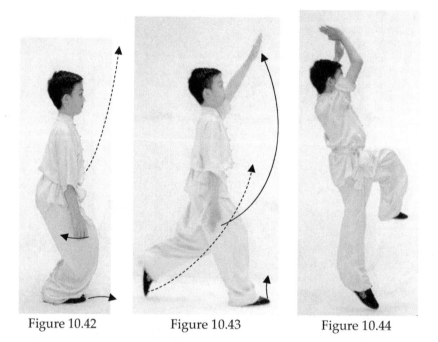

Figure 10.42   Figure 10.43   Figure 10.44

Step 4: Practice the Whole Movement

In reference to our previous description of this movement in the 'Practice Method.'

It's essential to acknowledge that the 'Jump, Front Straight Kick' is a relatively challenging technical maneuver for beginners. Therefore, it should be tackled methodically without rushing the learning process. Beginners should focus on establishing a solid foundation rather than fixating on achieving maximum jump height, perfecting the jump angle, or attaining top speed.

During the initial stages of learning, giving precedence to landing with the left foot is recommended. Wait until a specific foundation and a comfortable jump height have been attained before attempting to land with the right foot. This gradual approach aids beginners in developing the essential coordination and stability necessary for mastering this technical movement, ensuring a safer and more effective learning experience.

Step 5: Physical Fitness Exercises

The 'Jump, Front Straight Kick' requires good jumping ability, explosive power, and flexibility to execute the aerial kicking leg technique. Therefore, engaging in specific basic exercises is crucial to build a foundation for mastering the entire movement. As mentioned earlier, 'Leg Stretching' and 'Kicking' exercises are essential. During regular practice, it is beneficial to include activities such as 'front leg stretching,' 'higher leg stretching,' 'front straight kick,' and other exercises that focus on flexibility and warm-up. Incorporating alternating exercises for 'Leg Stretching' and 'Kicking' can enhance leg flexibility and joint agility, resulting in faster and easier kicks. Additionally, practitioners can include 'Strength Training' exercises to improve jump power and stability.

In 'Competitive Wushu' Competitions, deduction points are assigned for the following errors:

- Toes of the slapped foot below shoulder height.
- Missed slap.

4. Téng Kōng Bǎi Lián or Jumping Lotus Kick

'Téng Kōng Bǎi Lián,' (腾空摆莲) or 'Jumping Lotus Kick' in English, is a rotational jumping movement in Chinese Wushu routines. It involves both upward height in the air and rapid spinning of the body, making it a more challenging jump compared to a straight jump. The key aspect of this movement is the simultaneous execution of rotation and an outside kick. The shape formed by the body in the air resembles a lotus, hence the name 'Lotus Kick.'

Practice Methods:
(1) Step Forward, Jump Lotus Kick

Preparation Posture: Stand straight with your feet together and look straight ahead (Figure 10.45).

Movements:
- Rotate your upper body to the right. Take a large step forward to the right corner with your right foot. Allow your right heel to touch the ground first while naturally swinging your arms to both sides of your body. At this point, your body's weight should be between your legs, slightly leaning your upper body backward, and preparing to jump (Figure 11.46).

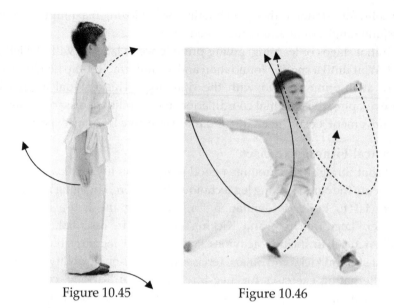

Figure 10.45   Figure 10.46

- Continue from the previous movement.
- After stepping to the right corner, quickly push your left foot onto the ground, shift your weight forward by driving your right foot, and then jump up. Simultaneously, kick your left foot up and swing your arms forward and upward from the sides. Hit the back of your right hand above your head with your left palm. Additionally, rotate your body to the right and maintain a straight-ahead gaze (Figure 10.47).

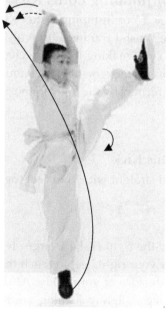

Figure 10.47

- Continue from the previous movement.
- After jumping, when your body is almost at the highest point in the air, perform a crescent-like kick with your right leg, kicking from the inside (left) to the outside (right). Pat your right foot in front of your head with your palms, first with your left hand and then your right hand. Bend your left knee and bring it to the inside of your right leg, or keep it extended on the left side of your body. Tilt your upper body forward slightly, while keeping your eyes focused on your hands (Figure 10.48). Land with your left foot first, followed by your right foot.

Figure 10.48

Generally, there are two postures of your legs in the air: One posture involves bending the left leg while controlling the left knee close to the core of the body. The other posture entails straightening the left leg to the left side of the body, with both legs almost forming a horizontal split in the air. Whichever method you choose, the movement should involve at least one full circle in the air. The training for this technique is typically divided into two steps: The first step involves practicing stepping forward and walking in a circular path. The second step consists of jumping and executing the lotus kick in the air.

1) Control of the left knee in the core: Focus on controlling the left knee as the central point. After stepping on your right foot, swing the left leg upward and inward in a crescent motion. Ensure your left knee close your chest. Simultaneously, initiate a turn of your upper body to the right. When jumping, execute a circular kick with your right foot and pat it with your palms. Aim to complete at least one full circle in the air.

2) Straightening the left leg on the left side of the body: In this method, the left leg is straightened and extended to the left side of the body, creating a nearly horizontal split in the air. After stepping on your right foot, straighten the left leg and initiate a turn of your upper body to the right. Jump, executing a circular kick with your right foot and patting it with your palms. Similar to the first method, aim to complete at least one full circle in the air.

The 'Jumping Lotus Kick' is characterized by the left leg swinging upward and inward after stepping on the right foot, resembling a crescent inside kick. As you push your right foot to the ground, initiate a turn of your upper body to the right. Upon jumping, execute a circular motion with your right foot, kicking it out while patting it with your palms. The entire movement requires high coordination and cooperation in the air to create a beautiful and graceful Wushu image. It places specific demands on jumping ability, including abdominal muscle, waist and leg strength, and coordination.

(2) Circle Walking, Jump Lotus Kick

Preparation Posture: Stand with your feet together. Hold your fists on your waists. Look straight ahead (Figure 10.49).

Movements :

- **Push the Palm in a High Empty Stance:**

Begin from your initial stance. Rotate your body to the left, approximately 45 degrees. Slightly advance your left foot to the left to establish a left-high empty stance. Simultaneously, extend your right palm forward from your right waist, maintaining it at shoulder height. Ensure your fingers face upward and tilt your palm to the left. Concurrently, extend your left hand backward with your fingers facing upward. Keep your focus on your extended right hand. (Figure 10.50).

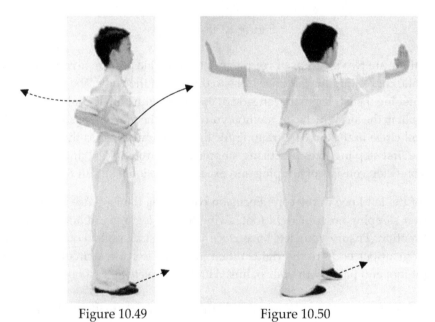

Figure 10.49　　　　　　　Figure 10.50

- **Step Forward:**

Keep your arms straight. Take a half step forward to the left with your left foot. Maintain your gaze on your right hand (Figure 11.51).

- **Circle Walking:**

  Proceed with the 'Circle Walking' motion. Take a substantial step forward with your right foot, slightly to the right in a circular path. Ensure that your right toes are slightly pointed outward, and your right knee is slightly bent. At the same time, move your right palm back to your right waist with the palm facing up. Swing your left arm forward from your left hip, with the palm facing outward. Direct your gaze to your left palm (Figure 11.52).

| Figure 10.51 | Figure 10.52 |

- **Jump:**

  Continue from the previous movement. With determination, push your right foot into the ground, maintaining your forward momentum. Then, leap into the air, rapidly bending your left knee and raising it in front of your body.

  Simultaneously, propel your right palm from your right waist, directing it through the inside of your left forearm and upwards with your right arm fully extended, palm facing up.

  As this occurs, swing your left arm back toward the front of your abdomen, following the path of your right arm, and continue the motion to the left side of your body.

  Now, swiftly turn your head to the left and lean your right shoulder forward. In mid-air, your right palm should be positioned on the right side above your head, while your left palm is slightly lower than your left shoulder on the left side of your body (as shown in Figure 10.53).

  Extend your right leg fully throughout this entire movement, keeping your left knee as high as possible. You should sense forward propulsion in addition to the upward jump, facilitating a smooth transition to the next jump movement.

- **Land:**

Continuing from the previous movement: Land your right foot first, ensuring that the right toes are pointed forward (Figure 10.54). Next, allow your left foot to land slightly in front of your body and the toes point to the right. Keep your left arm steady and extend your right hand downward to the right. Direct your gaze to the right (Figure 10.55).

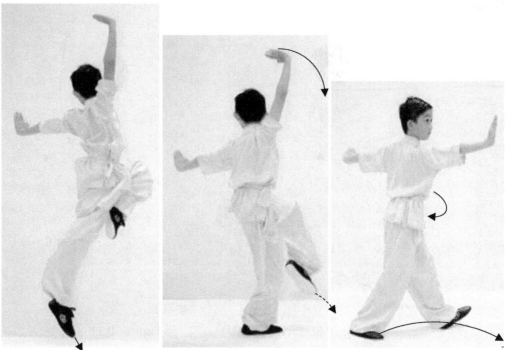

Figure 10.53   Figure 10.54   Figure 10.55

- **Stride Right Foot to the Right Side**

Continue from the previous movement. After your left foot lands, immediately step your right foot forward to the right corner, positioning your toes outward. This step should follow a circular path.

Simultaneously, rotate your body to the right and allow your arms to swing down to the back or both sides of your body naturally. Keep your gaze directed straight ahead, preparing for the next jump (Figure 10.56).

- **Jump Up**

Continue from the previous movement. Start by pushing your left foot to the ground first, swiftly shifting your weight forward. Then, push off the ground with your right foot to propel yourself into a jump.

As you jump, kick your left foot up and swing your arms forward and upward, guiding your body's upward motion. Bring the back of your right palm in contact with your left palm above your head (create a hitting action) and simultaneously rotate your body to the right (Figure 10.57). Your body should now be at the highest point in the air.

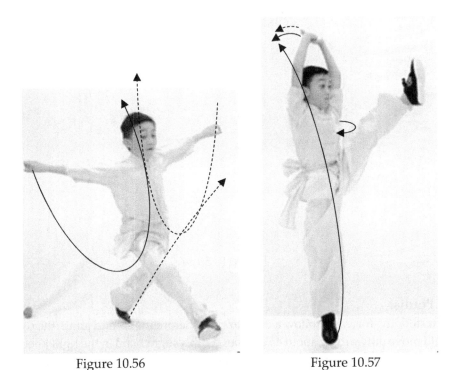

Figure 10.56   Figure 10.57

- **Lotus Kicks in the Air**

Continue from the previous movement. After the jump (when your body is nearly at its peak in the air), perform a circular motion by kicking your right leg from the inside (left side) to the outside, in sync with the left leg's swing. Pat your right foot in front of your head with your palms, initiating with the left hand and followed by the right hand. At this point, you can choose to either bend your left knee and move it inside your right leg or keep it stretched to the left side of your body, following the previously mentioned method. Slightly tilt your upper body forward. Maintain your focus on your hands (Figure 10.58).

- **Land**

Begin by landing your left foot first, followed by your right foot. As you progress and attain a higher skill level, you have the option to land with your right leg, both feet, or connect to a 'Falling Split' or a 'Sitting Cross Legged Stance' technique.

The dashed lines (solid and dotted) above of the 'Lotus Kick' route are the same as the previous 'Step Forward, Jump Lotus Kick.' If needed, you can go back to review it.

Figure 10.58

Key Points:
(1) When stepping forward, follow a circular path. Before the second jump, the right foot should move outward by about 45 degrees, with a slight bend in the right knee. While jumping, focus on kicking inward with your left leg, but do not overdo it.
(2) As you kick your right foot outward, your right leg should form a fan shape, and tilt your upper body slightly forward. Pat your right foot, aiming to do so in front of or near your face. Both hands should take turns patting your right foot. The patting should be continuous, precise, and produce a loud sound.
(3) At the moment of patting, you have the option to either bend your left knee and pull it back inside the right leg or extend your left knee to the left side of your body.
(4) As you complete the movement, focus on these actions: 'push the ground, jump, twist your waist, and rotate your body.' Ensure that the left leg's inward swing and the right leg's outward kick are consistent and well-coordinated.

Common Errors and Corrections:
(1) Running forward in a straight line rather than forming an arc.
(2) Incorrect jump angle, where the angle between the thigh and lower abdomen is either too small or too large, and the right foot doesn't turn outward (Figure 10.59).
(3) Inadequate jump height and insufficient body rotation, necessitate practice in achieving a full 360-degree jump to the right (Figure 10.60).
(4) Issues with 'patting,' such as patting too low, inaccuracy, timing issues, or even missing the pat. Additional practice is needed for the 'outside kick' with patting.

(5) Limited range of the outward swing and the left leg not kicking inward. Therefore, additional practice is required for 'left leg inside kick,' 'left leg moving in,' and 'right hip opening' exercises.

| Figure 10.59 | Figure 10.60 |

Practice Steps:

Step 1: Focus on Stretching and Kicking (Inside Connecting to Outside Kick)

The 'Jumping Lotus Kick' is a dynamic jumping movement in Wushu that incorporates two different kicking techniques. To master these techniques thoroughly, it's essential to practice the individual leg techniques without the jumping component. These exercises are designed to enhance waist and leg flexibility, improve hip agility, and increase the range of motion in your legs. Additionally, they prepare you to seamlessly combine both inside and outside kicks while rotating in a full circle. Here are the details:

- Begin by facing forward and step to the right with your right foot, positioning your toes slightly outward (Figure 10.61, 10.62). Rotate your body to the right and perform an 'inside crescent kick' with your left foot directed toward your right shoulder (Figure 10.63). Next, land your left foot in front of your right foot, with your toes pointing slightly inward (Figure 10.64).

Figure 10.61

Figure 10.62

Figure 10.63

Figure 10.64

- Continue to rotate to the right and execute an 'outside crescent kick' with your right foot (Figure 10.65). After completing both kicks, your body should have made almost a full circle to the right (Figure 10.66).

Figure 10.65   Figure 10.66

Practicing 'Combined Leg Kicks' (starting from an inside kick and transitioning into an outside kick) can closely simulate the movements in the air. Incorporating rotation into this practice can help you efficiently master aerial techniques. Begin with slower kick speeds and progressively increase your speed as you gain proficiency over time.

Step 2: Jump and Swing Your Left Leg Inward

- Begin by assuming a side stand position (Figure 10.67). Take a significant step forward with your right foot, placing it on the right corner while ensuring your right heel touches the ground. Strive for a jump angle of over 90 degrees between your right thigh and your torso to practice effectively. Rotate your right toe outward by 45 degrees to facilitate body rotation. As you take this step forward, swing your arms backward to enhance your body's strength and speed (Figure 10.68).
- As soon as your right foot firmly contacts the ground, swiftly push off from the surface, propelling yourself upwards, and execute a rapid turn to the right. At the same time, swing your left leg upward to the right, elevating your left knee as high as possible to facilitate the body's rotation. While in mid-air, perform a backward strike with your right palm, meeting your left palm. Lastly, shift your gaze towards

the left (Figures 10.69 and 10.70). It's important to remember to straighten the left leg slightly first before inwardly bending the knee during your turn.

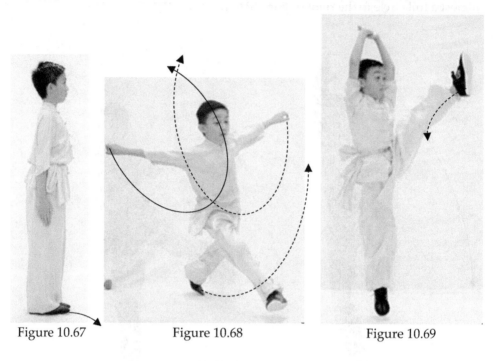

Figure 10.67   Figure 10.68   Figure 10.69

Figure 10.70

Begin by aiming for a slightly smaller right turn of approximately 90 degrees, and then progressively increase it to 180 degrees, 270 degrees, and finally a full 360-degree rotation. If your left leg is less flexible, and you find it challenging to swing your left leg upward, you have the option to bend your left leg while turning and jumping.

While airborne, concentrate on raising your head and waist, inhaling deeply, and maintaining an upright posture. Keep in mind that any deviations in any direction can impact the flawless execution of the aerial movement.

Step 3: Practice the Whole Movements:

Referring to the detailed practice method mentioned earlier, especially for beginners, it's important to approach it systematically without rushing the learning process. Beginners should concentrate on establishing a solid foundation rather than solely aiming for maximum jump height.

In Competitive Wushu, Deduction Points Include:

- Toes of the slapped foot below shoulder height.
- Missed or inaudible slap.

Continuous Total Movements of 'Jumping Lotus Kick'

5. Téng Kōng Xuànfēng Jiǎo Jump Tornado Kick

'Téng Kōng Xuànfēng Jiǎo,' (腾空旋风脚) translated as the 'Jump Tornado Kick' in English, is one of the fundamental jumping movements in Chinese Wushu. This term describes a dynamic kicking technique that involves jumping and spinning in the air while executing a kick, known for its acrobatic and impressive nature. It demands agility, balance, and precise control. Typically, it includes a sequence of actions such as running forward, jumping with an arm swing, performing an inward crescent kick with the body spinning, and then landing. The quality of this movement relies on factors like jump height, landing technique, and the degree of rotation in the air. There are three ways to land, ranging from simple to complex: 1) Landing with the left foot first, followed by the right foot; 2) Simultaneous landing with both feet; 3) Landing with the right foot only.

To execute a beautiful and elegant 'Tornado Kick,' you must possess excellent jump ability, muscular waist and abdominal muscle strength, complete body coordination, and leg flexibility. These elements are crucial for mastering this technique.

Practice Methods:
(1) Step Forward and Perform a Tornado Kick

Preparation Posture: Start by standing straight on your right leg and place your left foot in front to form a left-high empty stance. Meanwhile, push your left palm to the left and place your right palm above your head to create a 'Flash palm.' Then, look to the left (Figure 10.71).

Movements:
* **Step Forward:**

Step to the left with your left foot while keeping your left arm steady and pushing it to the left. Extend your right arm backward with all fingers pointing upward. Maintain your gaze to the left (Figure 10.72).

Figure 10.71   Figure 10.72

Proceed by stepping forward with your right foot, turning your toes inward at an angle of over 90 degrees, preparing for the jump. Simultaneously, swing your left arm downward, bending it to chest level. In coordination, swing your right arm upward and forward to the right, rotating your upper body to the left. Additionally, bend your knees slightly and lean forward. Direct your gaze toward the right corner (Figure 10.73).

Figure 10.73

- **Jump:**

  Continuing from the previous action without pause, shift your weight entirely onto your right leg, bending your right knee as you push off the ground with your right foot to initiate the jump. Simultaneously, lift your left leg and swing it upward to the upper left while rotating your body in the same direction to the left (Figures 10.74 and 10.75).

| Figure 10.74 | Figure 10.75 |

Important Note:

The rotational power generated during the jump in the air originates from the ground reaction force and is transmitted through a series of coordinated actions, including 'swinging arms while stepping forward,' 'waist twisting,' and 'body turning.' As the left foot moves to the left, the left hand swings upward from the front, while the right arm straightens and swings backward. Simultaneously, step forward with your right foot, ensuring that the tiptoes face inward, the knee is slightly bent, and your body turns to the left by approximately 180 degrees. This preparatory movement accumulates energy for the explosive jump. Additionally, lift and swing your left leg upward to the upper left. Then, swing your arms diagonally from the right lower corner to the upper left side, allowing your body to spin around with the momentum generated by the arms.

- **Kick in the Air:**

  Continuing from the previous jump movement, swing your arms down and then upward to the upper left. Allow your body to spin around. While jumping, execute an inward kick with your right leg, and pat the sole of your right foot with your left palm in front of your face ((Figure 10.76). Allow your left leg to drop naturally (Figure 10.77) or keep it beside your right leg (Figure 10.78).

| Figure 10.76 | Figure 10.77 | Figure 10.78 |

Important Note: During the moment of the jump, create friction with the ground using your right sole while twisting your waist and turning your hips. Apply powerful force to push off the ground. Simultaneously, straighten your hips, right knee, and right ankle, and swing your right leg from the bottom to the top, moving from the outside to the inside to create a fan shape. As the body completes a 180-degree rotation, keep your right leg as close as possible to your body. Turn your right foot inward when spinning your right leg around the hip to 180 degrees. Your left hand's palm should strike the sole of the right foot in front of your face. The striking action occurs after a 270-degree turn.

- **Land:**
    After the patting action, you can either land first with your left foot and then your right foot or land on both feet simultaneously (Figure 10.79).

Figure 10.79

Key Points:

(1) When kicking your right leg inward, keep it close to your body and ensure that your right knee is straight, forming a fan shape with your kick.

(2) The patting point should be close to your face. As your left leg swings inward, it should extend and leave the ground at the moment of the right kick.

(3) For beginners, the left leg can naturally drop after the right kick. As you become more proficient in jumping, gradually lift your left leg, bend the knee close to your chest, or stretch it out to the side of your body.

(4) The swinging of your arms, the force applied to the jump, and the inward kick should be consistent and coordinated. The rotation of your body should not be less than 360 degrees.

Common Errors and Corrections:

(1) Lack of upper and lower body connection and insufficient rotation. To improve your body's rotation ability, practice the movement of 'turning left 360 degrees jump' without using your legs (Figure 10.80).

(2) Bending your knees and dropping your hips while your legs swing. To correct this, practice leg techniques like 'turn and swing outward with your left leg' and 'turn and kick inside.' Emphasize the correct posture of keeping your knees extended.

(3) Leaning backward after jumping. Practice 'lift the left knee, turning 360 degrees, jump with the right leg' to emphasize jumping straight up with your head held high.

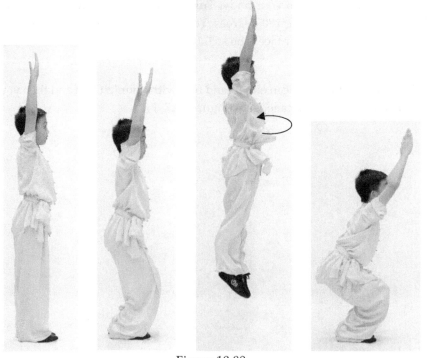

Figure 10.80

(2) Running Forward and Perform a Tornado Kick

Once you have mastered the 'Step Forward, Jump, Tornado Kick,' you can incorporate a 'Skip Step' to further enhance the movement. Additionally, you can introduce the more challenging landing with the right leg (Figure 10.81).

Figure 10.81

The dashed lines (solid and dotted) above of the 'Tornado Kick' route are the same as the previous 'Step Forward, Jump Tornado Kick.' If needed, you can go back to review it.

Practice Steps

Step 1: Step forward, practice 'Inside Crescent Kick' and turn left about 90 degrees' (Figure 10.82 (1) (2)(3) (4)).

Figure 10.82 (1)

Figure 10.82 (2)

Figure 10.82 (3)

Figure 10.82 (4)

Step 2: Practice 'Jump Up and Inside Crescent Kick' while staying in place, following the movements shown in Figure 10.83 (1), (2), and (3). (3)).

| Figure 10.83 (1) | Figure 10.83 (2) | Figure 10.83 (3) |

Step 3: Take a step forward and practice the 'Jump Up, Turn, Inside Crescent Kick' as depicted in Figure 10.84 (1,)(2),(3),(4),(5),(6),(7),(8).

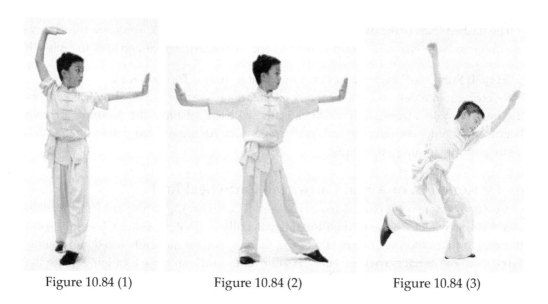

| Figure 10.84 (1) | Figure 10.84 (2) | Figure 10.84 (3) |

Figure 10.84 (4)   Figure 10.84 (5)

Figure 10.84 (6)   Figure 10.84 (7)   Figure 10.84 (8)

The dashed lines (solid and dotted) above of the 'Tornado Kick' route are the same as the previous 'Step Forward, Jump Tornado Kick.' If needed, you can go back to review it.

Step 4: Running-Forward and Perform a Whole 'Jump, Tornado Kick.'
Referring to the detailed practice method mentioned earlier, especially for beginners, it's important to approach it systematically without rushing the learning process. Beginners should concentrate on establishing a solid foundation rather than solely aiming for maximum jump height.

6. Cè Kōng Fān or Aerial Cartwheel, Cartwheel Roll

'Cè Kōng Fān,' (侧空翻) translated as the 'Aerial Cartwheel,' and also known as the 'No-Handed Cartwheel,' is one of the fundamental skills in Contemporary Chinese Wushu. It serves to strengthen your upper body and prepare you for more advanced movements. To practice the aerial cartwheel safely, it's crucial to find a suitable location. Ensure that you engage in stretching exercises before starting to prevent injuries. Do not attempt this on a hard surface. It is best to practice on grass outdoors or use gymnastic mats indoors.

Practice Methods:

Preparation Posture: Stand straight with your feet together and look straight ahead. After assuming this position, take a moment to focus, sink your Qi to your Dantian, adjust your breathing, and prepare yourself.

Movements:

- Start by taking a few running steps forward, typically two steps (beginning with the left foot, followed by the right foot), and then add one 'skip step' on the right foot. These running steps are essential for building momentum and motivation as you learn (Figures 10.85, 10.86, and 10.87). While running forward, let your arms swing naturally from behind your body. This movement assists your left foot in pushing off the ground for the upcoming jump. Keep an upright posture throughout your practice.

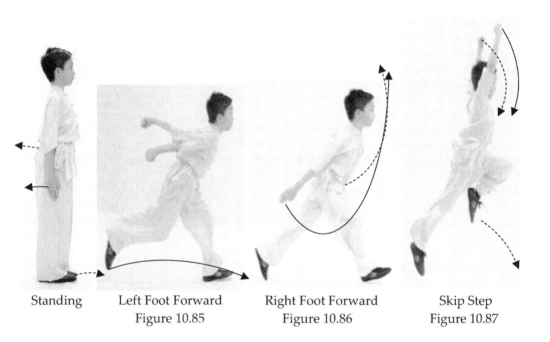

Standing	Left Foot Forward	Right Foot Forward	Skip Step
	Figure 10.85	Figure 10.86	Figure 10.87

- After the right foot takes a 'skip step,' first, land your right foot, then drop your left foot forward, and powerfully push it into the ground (Figure 10.88).
- Following this, swing your right leg from backward, up and forward, bending forward and flipping to the left in mid-air (Figures 10.89, 10.90). Remember to inhale and briefly hold your breath as you push off the ground with your left foot. Then, swing your arms and kick your right leg backward and upward simultaneously, fully extending your legs and separating them in mid-air.

Figure 10.88

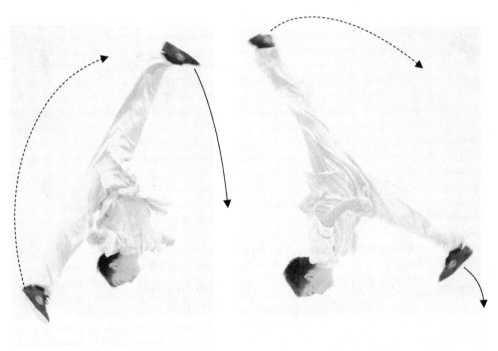

Figure 10.89   Figure 10.90

- First, land with your right foot, followed by your left foot (Figure 10.91). Straighten your head and chest as you land. Typically, especially for beginners, it's advisable to bend your right knee slightly while landing to prevent any potential harm to your right knee or right ankle. Once you've mastered the movement, you can work on extending your right knee to refine your technique.

Figure 10.91

Practice Step:

Step 1: Practice the 'Back Swing Kick' with your right leg to develop the strength needed for your back swing. You can practice this with a chair (Figure 10.92) or perform it freehand in place (Figure 10.93). Commonly, you can practice alternately with both legs.

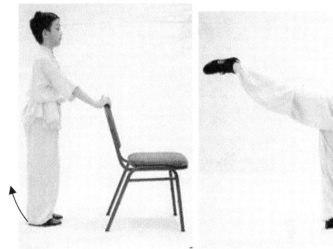

Figure 10.92

Figure 10.93

Step 2: Practice a regular two-handed cartwheel in place (Figure 10.94) to perfect the form of the movement and enhance the speed of your swinging leg (right leg).

Figure 10.94

Step 3: Next, practice a one-handed cartwheel in place (Figure 10.95). This exercise will bring you closer to your goal and help you understand how to generate momentum during the cartwheel without relying on your hands.

Figure 10.95

Step 4: Practice a regular two hands cartwheel in the running forward (Figure 10.96).

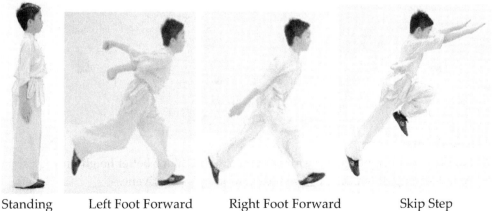

Standing   Left Foot Forward   Right Foot Forward   Skip Step

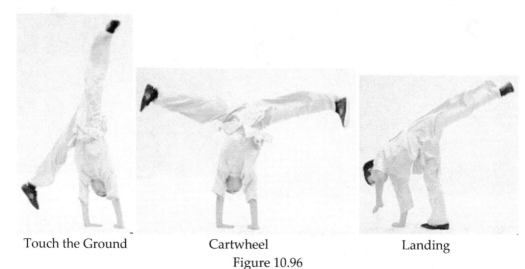

Touch the Ground   Cartwheel   Landing

Figure 10.96

The dashed lines (solid and dotted) above of the 'Cartwheel' route are the same as the previous. If needed, you can go back to review it.

Step 5: With the protection and assistance of your teacher or teammate, focus on understanding the technical requirements of the movement and gradually transition to performing it independently. When starting, have your helper stand sideways behind you. While you're in the air, the assistant should place their right hand on your left hip joint to aid in accelerating your rotation. As you complete the move, their left hand can support your right hip to maintain balance. If you're unable to execute the aerial cartwheel and complete the rotation, the helper can catch you if needed (Figure 10.97).

Figure 10.97

Key Points:
(1) Maintain an upright body posture as you run to achieve better height in your aerial. Avoid leaning down, as it will reduce your jump's effectiveness.
(2) Do not attempt this move if you feel uncomfortable, as it can lead to injuries.

(3) Remember that the momentum in an aerial comes from your legs. The force generated when kicking your legs should keep them straight rather than curling, which would slow down the movement.

(4) Initiate the kick with your back leg first, followed by your front leg, to get your legs over your head faster.

(5) Visualize the skill in your mind and focus on every detail before practicing. If you think you might fall on your head, place your hands down for safety. Safety always precedes the risk of injury.

(6) Swing both of your legs over your head. Begin by whipping up your rear leg and then launch off your leading leg, ensuring both legs are above your head during the movement.

7. Xuán Zi or Butterfly kick

The 'Xuán Zi' (旋子), translated as 'Butterfly' or 'Butterfly Kick' in English, is a fundamental jumping movement in Contemporary Chinese Wushu. It is named after how all limbs extend from the body, resembling the butterfly's wings during the kick's peak. Typically, this movement involves a rotation from right to left. As the left foot lands behind and prepares for the jump, the upper body leans forward, and the waist swings from the left to the rear. Simultaneously, the arms rotate horizontally from right to left. When the left foot pushes off the ground, the right leg initially swings backward, followed by the left leg swinging back upward. This horizontal body rotation occurs with momentum in the air, and the landing occurs sequentially. The butterfly kick is foundational and steppingstone for more advanced exercises like the 360 and 720-degree butterfly turns.

Practice Methods:

(1) Spin From Standing Position

Preparation Posture: Start by standing upright and placing your feet apart. Rotate your body to the right, lifting your left heel off the ground so your body faces the right corner. Extend your left arm upward towards the upper right corner of your body while allowing your right arm to hang naturally behind your body (Figure 10.98).

Slightly raise your left leg in preparation for the upcoming sequence. Keep your focus on your left hand (Figure 10.99).

Sequence of Movement:

• Step back with your left foot, making sure it firmly touches the ground. Lean your upper body forward at the waist level and swing your waist to the left. At the same time, straighten your arms and swing them to the left (see Figure 10.100 (1), (2), (3)).

• Push off the ground using your left foot to propel yourself into the air. Simultaneously, rotate both legs upward and to the upper left. Extend your feet, spreading your legs apart, resembling the graceful motion of a butterfly (see Figure 10.101 (1), (2)).

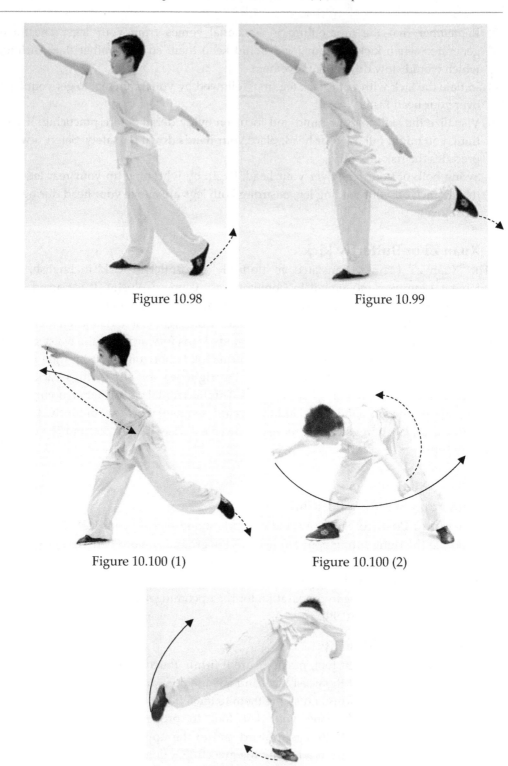

Figure 10.98

Figure 10.99

Figure 10.100 (1)

Figure 10.100 (2)

Figure 10.100 (3)

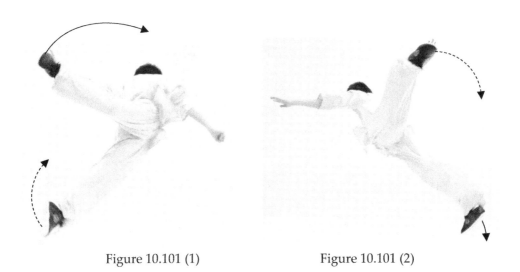

Figure 10.101 (1)   Figure 10.101 (2)

- Subsequently, land first on your right foot and then your left foot (Figure 10.102).

Figure 10.102

Key Points:
(1) The 'Butterfly Kick,' while relatively straightforward, still demands practice to develop strength and precision. Consistent practice for a few minutes daily will lead to noticeable improvements.
(2) For beginners, having a qualified person assist you can be highly beneficial. They can support you by holding your arm and guiding you through the rotation as you learn the movement.

(2) Take Three Run-Ups, Turn Around, and Connect to the 'Butterfly Kick'

Preparation Posture: Begin by standing upright and positioning your feet apart. Rotate your body to the right, lifting your left heel off the ground so that your body faces the right corner. The entire movement resembles a 'Spin from Standing Position' as shown above (Figures 10.103 (1), (2)).

Figure 10.103 (1)   Figure 10.103 (2)

Sequence of Movement:

- **Step Left Foot:** Step back with your left foot, ensuring complete contact with the ground. Simultaneously, rotate your entire body to the left. Lean your upper body forward and swing your waist to the left. Extend your arms and swing them horizontally to the left (as shown in Figure 10.104 (1), (2), (3)).

Figure 10.104 (1)   Figure 10.104 (2)   Figure 10.104 (3)

- **Step Right Foot:** Continue from the previous movement. As your left foot contacts to the ground, promptly step forward with your right foot while maintaining the rotation of your entire body and arms to the left (Figure 10.101 (1), (2)).

Figure 10.101 (1)   Figure 10.101 (2)

- **Swing the Left Leg and Turn the Right Foot in:** Swing the left leg and turn the right foot in: Continue from the previous movement. As you step your right foot forward, slightly swing your left leg to the left to assist with the rotation of your entire body but keep the swing relatively low. Simultaneously, pivot your right foot inward around 90 degrees. Also, swing your arms above your head, moving from left to right in a clockwise direction in one circle. Then, position your left arm in front of your right shoulder, pointing to the right (opposite of the forward direction), and place your right arm behind your body (Figure 10.102).

Figure 10.102

- **Turn and Prepare to Jump:** Continue from the previous movement. As you move your left foot back, ensure it makes complete contact with the ground. Lean your upper body forward at waist level and swing your waist to the left. Simultaneously, straighten your arms and swing them to the left in preparation for the jump (Figure 10.103 (1) (2) (3)).

Figure 10.103 (1)   Figure 10.103 (2)   Figure 10.103 (3)

- **Jump Up and Perform a Butterfly:** Push off the ground using your left foot, propelling yourself into the air. Simultaneously, rotate both legs upward and to the upper left. Extend your feet, spreading your legs apart, resembling the graceful motion of a butterfly (Figure 10.104 (1) (2)).

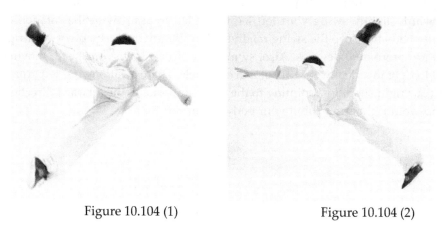

Figure 10.104 (1)   Figure 10.104 (2)

- **Landing:** Land first on your right foot and then your left foot (Figure 10.105).

Figure 10.105

Practice Steps:

Step 1: Swallow Balance Practice:

* Stand on your right leg, lift your left leg backward and lean forward horizontally at the waist. Slightly lift your head and stretch your chest. Hands are on both sides of your body. Try to extend the time. Practice your legs alternately (Figure 10.106, 107).

| Figure 10.106 | Figure 10.107 |

Step 2: Keep Swallow Balance by Raising the Heel and Rotating to the Left

* Maintain the 'Swallow Balance' posture by standing on your right leg and lifting your right heel off the ground. Use the sole of your right foot as an axis to rotate your body to the left, following the inertia of the swing. Slightly turn your upper body and eyes to the left. This exercise serves as a fundamental practice for improving jumping and spinning abilities. It enhances swing strength and balance skills (Figure 10.108 (1)).

| Figure 10.108 (1) | Figure 10.108 (2) |

- Practice the left leg and right leg alternately (Figure 108 (20).

Step 3: Protection and Help:

The assistant positions himself to your left, holding your left wrist with his left hand and your left abdomen with his right hand (Figure 10.109). Get ready.

As you lean forward, lift your left heel, and push off the ground, the helper supports your left waist upward with his right hand, aiding in your rotation in the air. Simultaneously, the assistant should gently pull your left hand to the left using his left hand to enhance the speed and strength of your spin (Figure 10.110 (1) (2) (3)). It's crucial to actively cooperate with your assistant during your practice of jumping and spinning.

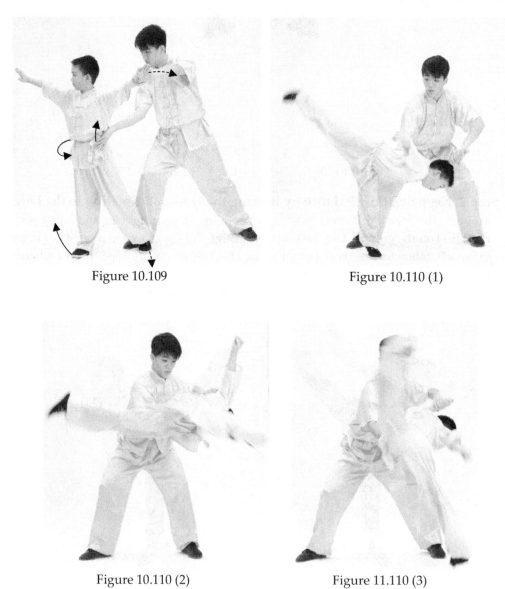

Figure 10.109   Figure 10.110 (1)

Figure 10.110 (2)   Figure 11.110 (3)

Step 4: Spin from Standing Position

- **Lean forward and swing:** Start by bending your upper body forward and shifting your weight from your right to your left leg, all while letting your arms naturally swing with your body (Figure 10.111 (1) (2)). Remember that leaning your upper body forward is crucial for greater upward force. The swinging motion provides the power required for the horizontal rotation in the air. Remember to hold your breath during this phase, preparing to release the force.

Figure 10.111 (1)   Figure 10.111 (2)

- **Spin Up:** Push off the ground with your right and left feet alternately. Vigorously swing your arms and hands to the left while coordinating this motion with your upper body. Simultaneously, swing both feet upwards to execute the 'butterfly kick' in the air (Figure 10.112). To achieve greater height, lift your head as it will elevate your upper body. Extending and separating your legs aids in making the movement more graceful and buoyant. The critical aspect is twisting your waist to the left during the upward spin.

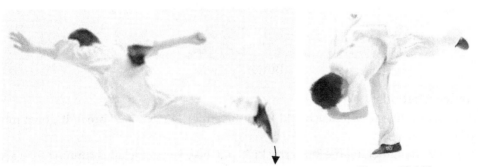

Figure 10.112   Figure 10.113

- **Land:** Upon landing, your body should touch down naturally. Start by allowing your right foot to land first and absorb the impact by bending your knees. Subsequently, your left foot follows suit, making a smooth landing (Figure 10.113).

Step 5: Practice the Complete Movement:

Now that you've practiced the individual components of the butterfly kick, it's time to put it all together into a fluid, continuous movement. Start with the initial posture, then flow through each step, from the lean and swing to the spin and landing. This practice will help you refine your technique and build the coordination needed for a successful butterfly kick. Be patient, and with consistent practice, you'll improve your skills.

8. 'Xuán Zi Zhuàn Tǐ,' Butterfly-twist

'Xuán Zi Zhuàn Tǐ' (旋子轉體), or the 'Butterfly Twist' in English, is one of the most challenging movements in Chinese competitive Wushu. It builds upon the foundation of the 'Butterfly Kick' and typically involves spinning in a complete circle or multiple circles, such as 360 degrees, 540 degrees (1.5 circles), and 720 degrees (2 circles). Learning the butterfly twist should be a gradual process, with steps and progressions tailored to your physical condition and skill level. It's important to approach this advanced movement with patience and proper guidance to ensure safety and effectiveness in your training.

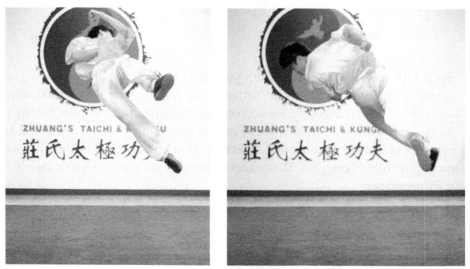

Butterfly Twist

Practice Methods:

The most effective way to teach and train the butterfly twist is to break it down into four steps:

(1) Begin by strengthening the 'butterfly kick' practice, which includes running forward and connecting the movements.

(2) Practice vertical turning circles by jumping in place. This step helps you experience the feeling of being in the air after jumping and teaches you how to turn your head and swing your arms (Figure 10.114 (1), (2)).

(3) Practice the 'Butterfly Twist' in place, focusing on how your body spins into a straight line in the air and how it twists. This step should be performed on a soft mat (Figure

276

10.115). The training method is similar to the butterfly kick movement. After jumping in place, aim to achieve a straight line in the air. Keep your arms in position, twist your body to the left, and look to your left side. After completing one full circle, land with your left foot first, followed by your right foot. The key elements are jumping, arm positioning, waist twisting, and head-turning to look at your left shoulder.

(4) Combine all the movements, starting with the initial posture, stepping, cross-leg positioning, turning, leg swinging, jumping, spinning, twisting, and landing.

| Figure 10.114 (1) | Figure 10.114 (2) |

These four practice steps provide a structured approach to mastering the butterfly twist. Remember to practice on a soft mat for safety and gradual progression. Each step contributes to your overall skill development in this complex movement.

Key Points:
(1) Achieving proficiency in the basic butterfly kick is essential before attempting the butterfly twist.

(2) After pushing off the ground with your left foot, raise your right leg while extending your arms, with the right arm reaching out. Simultaneously, twist your waist and keep your focus on your left side or shoulder.

(3) During the jump phase, emphasize pushing your right shoulder and using your waist as the axis for spinning. Engage your core muscles and slightly tighten your legs.

(4) Straighten your chest and waist, which adds beauty to your movement. The ideal butterfly twist extends your entire body in the air, creating a graceful and flowing motion.

(5) Typically, the left leg should be the first to initiate the jump, and it should also be the first to land during the butterfly twist.

In a 'Competitive Wushu' Competition, deduction points are applied based on specific criteria, including:

(1) The angle of the torso: If the angle of the torso during the twist exceeds 45°, it may result in deduction points. Ideally, the torso should remain relatively straight and aligned with the spin to achieve a clean and precise movement.

(2) Bent legs: If one or both legs are visibly bent at an angle of 45° or more while in the air, it can lead to deduction points. Straightened legs during the twist help maintain control and aesthetics in the performance.

These criteria are important for assessing the quality of the butterfly twist and ensuring that competitors demonstrate a high level of skill, balance, and technique during their performances. Deduction points are typically applied to encourage athletes to strive for greater perfection and precision in their movements.

Sun Peiyuan, a renowned Chinese Wushu athlete, executed a Butterfly Twist 720-degree maneuver during the Wushu Competition at the 19th Asian Games held in Hangzhou, China, in 2023, demonstrating a heroic posture

Chapter 11
Basic Movements (7)
Diē Pú Gǔn Fān - Tumbling
跌扑滚翻

In Chinese Wushu, 'Diē Pú Gǔn Fān' represents the sophisticated and intricate technique of tumbling, an essential component of this martial art. Each term in this phrase carries a significant meaning that collectively defines the essence of tumbling:

Diē (跌): This character translates to 'fall,' emphasizing the skill of controlled and deliberate falling as part of the tumbling process.

Pú (扑): Meaning 'pounce' or 'pounce forward,' this term indicates the action of bouncing or springing forward, an integral part of dynamic movements in tumbling.

Gǔn (滚): Referring to 'rolling,' this aspect involves executing rolls, which are foundational movements in the tumbling sequences.

Fān (翻): Translating to 'flip,' this character highlights the element of flipping, adding an acrobatic and complex dimension to the tumbling technique.

'Tumbling,' as a collective term in English, encapsulates these four elements – falling, pouncing, rolling, and flipping. It's a distinct and challenging discipline within Chinese Wushu that requires practitioners to master the art of falling safely and gracefully. Tumbling is not just about the execution of movements; it's about mastering them with finesse and without causing harm to oneself.

Endeavoring in tumbling cultivates the ability to manage falls proficiently and acts as a crucible for refining coordination, agility, balance, speed, strength, and suppleness. The routine encompasses various falling and rolling movements, each requiring precision and skill. Variations range from movements executed with a straight body, flexed posture, extended legs, bent legs moving forwards, backward, and sideways. Noteworthy examples include the 'Side-diving roll forward,' 'Carp flipping up,' 'Black dragon coils around the pole,' 'Pounce on the tiger,' and 'Jump with the back and buttock.'

'Tumbling' embodies physical grace, mental prowess, and technical acumen, showcasing the multifaceted dimensions of Chinese Wushu's techniques.

1. Qiǎng Bèi or Side-Diving Roll Forward

'Qiǎng Bèi' (抢揹), commonly referred to as the 'Side-Diving Roll Forward' in English, describes a maneuver characterized by the adept execution of a diagonal forward roll. This technique involves a lateral rotation where either the right or left shoulder, the posterior part of the body, and the left hip or right hip make contact with the ground. This contact ensures a smooth and continuous flow throughout the roll.

Accomplishing this motion involves a series of coordinated movements, encompassing foot pressure, controlled elevation through jumping, supporting actions, and the actual rolling itself. In certain instances, the technique can be performed without hand support.

For optimal safety and proficiency, practicing this technique on a cushioned surface such as a mat or a ground with a forgiving texture is advisable. This approach minimizes the risk of injury and allows practitioners to refine their execution of the 'Side-diving roll forward gradually.'

Practice Method: (using the right leg in front as an example)

Preparation Position: Begin by positioning yourself with the right foot placed in front and the left foot positioned at the back. Bend both knees slightly. Gently incline your upper body forward and direct your gaze downwards. Simultaneously, extend your right arm forward, poised to make contact with the ground (Figure 11.1).

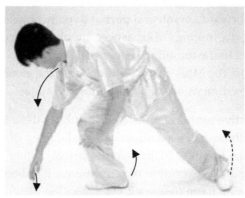

Figure 11.1

Movements:

- Initiate the movement by propelling your left foot rearward, executing a swift kick, and subsequently directing it towards the ground through the impetus of your right foot.

- Extend your right arm to contact the ground ahead of your right foot using either your right palm or forgoing hand contact altogether. In this instance, your right arm's outer aspect should be in touch with the ground. While executing this, lower your head and allow your upper body to curl inward.

- Concurrently, execute a bend in your right leg while extending your left leg backward. Follow this by initiating a fluid body roll forward (Refer to Figure 12.2).

- During the rolling action, utilize the outer section of your right arm, sequentially progressing from your right shoulder through your back, waist, and left hip, and concluding with the exterior of your left leg contacting the ground. Following the momentum of the roll, regain an upright position naturally (Figure 11.2, 11.3, 11.4, 11.5, 11.6).

Figure 11.2

Figure 11.3

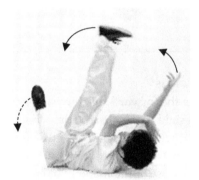

Figure 11. 4

Figure 11.5

Figure 11.6

Continuous Movement of 'Side-Diving Roll Forward'

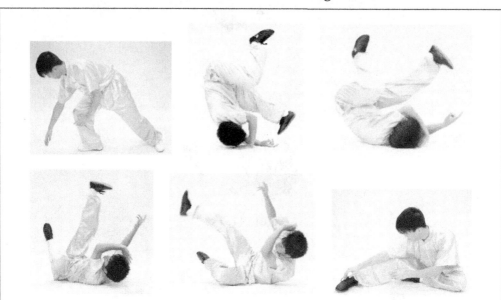

Key Points
1. During the forward roll, envision your body emulating the form of a sphere rather than a rigid plank. This approach facilitates smoother movement.
2. Pay particular attention to your left leg; execute a rapid and efficient bend, promptly followed by an impactful kick backward.
3. In the course of the maneuver, ensure a sequential progression of contact with the ground: initiate with the right shoulder, followed by the back, and culminating with the hip.
4. Execute the roll with agility and enthusiasm, enabling a swift rotation and prompt recovery to an upright position.

Practice Steps:
Step 1: Bend Knees and Hold Them in Place
- Begin by lying on your back with your arms and legs fully extended.
- Allow your body to relax naturally in this position (Figure 11.7).

Figure 11.7

- Bend your knees, drawing them toward your chest while maintaining an upright upper body. Hollow out your chest and lower your head.
- Simultaneously, swiftly employ your arms to grasp your calves (Figure 11.8).

Figure 11.8

- Engage in a repetitive exercise cycle: Grasp → Lie down → Grasp. This process serves two essential purposes. Firstly, it fosters a comprehensive comprehension of each bodily segment's placement during the rolling movement, enhancing coordination and body awareness. Secondly, it contributes to strengthening abdominal muscles, consequently rendering the body more compact and spherical in form.

Step 2: Practice Rolling Forward

- During the rolling motion, initiate by moving both shoulders forward in unison. This motion serves a dual purpose: firstly, it facilitates a deeper understanding of the correct head positioning, encouraging a tucked chin, a chest hollowed slightly, and the abdomen contracting. Additionally, it allows for the coordination of bending the knees and swiftly drawing the legs inward.
- In the initial stages of practicing this rolling technique, executing the movement gradually is advisable before progressing to a swifter pace. Begin by slowly lowering your head, then, as you gradually make contact with the ground, incrementally increase the speed of the roll until it culminates in a brisk rotation, eventually transitioning into a rapid rise to a standing position (Figure 11.9 (1)(2)(3)(4)(5)).

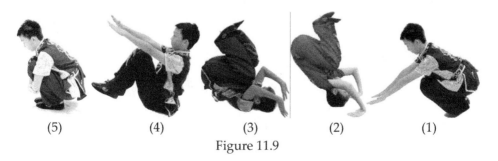

| (5) | (4) | (3) | (2) | (1) |

Figure 11.9

Step 3: Initiating Self-Protection with Hand and Arm Ground Contact

- When executing a forward 'side-diving roll' to your right side, it's wise to make initial contact with the ground using your right arm. This strategic placement mitigates the impact force between the shoulder and the ground, enhancing self-protection.
- It's important to note that the right arm should not extend too far from the body, especially for beginners. This is because the center of gravity tends to be less stable in novice practitioners. Extending the right arm too far from the body can lead to complications such as a failed roll or an unstable standing stance. Hence, keeping the right arm relatively close to the body is advisable for smoother and safer execution.

Step 4: Mastering the Leaping Motion of the 'Side Diving Roll Forward'

- Once you've thoroughly absorbed the concepts and prerequisites outlined in the preceding 'Figures,' it's essential not to hurry or exert excessive pressure upon yourself during this phase. Begin by practicing the 'rolling' movement without incorporating the leap. Focus on enhancing the forward body angle and the impact of your movement. Gradually, allow your right hand and right shoulder to extend further from your body as you execute the rolling motion.
- Once you've attained proficiency in the movement, introduce the 'jump up' component of the 'side dive roll forward' (as depicted in Figure 11.10).
- It's natural for the body to require an adjustment period when learning this motion. You might experience heightened sensations within your internal organs or slight discomfort in the shoulder region. These sensations are within the realm of normalcy. As long as you adhere to the appropriate force application and maintain the correct action sequence, these sensations can be mitigated.
- Upon making contact between the shoulder and the ground, hold your breath momentarily and allow for a slight pause following exhalation; this can help alleviate any discomfort.

Continuing the Fluid Motion of Jumping up in the 'Side-Diving Roll Forward'

Figure 11.10

Common Errors and Corrections:

(1) Rolling in the Wrong Direction or Incorrect Sequence: One common error is initiating the roll facing forward or rolling sideways. To rectify this, focus on the proper body landing sequence. As you practice, ensure your right arm is tucked beneath your left armpit while your head turns to the left, bringing your chin close to your left shoulder. When rolling, adhere to the following order: first, your right shoulder contacts the ground, followed by your back, left waist, and left hip. Additionally, exert force toward your left leg while your right shoulder touches the ground to enhance the rolling speed.

(2) Lack of Tightness in the Roll: A mistake often observed is a lack of tightness in the roll. Counter this by emphasizing tucking your chin as closely as possible to your left clavicle. During the jump, consistently remind yourself to 'lower your head' or seek assistance from your instructor or a partner for reminders. Simultaneously, relax your chest, engage your abdominal muscles, and bend your knees to meet the technical requirements of the movement.

(3) Bumping the Back of the Head: 'Bumping the back of the head' commonly occurs due to a loose neck during practice and failure to lower the head and tuck the chin. To overcome this, dedicate time to refining your 'body-rolling' technique. Develop a feel for the conditions of proper body rolling and work on enhancing your rolling speed. Remember that achieving the rate is essential, as inertia alone won't suffice.

(4) Difficulty Standing Up After Rolling: The issue of struggling to stand up after rolling has multiple factors. Here are some ways to address this problem:

1) Ensure your body's center of gravity moves forward, particularly during the jump. The angle of gravity should lean on, and the forward force should exceed the rolling motion to enable a smooth transition to stand.

2) Check the landing point of your feet; they should naturally fall in front of your body as you bend your knees and roll forward. If mistakes occur, consciously bend your knees more, primarily upon landing close to your body.

3) Avoid delaying the upper body's ascent after rolling. Emphasize timely and coordinated movement to transition to a standing position successfully.

4) Remember, refining your technique requires dedication and practice. Addressing these common errors with the recommended corrections will improve proficiency in the 'Side-Diving Roll Forward' movement.

2. Lǐyú Dǎtǐng, Carp Flipping Up

'Lǐyú Dǎtǐng' (鯉魚打挺) or 'Corp Flip Up' refers to a specific movement or technique and is a fundamental tumbling maneuver in Chinese Wushu, characterized by a rapid transition from a supine position to an upright stance. This technique combines elements of falling, flipping, and agile movement, with applications in both defensive and offensive contexts.

There are two primary practice methods for mastering the 'Carp Flipping Up' technique: the 'Push Ground Method' and the 'Push Knees Method.' These methods offer distinct variations, allowing practitioners to choose based on individual preferences or specific training requirements. For beginners, it is advisable to start with the 'Push Ground Method' as it provides a solid foundation for technique. Subsequently, more advanced practitioners can explore the 'Push Knees Method.' Here's an illustration of both practice methods:

Practice Method:

(1) Push Ground Method:

Preparation Posture: Begin by lying on your back, facing upwards, and position your arms beside your body (Figure 11.11).

Figure 11.11

Movements:
- Start by straightening your legs and bringing them close to your chest, or if preferred, keep your knees slightly bent initially.
- Concurrently, bend your elbows and position your hands on either side of your head, with your fingers pointing towards your shoulders (Figure 11.12).

Figure 11.12

- Progress into the next part of the motion. Continue rolling your body backward until the weight is predominantly on your shoulders (Figure 11.13).
- Simultaneously, exert pressure against the ground using your palms and contract your elbows to ensure your upper back and neck make contact with the ground.
- Following this, execute a forceful kick upward (Figure 11.14).
- As you kick, your body will ascend into the air. Respond promptly by pushing your hands downward when you sense the upward momentum. This action is akin to performing reverse push-ups, demanding maximum effort (Figure 11.15).

Figure 11.13   Figure 11.14

Figure 11.15

- Build upon the preceding movements.
- Lower your legs and engage your back muscles to contract them, thereby storing muscle elasticity.
- Subsequently, extend your hips upwards and forwards.
- Having stretched your hips, energetically whip your legs backward and push against the ground using your palms (alternatively, you can employ head and neck support for whipping).
- Upon landing, stretch your feet and body, and extend your waist. Elevate your head and arms while directing your gaze upward (Refer to Figure 11.16).

Figure 11.16

(2) Push Legs Method:

Preparation Posture: Begin by lying on your back, facing upwards, and place your arms beside your body (Figure 11.17).

Figure 11.17

Sequence of Movements:

- Elevate your legs, keeping them straight, and draw them close to your chest. With your palms, grip your knees, getting ready for the next phase (Figure 11.18).

- Push your knees with your palms, flip your legs down and stretch your abdomen to get up (Figure 11.19). The practice is like 'Push ground method.'

Figure 11.18   Figure 11.19

Key Points:

(1) The buttocks should be lifted when lying on the back and moving your legs backward.
(2) Do not stop after moving the legs backward, follow the previous inertial, extend your hips up first, and then quickly forward. Try to increase the height of the hips.

(3) After extending your hips, speed up your legs' downward swing so that the supporting point of both feet falls behind the body. Therefore, you can have the strength to stand up quickly.

Practice Steps:
Step 1: Prepare Physical Fitness
- Practice 'push-ups' and strengthen the thrust of your arms (Figure 11.20, 11.21).

Figure 11.20	Figure 11.21

- Practice continuously bending and stretching the waist, abdomen, and hips by 'neck and shoulder standing up' (Figure 11.22, 11.23). Next, develop the flexibility at the core part into a bridge (Figure 11.24).

Figure 11.22	Figure 11.23

Figure 11.24

Step 2: Practice It from High to Low

- During practicing, gradually reduce the height of the equipment from easy to difficult. In practice, do not swing your legs too earlier or lean forward too much. Pay attention to self-protection and help (Figure 11.25, 11.26, 11.27).

Figure 11.25   Figure 11.26

Figure 11.27

Step 3: Practice with Somebody's Help

- The practice assistant kneels on the floor beside the practitioner, holding the practitioner's forearm in one hand and placing the other hand on his/her waist.
- During practice, as the practitioner extends their hip and kicks out, the assistant should provide a gentle pull to aid them in standing up. Over time, the assistant should gradually lessen the strength of this pull, allowing the practitioner to progressively achieve the ability to complete the movement independently (Figures 11.28, 11.29).

Figure 11.28

Figure 11.29

3. Wū Lóng Jiǎo Zhù or Black Dragon Coiling Around a Pole

'Wū Lóng Jiǎo Zhù' (烏龍絞柱), translated as 'Black Dragon Coiling Around a Pole,' is indeed a martial arts movement or technique. It involves the swift and decisive action of sweeping and coiling an opponent's legs while on the ground, facilitating a rapid standing up motion. This technique derives its name from the imagery of a dragon coiling around a pillar, emphasizing its speed and precision.

The movement itself incorporates a combination of sweeping and twisting actions, along with the coordinated use of the waist and legs, to ensure a consistent and effective execution. To master this intricate movement, dedicated practice is essential to refine its various components and achieve a fluid and proficient execution.

It's worth noting that 'Wūlóng Jiǎo Zhù' is likely associated with specific styles or schools of martial arts within the realm of Chinese Wushu. As with many martial arts techniques, there may be variations or interpretations of this technique depending on the lineage, tradition, and specific teachings within Chinese martial arts schools and systems.

Practice Methods:

Preparation posture:

- Lie on the left, slightly bend your left leg, touch the ground with the outside of your left leg, and straighten your right leg. Place your palms on the ground. Look in the right direction (Figure 11.30).

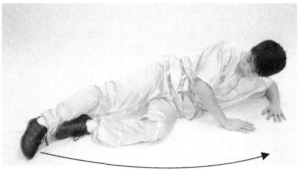

Figure 11.30

Movements:

- Keep your left leg still or as a support point. Tile your upper body backward, allow your right hand off the ground, and put it on the right side of your body.
- Next, straighten your right leg, use the back of your right foot as a force point, and sweep it horizontally to the left shoulder (Figure 11.31).

This is to kick your opponent's ankle with your right foot. Therefore, your right foot should be lower, and if you kick correctly, it can easily take your opponent off balance and fall to the ground. However, if the sweep is too high, it can only kick your opponent's calf, not let your opponent lose balance, and give you a chance to counterattack.

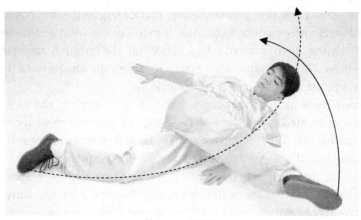

Figure 11.31

- Continue with the previous action. Keep your right leg sweeping horizontally. Tilt your upper body back to the ground. When your right leg is swept from your face to the right, the left leg should be swept immediately from the left and crossed with your right leg (Figure 11.32).
- At this moment, both legs should extend upward, and the support point should transfer to the upper back close to the shoulder blades.

Figure 11.32

- Continue the previous movement and accelerate your legs' twisting and coiling.
Let your legs rotate a circle that follows the counterclockwise. At the same time, the upper body should twist, straighten your waist, push your whole body up, and form a shoulder-arm standing state (Figure 11.33).

Figure 11.33

- Keep your whole body twisted and bring up, then push your shoulders and touch the ground quickly with your left palm. Meanwhile, the left forearm is supported to the ground to form a right shoulder-arm standing state (Figure 11.34).
- Hands on the ground and push your arms. Let your head coordinate with your push movement so that the body continues to rise into a hand-standing state (Figure 11.35).
- Pull your abdomen and hips in, drop your left leg down, then drop your right leg to form a stand-up position (Figure 11.36).

Figure 11.34   Figure 11.35   Figure 11.36

Key Points:

(1) Pay attention to your 'sweep' leg (s). In practice, the initial 'sweep' should be as large as possible so that your sweep leg (s) can be as close to the ground and your chest as possible. Then after sweeping through your face, gradually reduce the sweep range and accelerate it from big to small.

(2) In this movement, the 'coil around' is a core movement, and when you practice, the 'coil around' twisting force on the leg (s) should be based on accelerating the sweep to accelerate twisting and coil.

(3) In addition to the 'sweeping and coiling,' are the main movements. Another core is 'push up.' When coiling your legs, you should follow your actions to straighten your waist and push up your shoulders, head, and arms. All movements should be coordinated.

(4) To master this movement perfectly, you must practice some assistant movements and have the physical conditions associated with this movement. For example, shoulder-arm standing (Figure 11.37), head-hand standing (Figure 11.38), hand standing (Figure 11.39), and push hands standing with the help of your partner (Figure 11.40). These exercises effectively increase the strength of the arms, waist, and back. In addition, they can produce a good body sensation, facilitating faster and better mastery of the whole movement.

Figure 11.37   Figure 11.38   Figure 11.39   Figure 11.40

4. Zāi Bēi or Straight Forward (Backward) Falling

'Zāi Bēi,' a term in Chinese Wushu, translates to 'Tumbling' or 'Falling Like a Stone.' The component 'Zāi' (栽) refers to falling with a stiff body, typically indicating a lack of flexibility or control in the fall. 'Bēi' (碑) means large, erected stones or wooden columns, symbolizing the straight, rigid posture associated with this technique.

In martial arts, particularly in styles such as Drunken Boxing and Ditang Boxing, 'Zāi Bēi' describes a specific technique of tumbling or falling. The essence of this technique lies in maintaining a straight, stone-like posture while falling. This technique is often categorized into two types: straight-forward falling and straight-backward falling, both requiring the practitioner to emulate the rigid, upright position of a stone or column.

Practice Methods:
(1) Straight Forward Falling

'Straight forward falling' is usually used to contact the ground with the outside of your forearms or palms, and the author thinks both methods are similar. However, beginners can reach the ground with their forearms because the force area of the forearm is relatively large. And folding of the forearms can protect the torso and your face.

Preparation posture: Stand straight and keep your feet together. Bend your elbows inward to your chest. Allow your forearms to be almost parallel to your body. Sink your shoulders and drop your elbows. Hold your fist firmly. Stretch your body like a standing stone. Look straight ahead (Figure 11.41).

Movement:
• Straighten up, lift your heels, and fall forward. Look downward (Figure 11.42).

Figure 11.41   Figure 11.42

- After falling, support the ground with your toes and forearms or palms. Make your whole body into a straight line (Figure 11.43, 11.44).

Figure 11.43

Figure 11.44
Straight Forward Falling

Key Points:
(1) Do not hesitate to touch the ground at this moment.
(2) Never bend your knees, which can make injury.
(3) After you can handle this skill, try to touch the ground with your palms.
(4) If you touch the ground with your palms, pay attention to the elastic distribution of the arms and gradually counteract the inertia of falling.
(5) If your arm is not strong, do not practice; it will hurt your face.

(2) Straight Backward Falling)
'Straight backward falling' is usually used to touch the ground with your upper back close to the shoulder blade area. Most importantly, when your shoulders touch the ground, do not panic, and raise your head as much as possible to avoid hitting the back of your brain. It is a suggestion that when you want to learn this movement, you should choose a soft mat or carpet; the best thing is that someone can protect you next to your body. Do not forget that this is a dangerous movement. If your skills are not strong enough, do not try.

Preparation Posture: It is the same as the previous action. The difference is that your consciousness. Straighten up, lean backward, and fall (Figure 11.47).

Movements:
- After falling, support the ground with the upper back near the shoulder blade areas. Make your whole body into a straight line. (Figure 11.48).

Key points:

(1) The body should be straightened, legs clamped, head and neck straight, anus lifted in all processes.

(2) Hollow chest and pull back up. Waist and back muscles should be wrapped tightly.

(3) The body touches the ground, and the buttocks slightly protrude up.

Figure 11.48   Figure 11.47

Straight Backward Falling

5. Pū Hǔ or Pounce on the tiger

'Pū Hǔ' (撲虎) in English can be translated as 'Pouncing on the Tiger.' This term is often associated with martial arts and may refer to a particular technique, movement, or stance resembling the action of a tiger pouncing or attacking its prey. It's possible that "Pouncing Tiger" is used in various martial arts styles to describe a specific technique or form within their curriculum. The exact interpretation and application of "Pouncing Tiger" may vary depending on the martial art system in which it is practiced.

Practice Methods:

Preparation Posture: Stand with your feet together, bend your knees, and squat. Place your arms naturally behind your body. Look straight ahead (Figure 11.49).

Movements:

- Swing your arms forward and upward, pushing on the ground with your feet, jumping up like a tiger to pounce on the food.
- Keep your legs straight out and lift your head. When touching the ground with your palms, you should immediately bend your elbows slightly and make your entire body almost straight, close to the vertical line (Figure 11.50).

- When landing, both your hands touch the ground first, bend your elbows, support the floor with your arms, and allow your chest, abdomen, legs, and knees to touch the ground.
- Remember, jumping should be high, the landing should be light, and both knees should stretch. Allow the legs to be close or slightly apart, and the body should form a reverse bow shape.
- Then, to cushion the falling gravity, hands, chest, abdomen, and thighs land in the sequence (Figure 11.51).

Figure 11.49

Figure 11.50

Figure 11.51

Appendix
Physical Fitness Training Methods for Wushu Jumping Movements

A steadfast commitment to 'physical fitness training' is vital for nurturing and preserving the fundamental skills in the Chinese Wushu. Particularly in the field of Contemporary Wushu, the aim is to embody the principles of 'higher, faster, stronger,' advocating for 'high, difficulty, beauty, and innovation.' This entails fostering exceptional jumping abilities, nimble movements, and heightened overall strength. Presented here are simple yet effective physical fitness training methods that enhance your jumping prowess. You can seamlessly integrate these exercises into your training routine, tailoring them to your specific objectives and requirements.

1. Vertical Jumps

The 'Vertical Jump' uses your body weight to activate muscle groups by bending your hips, knees, and ankles until you lower to a quarter-squat position.

- Start by standing with your feet shoulder-width apart and your arms slightly in front of you. Squat to approximately a 45-degree angle, keeping your back straight and your knees aligned with your toes (Figure A1).
- Explosively jump as high as possible, using the power from your legs and core (Figure A2). Land softly on the balls of your feet, ensuring your whole foot touches the ground before immediately jumping again.
- Aim to perform three sets of 20 to 40 repetitions, with a brief rest between sets.

Figure A1   Figure A2

2. Jump Squats

'Jump Squats,' also referred to as 'Squat Jumps,' are a plyometric variation of the traditional squat. This dynamic strength training exercise is simple yet potent, fostering the simultaneous development of muscle strength and power. Performing jump squats continuously, without pauses, raises your heart rate, effectively transforming it into an excellent cardiovascular exercise. This movement engages numerous muscles, with a primary focus on the hip and lower body region.

- Stand with your feet shoulder-width apart, toes pointing forward, and arms extended behind you (Figure A3).
- Descend into a deep squat position, ensuring your thighs are parallel to the ground and your knees are aligned with your toes. Keep your back straight and engage your core. Propel yourself explosively into the air by pushing through your feet, simultaneously swinging your arms up and overhead. Strive for maximum height and complete body extension, maintaining straight legs and pointed toes (Figure A4).
- Land gently into the deep squat position, absorbing the impact by bending your knees and maintaining control.
- Repeat the sequence for three sets, completing 10 to 20 repetitions in each set.

Figure A3

Figure A4

3. Split Squat Jumps

The 'Split Squat Jump' is a bodyweight exercise crafted to target the quads, hamstrings, and glutes. This unilateral movement zeroes in on one leg at a time, enhancing balance and stability while presenting a formidable challenge to the muscles of the lower limbs.

Known for their high intensity, 'Split Squat Jumps' can be executed swiftly, providing a time-efficient option for training. This quality makes them particularly valuable for the dynamic jump movements in a Wushu Routine, enabling effective workouts and the acquisition of numerous benefits in a short period.

- Begin in a split stance with your right foot forward and left foot behind you in a lunge position. Keep your upper body upright and your core engaged. Lower your body into a deep lunge by bending both knees, ensuring that your front knee is aligned with your ankle and your back knee is hovering just above the ground (Figure A5).
- Explosively jump up into the air, propelling yourself as high as possible. While in mid-air, switch the position of your legs, bringing your left foot forward and your right foot back. Maintain the same posture opposite the starting position (Figure A6).
- Land softly with your left foot forward and immediately lower yourself into the lunge position.
- Repeat the movement for three sets, performing 10 to 20 repetitions on each leg.

| Figure A5 | Figure A6 |

4. Knee Tuck Jumps

'Knee Tuck Jumps' offers a comprehensive full-body training exercise, activating muscle groups across your body, including the glutes, hamstrings, hip flexors, quadriceps, obliques, calves, and lower back muscles. Incorporating 'Knee Tuck Jumps' into high-intensity interval training can elevate cardiovascular fitness and power output. Regular practice can further boost your performance in various plyometric exercises like squat jumps, box jumps, burpees, lunges, and depth jumps.

- Begin by standing straight with your feet shoulder-width apart, toes pointed slightly outward. Place your arms slightly in front of you. Bend at your knees and hips, lowering yourself slightly to engage your hamstring muscles (Figure A7).
- Jump straight up, using the power of your lower abs and legs to bring your thighs toward your chest. Flex your abs and use your hands to grab and hold onto your knees as you tuck them in (Figure A8).
- When landing, focus on landing on your toes first to minimize impact on your knees and ankles. Keep your knees slightly bent. Immediately move into the next jump without pausing.
- Perform Knee Tuck Jumps for 20 seconds, then rest for 10 seconds. Repeat this sequence eight times, resulting in a 4-minute exercise session.

Figure A7   Figure A8

5. Box Jumps

'Box jumps' entail jumping from the floor onto an elevated surface or box. This exercise is an excellent method for boosting explosive power, strengthening the lower body, enhancing vertical jump height, and overall improving athletic performance.

- Stand in front of the box with your feet about shoulder-width apart. Position yourself 1-3 feet away from the box to start (Figure A 9).
- Jump up explosively, using your arms for balance and coordination. Let your arms swing forward naturally as you jump. Focus on landing on the middle part of the box. Now, keep your knees bent and aim to land on the balls of your feet. This helps

absorb the impact and minimize the risk of injury. Maintain proper balance and alignment in your upper body once you land on the box (Figure a10).

- Fully extend your legs and stand up straight on the box to regain control and stability. Jump back down from the box carefully. Repeat the required repetitions, maintaining a safe distance from the box.

- Ensure you have enough space and a sturdy box for this exercise. Start with a box height that is comfortable for you. Usually, the height of the box should be slightly lower, then gradually increasing the height as you become more proficient and confident (Figure A11, A12). Focus on proper form, using your leg muscles to generate power for the jump.

Figure A9   Figure A10

Key Points:

(1) Maintain a fixed position with your head and neck while jumping. Avoid looking down at the ground and instead focus your eyes on a specific spot on the top of the box. This helps with balance and stability.

(2) Use a stable and secure box or surface for performing box jumps. Avoid using an unstable or unsafe box that could increase the risk of falling or injury. Choose a box height appropriate for your current fitness level and abilities.

(3) Avoid jumping back down too hard to the ground when landing, as this can place excessive pressure on the knees. Instead, lightly jump down from the box and bend the knees to reduce impact and protect your joints, maintaining a smooth and controlled movement pattern.

(4) The number of repetitions and sets for box jumps can vary based on your fitness level. Beginners should start with a shorter box and perform 3-4 properly executed jumps. As you progress, gradually increase the number of repetitions per set to 20. Aim for 3-4 sets of 20 jumps each to create an effective workout. Take a 60-90 second rest between sets to allow for proper recovery before starting the next set.

6. Hurdle Jumps

Hurdle jumps are an effective plyometric exercise that combines leg work with cardiovascular conditioning, helping to increase strength and explosiveness by exerting maximum force in short intervals. This exercise involves stretching and contracting the muscles at a high pace, making it an intense and impactful movement that can greatly enhance your overall physical capabilities. Regular practice of hurdle jumps can improve strength, muscle control, balance, kicking ability, jumping power, speed, and even bone density. Here's how to perform hurdle jumps:

- Begin by standing in front of the hurdle with your feet shoulder-width apart. Position your body approximately 1-3 feet away from the hurdle. Keep your chest up, shoulders relaxed, and gaze forward.
- Bend your knees slightly and engage your core muscles. Explosively jump upward and forward, driving your knees toward your chest to clear the hurdle. Emphasizing a powerful double arm swing to generate momentum (Figure A11).
- Focus on landing softly and with control, actively engaging your leg muscles to absorb the impact. Keep your legs strong and active throughout the exercise. Immediately transition into the next jump, clearing the next hurdle with the same technique.

Figure A11

Key Points:

(1) Always warm up thoroughly before performing hurdle jumps or any plyometric exercise. Gradually increase the intensity and difficulty of the exercise over time as your strength and jumping ability improve.

(2) Start with a height that is appropriate for your current fitness level and gradually increase it as you gain strength and confidence. Always prioritize safety by using stable and properly set-up hurdles.

(3) Remember to maintain proper technique throughout the exercise, including a controlled landing and active leg engagement. If you experience any pain or discomfort during or after the exercise, consult with a qualified fitness professional to assess your technique and make any necessary adjustments.

7. Frog Jumps

The 'Frog Jump' is a dynamic, mimicking movement that targets the lower body muscles, including the quadriceps, hamstrings, ankles, and glutes. This exercise imitates the powerful release of energy seen in a frog's leap, reminiscent of a catapult or an archer's bow, resulting in a swift extension of the ankle joint that propels individuals forward. Additionally, 'Frog Jump' engages the core muscles for stabilization and present a cardiovascular challenge due to their dynamic and repetitive nature. Incorporating 'Frog Jump' into your Wushu training routine can significantly enhance overall lower limb strength, agility, and endurance.

- Begin in a squat position with your knees bent, feet parallel, and weight on your balls. Keep your arms behind you (Figure A12).
- Using the strength in your hips, quadriceps, and biceps, jump forward while swinging your arms forward, but avoid jumping too high (Figure A13, A14).
- Land softly and return to the squat position (Figure A15).
- Repeat the frog jumps, moving forward with each jump.

| Figure A15 | Figure A14 | Figure A13 | Figure A12 |

8. Burpees

The burpee, a squat thrust with an added stand between repetitions, is a comprehensive full-body exercise commonly incorporated into strength training routines. While the movement primarily engages anaerobic energy systems, performing burpees in succession over an extended period can transition into an effective aerobic exercise. This two-part exercise involves combining a pushup with a dynamic leap into the air. Executing multiple burpees consecutively poses a challenge, yet this versatile workout delivers notable benefits. It proves to be an excellent choice for developing strength and endurance, burning calories, and improving cardiovascular fitness.

- Begin by standing straight (Figure A16).
- Drop into a deep squat, bringing your glutes to your calves and placing your hands on the floor in front of you. Shift your weight to your arms and press the floor away (Figure A17).
- Kick your feet back behind you (Figure A18). Keep your core engaged, hips elevated, and energy directed back through your inner heels.

| Figure A16 | Figure A17 | Figure A18 |

- Perform a low push-up, aiming for a deep descent (Figure A19).
- Jump or step your feet forward, creating a squatting position and bringing your glutes close to your heels (Figure A20).
- Propel yourself upward with as much force as possible, aiming for maximum height, and then land softly back into the squat position (Figure A21).
- Repeat the sequence for 15-20 repetitions per set.

Figure A19

| Figure A20 | Figure A21 | Figure A22 |

9. Heels Raises

The 'Heel Raise' is a simple and convenient exercise within the Wushu fitness practice method, designed to sustain the vitality of your calf muscles. It specifically targets the gastrocnemius and soleus muscles in the calf region, fostering more robust and stable ankles. Incorporating 'Heel Raises' into your regular Wushu training can result in more sculpted calves and increased calf strength, contributing to enhanced jumping capabilities in Wushu.

- Stand with both feet flat on the floor. If needed, you can steady yourself by placing your hand on a ledge, wall, or table for support (Figure A23).
- Raise your heels off the floor as far as possible, lifting yourself onto your toes while keeping your knees straight (Figure A24). Hold this position for 5-10 seconds.
- Slowly lower your heels back down to the floor.
- Repeat this exercise for 30-50 repetitions each time. Aim to complete 2-4 sets, with a short rest in between each set.

- As your strength improves, you can challenge yourself further by standing on one foot at a time and raising that heel off the floor (Figure A25, A26). .

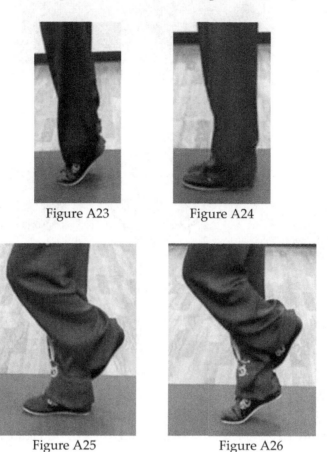

Figure A23   Figure A24

Figure A25   Figure A26

10. Heels Raise with Dumbbells

In the 'Heel Raise with Dumbbells' exercise, the gastrocnemius and soleus muscles in the shin play a pivotal role in plantar flexion, extending the foot downward. As you lift your heels, maintaining contact between the ball of your foot and the supporting surface, these muscles contribute significantly to lifting the entire body. This action provides the essential push needed for propelling the body forward and upward. From building more muscular calves to fostering stable ankles, this exercise enhances ankle strength and stability.

- Start by standing with a dumbbell in each hand. Position your feet shoulder-width apart or feet together and place your toes on a slightly raised platform or step. Ensure that your heels are on the floor and your weight is evenly distributed. Hold the dumbbells at your sides, with your arms extended down and palms facing your body (Figure A27).

- Slowly raise your heels off the floor, lifting yourself up onto your toes. Focus on contracting your calf muscles and hold the raised position briefly (Figure A28).
- Lower your heels back down in a controlled manner until they touch the floor.
- Repeat the exercise for the desired number of repetitions, following your fitness level and ability.
- You can adjust the weight of the dumbbells and the number of sets and repetitions according to your capabilities and progress over time.

Figure A27   Figure A28

11. Leg Raises

The leg raise is a highly effective strength training exercise primarily targeting the iliopsoas, the anterior hip flexor muscles. Additionally, the exercise engages the abdominal muscles, playing a crucial role in stabilizing the body during movement. Leg raises are beneficial for strengthening the rectus abdominis and the internal and external oblique muscles. Here's how to perform leg raises:

- Lie flat on your back on a mat or a flat surface, keeping your legs fully extended and your arms by your sides, palms facing down or inward. Engage your core muscles by drawing your navel towards your spine and pressing your lower back into the ground (Figure A29).
- Inhale and lift your legs off the floor, aiming to raise them around 45 degrees. Simultaneously, bring your chin toward your chest and lift your upper body around 45 degrees. Keep your legs straight and your feet flexed throughout the movement (Figure A30).

- Pause at this position for a moment, then exhale as you slowly lower your legs back down to the starting position. Maintain control throughout the decent. Avoid letting your legs touch the ground between repetitions to keep tension on the muscles.
- Aim for 2-3 sets of 10-15 repetitions, adjusting the numbers based on your fitness level and comfort.

Figure A29   Figure A30

12. Push Up

The push-up is a classic exercise that targets the muscles of the chest, shoulders, and arms. Here's how to perform a push-up with proper form:

- Start in a plank position, with your hands placed at shoulder width or slightly wider than your shoulders. Your body should form a straight line from your head to your heels. Engage your core by drawing your navel toward your spine and keep your abs tight throughout the exercise (Figure A31).

Figure A31

- Bend your elbows and lower yourself down towards the ground until your elbows are at a 90-degree angle, and your chest is just above the floor. Keep your elbows tucked in close to your sides, pointing slightly backward (Figure A32).

Figure A31

- Pause for a moment in the lowered position, then push through your hands to extend your arms and return to the starting position. Avoid locking out your elbows at the top; instead, keep them slightly bent (Figure A32).

Figure A32

- Repeat the exercise for the desired number of repetitions, focusing on maintaining proper form and control throughout the movement.

As you perform push-ups, it's important to maintain a strong, stable core and avoid sagging or arching your back. If full push-ups are challenging, you can modify the exercise by performing them on your knees or against an elevated surface like a bench or wall. Remember to listen to your body and work within your fitness level. Gradually increase the number of repetitions or progress to more challenging variations as you build strength and improve your form.

13. Hanging Knees Raise

The 'Hanging Knee Raise' is a targeted lower abdominal workout that isolates the abdominal muscles, contributing to developing a strong core. Additionally, this exercise provides benefits for grip strength and forearm stability.

- Begin by grabbing a pull-up bar with a wide grip, ensuring your hands are shoulder-width apart or slightly wider. Hang from the bar with your arms fully extended and your feet off the ground. Engage your core by drawing your navel toward your spine and keeping your abs tight throughout the exercise (Figure A33).
- Slowly lift your knees toward your chest, focusing on using your abdominal muscles to initiate the movement. Keep your legs together and avoid swinging or using momentum.
- Continue lifting your knees until they reach your chest or as high as you can comfortably. Hold the position briefly, squeezing your abs at the top (Figure A 34).
- Slowly lower your knees back down to the starting position, maintaining control and preventing any swinging motion.
- Repeat the exercise based on your fitness level and comfort, making adjustments as needed.

Figure A33   Figure A34

It's important to avoid using momentum or excessive swinging during the exercise to ensure that the abdominal muscles are effectively engaged. If you find it challenging to lift your knees all the way to your chest, you can start with smaller knee raises and gradually increase the range of motion as your strength improves. Remember to listen to your body and work at your own pace. Adjust the difficulty level by performing fewer or more repetitions based on your fitness level. As you progress, you can also explore variations such as straight leg raises, or side knee raises to target different areas of the abdominal muscles.

14. Hanging Legs Raise

The hanging leg raise is an advanced exercise that targets the abdominal muscles, particularly the lower abs. Here's how to perform it correctly:

- Begin by grabbing a pull-up bar with a wide grip, ensuring your hands are shoulder-width apart or slightly wider. Hang from the bar with your arms fully extended and your feet off the ground. Engage your core by drawing your navel toward your spine and keeping your abs tight throughout the exercise (Figure A35).
- Slowly lift your legs, keeping them fully extended, toward your chest. Focus on using your abdominal muscles to initiate the movement and avoid using momentum or swinging.
- As you lift your legs, allow your upper back to slightly round backward to create balance and stability. This will help prevent swinging and ensure that your abs are doing the work.
- Continue raising your legs until your toes touch the bar or reach the highest point you can comfortably achieve (Figure A36).

- Slowly lower your legs back down to the starting position, maintaining control and preventing any swinging motion.
- Repeat the exercise for the desired number of repetitions, focusing on maintaining proper form and controlled movement throughout.

Figure A35

Figure A36

It's important to note that the hanging leg raise requires considerable core strength and stability. If you cannot lift your legs all the way to your chest initially, start with more minor knee raises or bent-knee variations and gradually work your way up to straight leg raises.

As with any exercise, listening to your body and working within your capabilities is essential. If you experience any pain or discomfort, modify the exercise or seek guidance from a qualified fitness professional.

Remember to prioritize proper form and controlled movements over the number of repetitions. This will ensure that you're effectively targeting your abdominal muscles and minimizing the risk of injury.

15. V Sit-Up

The V sit-up is an effective exercise that targets the abdominal muscles, including the rectus abdominis, transverse abdominis, hip flexors, and obliques. Here's how to perform it correctly:

- Start by lying on your back with your legs extended straight and your arms extended overhead, resting on the floor. You can use a yoga or exercise mat for added support and comfort. If you have occasional back pain, you can place a rolled towel under the arch of your back, just above your hips, for additional support (Figure A37).

- Engage your core by drawing your navel toward your spine and keeping your back neutral throughout the exercise. This will help protect your lower back and maintain proper form.
- Simultaneously lift your legs and upper body off the floor, aiming to create a V shape with your body. Keep your legs straight and your toes pointed. At the same time, reach your arms straight forward or up toward your feet, depending on your comfort level and flexibility.
- Pause for a moment at the top of the movement, feeling the contraction in your abdominal muscles (Figure A38).
- Slowly lower your arms and legs back down to the starting position, maintaining control and avoiding any sudden or jerky movements.
- Repeat the exercise for the desired number of repetitions, focusing on maintaining proper form and engaging your core throughout. Avoid using momentum to swing into each repetition, as this reduces the effectiveness of the exercise.

Figure A37

A38

As with any abdominal exercise, working within your capabilities as far as possible. If you experience any discomfort or strain in your lower back, consider reducing the range of motion or modifying the exercise to a level that is more comfortable for you.

Remember to breathe continuously throughout the exercise and engage your core muscles to stabilize your body. Gradually increase the number of repetitions as your strength and technique improve.

Moreover, stair running is an excellent choice for those seeking a high-intensity workout that enhances speed, power, and cardiovascular endurance. Incorporating stair running into an agility training program offers particular advantages, fostering rapidity and foot speed while serving as an exceptional start-up movement workout.

Stair running targets explicitly some of the body's major muscle groups, including the glutes, quadriceps, and calves, which are also engaged during lunges and squats. Serving as a plyometric exercise, stair running stimulates the muscles to exert maximal force within short intervals, facilitating rapid extension and contraction. Ascending stairs involves working against gravity, thus promoting strength and power development.

During stair running, your heart rate rapidly accelerates, leading to faster breathing to intake more oxygen. This process enhances your VO2 max—the maximum volume of oxygen you can utilize during intense physical activity.

If you're new to stair workouts, it's crucial to start gradually, progressively increasing the duration and intensity of your sessions. Pushing too hard initially may lead to unnecessary muscle soreness. Follow these gradual guidelines as you steadily build up your routine:

- Ensure a comprehensive warm-up before initiating your stair running workout. A brisk 5 to 10-minute slow running on a level surface can stimulate blood circulation and loosen your muscles.
- During the initial stages, refrain from running the stairs. Instead, commence by walking up the stairs, focusing on taking one step at a time. Gradually progress to a jogging pace, maintaining a centered weight with your head and eyes forward, avoiding looking down at your feet.
- Introduce running around the second week, considering the option of taking one or two steps at a time.
- Use the descent back to the starting point as your designated rest interval before proceeding to the next set.
- Increase your sets to approximately 10 per workout, adjusting the number based on the length of your stairway. A 20- to 30-minute session can provide an adequate level of intensity.
- Incorporate stair running into your workout routine on high-intensity training days or as part of your interval training program.
- Restrict your stair workouts to a maximum of twice a week.

Stair Running

Chapter 12
Combination Movement Practice

In Chinese Wushu routines, 'Combined Movements' involve skillfully integrating various actions following specific rules. These combinations encompass 'hand techniques,' 'eye movements,' 'body techniques,' 'stances,' and the arrangement of other typical Wushu movements to create a seamless sequence of activities. To master 'Combined Movements,' a systematic approach is essential, starting with a fundamental understanding and progressively advancing to more intricate combinations.

A strong foundation in basic movements is vital for effectively organizing combination exercises or choreographing routines. By mastering fundamental actions and consistently practicing them, the quality of each movement can be significantly improved. This process enhances overall coordination, facilitates the mastery of crucial movement and transition points, and serves as the cornerstone for learning Chinese Wushu routines. It also offers a valuable means of refining more challenging movements.

This chapter introduces several typical combination actions for practitioners to practice. You can select combinations that suit your level and circumstances or use them as a reference for your training. It's important to emphasize that this chapter holds particular significance for beginners, as it builds upon the foundation established in previous chapters. Just as a knife must be sharpened before cutting wood, mastering fundamental movements is critical for progress. From this point onward, you will learn how to construct an introductory framework for martial arts. Remember that learning any Wushu routine or style depends on mastering basic movements, and the quality of your foundation will significantly impact your future progress. In essence, a strong foundation will yield double the results.

The Combination of 'Stance' Movement Exercises

1. The Combination of 'Bow Stance' and 'Horse Stance'

(1) The First Set of Movement Exercises

Movement Names: Push the Palm in a Bow Stance – Punch in a Twist Bow Stance - Punch in a Horse Stance – Hold the Fists on the Waist with Feet Together

Preparation Posture: Begin by standing upright with your feet together and clench your fists at your waist. Keep your gaze directed straight ahead, ensuring that your body maintains proper alignment ((Figure 12.1).

In the Long Fist categories, which encompass hand forms and various weapons like saber, sword, spear, and staff, it is crucial to adhere to specific fundamental criteria for the body form. These criteria include:

321

Maintaining an upright head position. Elevating the chest. Keeping the waist straight. Engaging the abdominal muscles. Gathering the buttocks. Relaxing the shoulders. Lowering the elbows.

Following these fundamental guidelines ensures proper posture and body alignment, essential for effective execution and performance in Long Fist techniques and forms.

Push the Palm in a Bow Stance (弓步推掌)

Begin by stepping your left foot to the left, forming a left bow stance. Simultaneously, transform your left fist into an open palm and execute a powerful push to the left from your left waist. Keep your fingers pointing upward and maintain your focus on your left hand (Figure 12.2).

Figure 12.1   Figure 12.2

Punch in a Twist Bow Stance (拗弓步衝拳)

While keeping your bow stance steady and motionless, swiftly rotate your upper body to the left. Execute a powerful forward punch with your right fist in a straight line from your right waist. Make sure the heart of your fist faces downward. Simultaneously, retract your left fist back to your left waist. Maintain your gaze fixed straight ahead as illustrated in the Figure (12.3). Remember that punching forward and pulling back should use the same force simultaneously.

Punch in a Horse Stance (馬步衝拳)

Connect to the previous movement. Rotate your upper body to the right, forming a horse stance. Simultaneously, draw your right fist to your right waist and deliver a forceful left punch to the left. Direct your gaze to the left (Figure 12.4).

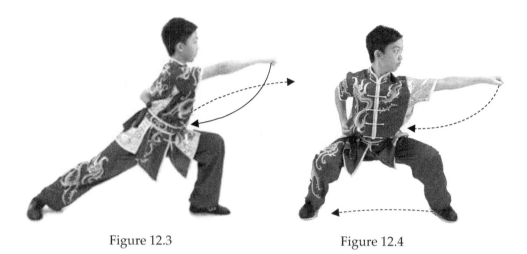

Figure 12.3   Figure 12.4

Hold the Fists on the Waist with Feet Together (并步抱拳)

Begin by moving your left foot back to align with the inside of your right foot, pull your left fist to your waist, adopting the 'holding the fists with feet together' stance. Direct your gaze to the left (Figure 12.5).

Figure 12.5

323

You could continue practicing the same movement in a different direction if you needed.

'Bow Stance' and 'Horse Stance' Combination Exercises for Continuous Movement

(2) The Second Set of Movement Exercises

Movement Names: Brush the Hand and Punch in a Twist Bow Stance - Punch with a Horse Stance - Push the Palm with an Aligned Bow Stance - Pound the Fist with a Half Squat Stance and Feet Together - Jump and Turn Around, Uphold Palm and Punch with a Horse Stance - Hold the Fists on the Waists, with Feet Together.

Preparation Posture: Stand upright with your feet together and clench your fists at your waist. Direct your gaze straight ahead (Figure 12.6).

Brush the Hand and Punch in a Twist Bow Stance (拗弓步摟手衝拳)

Begin by rotating your upper body slightly to the right while stepping your left foot to the left, forming a higher right bow stance. Transition your left fist into an open palm by inwardly rotating your left wrist. Extend your left arm from your waist to the right shoulder corner, emphasizing the left palm facing outward. Keep your upper body upright, focus on the left palm, and direct your gaze towards your left palm (Figure 12.7).

Please note that this move is a transitional action, and there should be no pause in your motion, whether you are in a right bow stance, or your waist is in motion. Precision is crucial in executing this movement, with every part of your body adhering to the rule's requirements, including hand form, footwork, body form, and internal aspects.

Figure 12.6   Figure 12.7

After extending your left palm to the right corner, swiftly turn your body to the left and shift your weight to your left leg, forming a left bow stance. Simultaneously, execute a horizontal brushing motion with your left palm towards the left, following a circular path until it reaches your left waist. The focal point of force should be on the left palm. As your upper body turns left, draw your left palm to your left waist, palm facing up, while forcefully punching your right fist forward in a straight line. Ensure that the force point is on the front surface of your right fist, targeting an imaginary opponent's face. Maintain a forward gaze (Figure 12.8).

Figure 12.8

Key Points:
(1) Engage your right foot by pushing it forward while twisting your waist to the left and extending your right knee.
(2) The punch should involve a twisting of the waist, pushing of the shoulders, and a sinking of the buttocks.
(3) The execution of the punch and the formation of the bow stance should coincide.

Common Errors:
(1) Avoid bending your right knee excessively or lifting the outside of your right foot off the ground. Ensure that your waist is not too loose, the punch is not weak, and your left thigh remains parallel to the floor.
(2) Concentrate on ensuring that the force point of the punch is accurate.
(3) Avoid lifting your shoulder or using stiff and awkward strength while punching.

Suggestions:
(1) Begin by practicing 'pushing the ground with your right foot' while simultaneously 'twisting your body to the left,' forming a left bow stance. Pay close attention to mastering the effective extension of your rear knee. Next, execute a 'twist of your body to the right' to transition into a right bow stance and practice this movement.

Remember, in between the two bow stance practices, incorporate a brief pause by performing a horse stance. This means that after each bow stance practice, transition to the horse stance, hold it momentarily, and then proceed to the next twist in the opposite direction. This sequence allows for a well-rounded practice (Figure 12.9 (1)(2)(3)).

| Figure 12.9 (1) | Figure 12.9 (2) | Figure 12.9 (3) |

(2) Engage in single punching practice. You can practice punching in either a bow stance (Figure 12.10 (1)(2)(3)) or a horse stance (Figure 12.11 (1)(2)(3)), alternating from left to right.

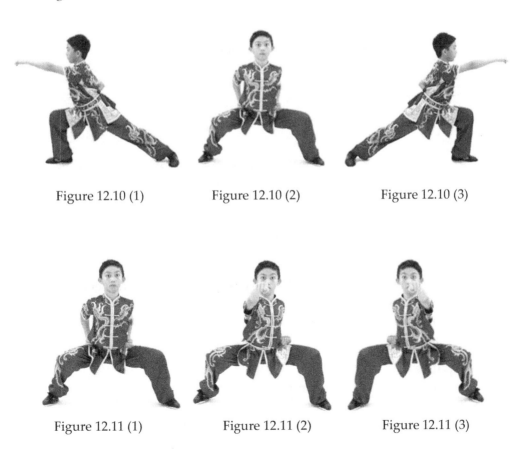

| Figure 12.10 (1) | Figure 12.10 (2) | Figure 12.10 (3) |

| Figure 12.11 (1) | Figure 12.11 (2) | Figure 12.11 (3) |

Punch with a Horse Stance (马步冲拳)

Transition smoothly from the preceding movement. Swiftly rotate your body to the right and lower yourself into a horse stance, bending both knees. At the same time, retract your right fist directly towards your right waist while extending your left fist to the left side, maintaining it at shoulder height. Ensure the striking force point remains on the front surface of your left fist, with the fist horizontally oriented. Keep your focus directed to the left (Figure 12.12).

Figure 12.12

Key Points:

(1) Generate power from your waist as you execute the movement. The body turn should be quick but avoid excessive up-and-down motion.
(2) When transitioning from the bow stance to the horse stance, use the left heel and the sole of your right foot as the axis for a rapid rotation.
(3) Maintain an open chest and slightly pull your right shoulder back.

Common Errors:

(1) Ensure that your thighs are parallel to the ground. Avoid pointing your toes inward or outward and collapsing your knees inward.
(2) Avoid shrugging your shoulders and lifting your elbows. Do not protrude your buttocks outward.

Suggestions:

(1) Focus on practicing the horse stance in isolation, emphasizing proper alignment and stability.
(2) Incorporate exercises that involve transitioning between the bow stance and the horse stance to improve your agility and coordination.

Push the Palm with an Aligned Bow Stance (顺弓步推掌)

Transition smoothly from the previous movement. Transfer your body weight onto your left leg and take a step forward with your right foot, creating a right bow stance. Before stepping, ensure that your left foot turns outward to facilitate the movement of your right foot. At the same time, retract your left fist to your left waist, convert your right fist into an open palm, and push it forward from your right waist. Concentrate the force on the right palm. Keep your gaze forward (Figure 12.13). Perform the stepping and pushing actions simultaneously.

Pound the Fist with Half Squat Stance and Feet Together (并腿半蹲砸拳)

Transition smoothly from the previous movement, maintaining an upright upper body. Apply pressure with your right foot against the ground as you shift your weight to the left side, simultaneously executing a 90-degree rotation to the left. Raise your right leg, bring it to the left leg's inner side, and then forcefully stomp it down. This should result in a half-squat position with your feet together and all toes pointed forwards. Simultaneously, convert your right palm into a fist and strike the back of your right fist against your left palm, which should be positioned in front of your abdomen. The point of force should be on the back of your right fist. Keep your gaze focused on your right fist (Figure 12.14).

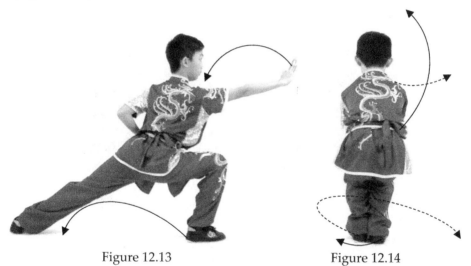

Figure 12.13   Figure 12.14

Key Points:
(1) Use the back of your right fist to strike your left palm, ensuring a firm and coordinated motion. Keep your armpits relaxed throughout the movement.
(2) The pounding action should be firm and synchronized with your breathing, known as 'condense Qi.'
(3) As you stamp your right foot to the ground, keep your heels firmly planted without lifting them. Maintain proper alignment and avoid protruding your buttocks.

329

Common Errors:
(1) Neglecting to coordinate the pounding and stamping simultaneously.
(2) Insufficient force in the pounding and stamping actions, resulting in the heels lifting off the ground.

Suggestions:
(1) Practice performing a full squat to increase flexibility in your ankles.
(2) Focus on practicing the specific action of 'pounding the fist,' emphasizing accuracy and generating a loud sound at the force point.

Jump and Turn, Uphold the Palm, and Punch with a Horse Stance
(跳转马步架冲拳)

Transition smoothly from the previous movement. Push feet firmly to the ground, then jump and rotate your body to the right 180 degrees. Upon landing, adopt a Horse Stance. Simultaneously, release your right fist into an open palm, and raise it above your head in a blocking position. Convert your left palm into a fist and punch horizontally to the left side from your left waist. Maintain your focus on the left fist (Figure 12.15).

Figure 12.15   Figure 12.16

Key Points:
(1) Pay meticulous attention to the openness of your shoulders during this action. If you feel any tightness or stiffness in your right arm, work on extending your shoulders more.
(2) When executing the jump and turn, emphasize agility in your movements, maintaining coordination throughout the entire sequence.
(3) Ensure that the right palm provides upward support, and both arms extend outward to achieve the objective of 'releasing a long strike far.'

Common Errors:

(1) Lack of coordination in the landing, with feet not touching the ground simultaneously, which results in instability and loss of balance.

(2) After performing the movement, failure to maintain an open posture, a lack of upper body strength for support, and not effectively delivering a punch; instead, simply placing the right fist to the right without a clear point of force.

Hold the Fists on the Waists, with Feet Together (并步抱拳)

Apply pressure with your right foot against the ground and rise to a standing position. Bring your right foot towards the left, aligning your feet together. Simultaneously, move your fists on your waists, palms facing upward. Maintain a forward gaze (Figure 12.16).

This exercise will focus on seamlessly transitioning between the Bow Stance and the Horse Stance continuously. The key is to maintain fluidity and control throughout the movements. Remember to breathe naturally throughout the exercise and maintain a steady and relaxed demeanor.

Continue practicing the same movement but in a different direction if you needed.

'Bow' and 'Horse Stance' Combination Exercises for Continuous Movement

2. The Combination of 'Empty Stance,' and 'Crouch Stance'

Movement Names: Thread the Palm with Knee Lifted – Thread the Palm in a Crouch Stance - Pick Up the Palm in an Empty Stance

Preparation Posture: Stand upright with your feet together and clench your fists at your waist. Direct your gaze straight ahead (Figure 12.17).

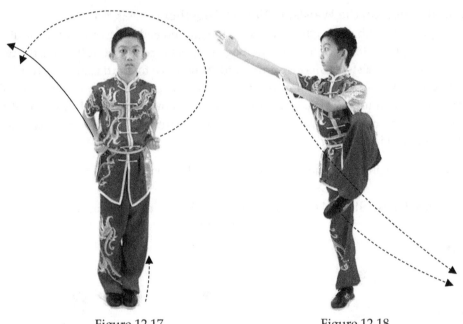

Figure 12.17   Figure 12.18

Thread the Palm with Raise the Knee (提膝穿掌)

Transform your left fist into an open palm while turning your upper body to the right and swinging your left palm from your left waist downward, passing it through the left side and guiding it upward to the right in a circular path. As your left palm reaches shoulder height on the right, slightly bend your left elbow and press your left palm somewhat with your palm facing downward. At the same time, bend your left knee, raising it in front of your body. Simultaneously, convert your right fist into an open palm, ensuring your palm faces upward. Thread it over the back of your left palm, moving it to the upper right side with your palm tilted upward. During this motion, bring your left palm towards your right elbow, tilting the palm downwar. Slightly lean your upper body to the right and maintain your gaze towards your right palm (Figure 12.18).

Thread the Palm with a Crouch Stance (仆步穿掌)

Squat the right leg fully while extending your left leg to the left to form a left-crouching stance. Simultaneously, thread your left palm from the chest downward along the inside of your left leg to the instep of your left foot, with the thumb side facing up. Maintain your right arm but position your right palm as a vertical palm behind your body, fingers tilted upwards. The arms should form a tilted line, with the right arm higher than your head and the left arm lower than your shoulder, almost parallel to the left leg. Lean your upper body slightly toward your left foot. Gaze at your left palm (Figure 12.19).

Figure 12.19

Scoop the Palm Strike Upward in an Empty Stance (虚步挑掌)

Shift your weight to the front leg, stepping forward with your right foot to assume a right empty stance. Simultaneously, circle your right palm downward. As it passes through your right hip, snap your right wrist upward to raise your right fingers to shoulder height while keeping the arm slightly bent and the wrist cocked. At the same time, straighten your left arm and swing it upward behind your body in a circular motion. When your left arm reaches the upper left position, transform your left palm into a hook hand. Snap your left wrist downward with the tips pointing downward, slightly higher than your shoulder. Keep your gaze fixed straight ahead (Figure 12.20).

Figure 12.20

333

Hold the Fists on the Waists, with Feet Together (并步抱拳)

Apply pressure with your left foot against the ground and rise to a standing position. Bring your left foot slightly towards the right, aligning your feet together. Simultaneously, place your fists on your waists, with your palms facing upward. Look to the left (Figure 12.21).

Figure 12.21

Continue practicing the same movement but in a different direction if you want.

'Empty Stance,' and 'Crouch Stance' Combination Exercises for Continuous Movement

3. The Combination of 'Empty Stance,' 'Crouch Stance' and 'Rest Stance'

Movement Names: Tiao Palm with a Left Empty Stance - Swing Palm with a Left Crouch Stance - Turn Left with Dancing-Flower Hands (8 hands) - Double Push Palms Out with a Left Rest Stance - Tiao Palm with a Right Empty Stance - Swing Palm with a Right Crouching Stance - Turn Right with Dancing-Flower Hands - Double Push Palms Out with a Right Rest Stance - Hold the Fists on the Waists, with Feet Together

Preparation Posture: Begin by standing upright with your feet together and clenching your fists at your waist. Direct your gaze straight ahead, ensuring that your body maintains proper alignment (Figure 12.22).

Tiao Palm with a Left Empty Stance (左虚步挑掌)
Movement 1:
Rotate your body to the left and step backward with your right foot, assuming a left bow stance. Simultaneously, release both fists and open your hands into the palms. Extend your right hand forward circularly with the tiger's mouth facing upward (vertical palm) while positioning your left palm naturally under your right armpit, ensuring the tiger's mouth is facing inward. Direct your gaze towards your right palm (Figure 12.23).

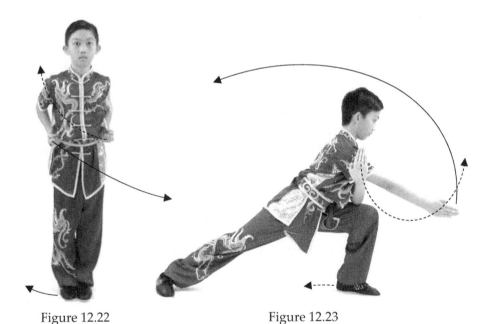

Figure 12.22   Figure 12.23

Movement 2:
Continue from the previous movement, maintaining your position and focus.

Apply pressure with your left foot, firmly planted on the ground. Simultaneously, shift your weight backward and draw your left foot slightly back, creating a left empty stance. While transitioning into the empty stance, circle your right arm up and back, extending it towards the rear at shoulder height. Now, transform your right palm into a hook hand, with the tip-down and positioned at or slightly above shoulder level.

At the same time, swing your left palm from your right armpit, bringing it down and forward. When your left palm reaches the height of your abdomen, flick it upward, allowing the fingertips to point upward. Slightly bend your left elbow, keeping your left arm at approximately shoulder height. The force point of this movement should be at the tip of your left fingers and the tip of your right hook. Maintain your focus on your left palm (Figure 12.24).

Figure 12.24

Key Points:
(1) When performing the Tiao palm, emphasize flipping your left wrist upward, creating a slight bend in your left elbow.
(2) Pay close attention to the alignment of your right thigh, aiming to maintain it as parallel to the ground as possible.

Common Errors:
(1) Avoid protruding your buttocks and excessive forward leaning of your upper body. Maintain a balanced and stable posture.
(2) Ensure that your hook hand maintains a firm grip, and the force is effectively transferred to the tips of your left fingers.

Suggestions:
(1) Dedicate time to practice the transition between different stances, with a particular focus on mastering the empty stance.
(2) Focus on the sensation of flipping your palm upward during the movement, ensuring a smooth and controlled execution.

Swing the Palm with a Left Crouch Stance (左仆步摆掌)
Continue from the previous movement, maintaining your position and focus.

Shift your body to the right and lower yourself into a left crouch stance. This involves entirely squatting down with your right leg while keeping your left leg stretched to the left. While forming the crouch stance, rotate your right arm inward to form a counter-hook hand with the tip of the hook facing upward. Simultaneously, circle your left palm up to the right side of your chest, moving it close to your right shoulder. The tiger's mouth faces inward, and your fingers are pointing upward. As you circle your left hand to the right, let your eyes follow the movement to the right. As you conclude the action, turn your head to the left, looking either at your left foot or straight ahead (Figure 12.25).

Figure 12.25

Key Points:
(1) In the crouch stance, ensure that you squat down fully and stretch your left knee, applying slight pressure to keep it pressed down.
(2) While rotating your right arm inward, be mindful not to tense your right armpit.

Common Errors:
(1) Avoid lifting the outside of your left foot and the heel of your right foot off the ground. Maintain a stable stance.
(2) Ensure that the back of your right thigh and calf are close together, and that your right knee does not collapse inward.

Suggestions:
(1) Incorporate stretching exercises to improve your flexibility in the crouch stance.
(2) Practice transitioning smoothly into and out of the crouch stance (left to right) to enhance your overall technique and control.

Turn Left with a Dancing-Flower Hand (8 figure) (左转身舞花手)
Movement 1:
Continuing from the previous movement, maintain your position and focus.

Push your right foot against the ground and shift your weight forward, transitioning into a left bow stance. Simultaneously, brush your left hand from the inside of your left leg, passing it through your left foot, and extend it to the front of your head. Your palm should be stretched out, with the outside of the little finger facing upward. As you perform this motion, transform your right hook hand into a palm, lowering your right arm and aligning it parallel to your right leg, with the palm facing upward. Keep your eyes focused on your left palm as you execute this movement (Figure 12.26).

Figure 12.26

Movement 2:
Continue seamlessly from the previous movement, maintaining the flow.

Push your left foot against the ground, stand up, and step your right foot forward to the inside of your left foot. Rotate your feet 90 degrees to the left, with your toes pointing towards the opposite direction of the preparation posture, while turning your body 180 degrees to the left. Simultaneously, swing your right hand horizontally to the left in front of your left shoulder and rotate your left palm outward. Bend your left elbow and thrust your palm under your right forearm, crossing both arms in front of you. Your right arm should be positioned above your left, and both palms should face outward. Keep your gaze fixed on the direction of your left palm throughout the movement (Figure 12.27).

Movement 3:
Continue from the previous movement and maintain your position. Use the soles of your feet as the axis and rotate your entire body 180 degrees to the left, still keeping your feet together, and return to the direction of the preparation posture. As you rotate, use your right hand to perform a 'cloud swinging hand' above your face, which means following a clockwise direction. Draw your right hand backward (close to your face), to the right (without crossing over your right shoulder) and extend it until it reaches the upper right corner as you complete your left turn. Simultaneously, with your left hand, swing it downward and to the left as if you are brushing something away, until it reaches below the left corner. Both palms should be tilted upward during this movement. Keep your eyes focused on your right hand throughout the movement (Figure 12.28).

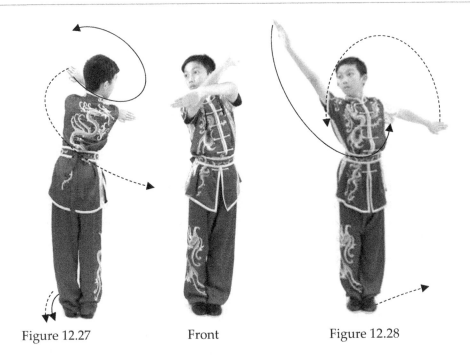

Figure 12.27   Front   Figure 12.28

Movement 4:

Connect smoothly from the previous movement without pausing.

Bend your right leg and step your left foot back, forming a right bow stance. Simultaneously, turn slightly to the right and circle your right arm from the upper right corner, down, and inside close to your body, while circling your left arm from below the left corner, moving to the left side, passing over the top, and inside in front of your chest. Cross your arms in front of your chest, with the left arm positioned above the right arm. All fingers should be pointing upward, and the palms should face outward. Look at your hands throughout the movement (Figure 12.29).

Figure 12.29

339

In fact, from Movement 1 to Movement 3, it constitutes an integrated sequence known as 'Dancing Flower Hand' or 'Figure 8' in official Wushu terms. This is a large 'Figure 8' movement in this combination group practice, which emphasizes using all of your arms, not just the wrists, as seen in the 'Small 8' variant. Regardless of whether you perform the larger or smaller version, the pivotal axis is your waist, which orchestrates the movement of your upper body and limbs. Your core should exhibit agility and flexibility, with your head consistently tracking the motion of your hands. Throughout this sequence, the whole body should maintain a state of relaxation, devoid of stiffness, yet remain stable to preserve balance during the turns.

When mastering this complex movement, it's recommended to begin with a systematic, step-by-step approach to comprehend the directions, orbits, and lines integral to the motion. Afterward, prioritize consistent practice to hone the movement, aiming for fluidity, circularity, and flexibility. Strive for seamless coordination among your hands, eyes, body techniques, and footwork while executing the action.

Double Push the Palms Outward with a Left Rest Stance (左歇步双撑掌)

Continuing from the previous movement, maintain your position.

Push your right foot against the ground and shift your weight onto your left leg. Cross your right foot behind your left leg, positioning it slightly to the left side. Squat down to form a left rest stance, ensuring your thighs are almost parallel. Simultaneously, extend both arms outward, straighten the arms, and push your palms to the left and right directions. Your right palm should be positioned in the upper right corner, while your left palm should be in the lower left corner. Focus on your left palm throughout the movement (Figure 12.30). Both your palms should maintain a horizontal supporting strength to the outside during the motion. Look to the left.

Figure 12.30

Key Points:
(1) Maintain your balance and keep your upper body upright before squatting down.
(2) Ensure the legs are tightly crossed together, maintaining a stable position.

Common Errors:

(1) Avoid sitting with your buttocks not resting on the rear calf.

(2) Ensure the distance between your feet is not too big, as it may affect the support of the rear leg for the front leg.

Suggestions:

(1) Practice the cross-legged sitting stance alternately, using your hands to hold the front leg and pull it inside for better flexibility.

(2) Focus on practicing the rest stance conversion to enhance your stability and coordination in this movement.

Tiao Palm with a Right Empty Stance (右虚步挑掌)

Movement 1:

Connect to the previous movement.

Turn to the right and step backward with your left foot to form a right bow stance. Simultaneously, extend your left palm downward from the outside of your left leg towards the right, placing it in front of your right knee straightly while keeping your thumb up. Push your right palm down under your left armpit, with the palm facing outward. Maintain your gaze on your left palm (Figure 12.31).

Figure 12.31

Movement 2:

Continue from the previous movement. Apply pressure with your right foot, firmly planted on the ground. Simultaneously, shift your weight backward and draw your right foot slightly back, creating a right empty stance. While transitioning into the empty stance, circle your left arm up and back, extending it towards the rear at shoulder height. Now, transform your left palm into a hook hand, with the tip-down and positioned at or slightly above shoulder level.

341

At the same time, swing your right palm from your left armpit, bringing it down and forward. When your right palm reaches the height of your abdomen, flick it upward, allowing the fingertips to point upward. Slightly bend your right elbow, keeping your right arm at approximately shoulder height. The force point of this movement should be at the tip of your right fingers and the tip of your left hook. Maintain your focus on your right palm (Figure 12.32).

Figure 12.32

Swing Palm with a Right Crouching Stance (右仆步摆掌)

Build upon the previous movement by executing the same actions as in the 'Swing Palm with a Left Crouching Stance.' However, in this instance, perform these actions in a right crouching stance, as illustrated in Figure 12.33.

Figure 12.33

Right Turn with a Dancing-Flower Hand (右转身舞花手)

Continue the sequence from the previous movement.

This movement is a mirror image of the 'Turn Left with Dancing-Flower Hands,' but it is the same actions while turning to the right (Figures 12.34, 12.35, 12.36, and 12.37).

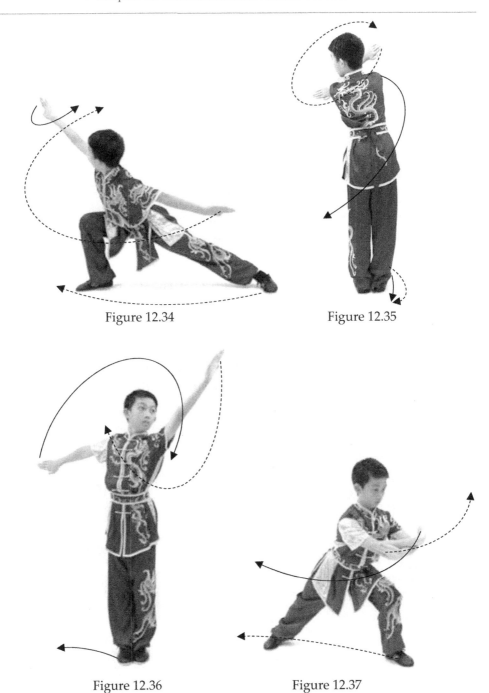

Figure 12.34

Figure 12.35

Figure 12.36

Figure 12.37

Double Push the Palms Outward with a Right Rest Stance (右歇步双撑掌)

Continue from the previous movement. Execute the same actions as in the 'Double Push Palms Outward with a Left Rest Stance,' but this time, perform them in the opposite direction, as shown in Figure 12.38 for specific hand and body positions.

Figure 12.38

Hold the Fists on the Waists, with Your Feet Together (并步抱拳)

Step your right foot to the right and bring your left foot close to your right foot. To form a 'Hold the Fists on the Waists, with Your Feet Together.'

'Empty,' 'Crouch' and 'Rest Stance' Combination Exercises for Continuous Movement

4. The Combination of 'Rest Stance' and 'Horse Stance'

Movement Names: Flash the Palm in a Rest Stance – Turn Around and Swing the Arms and Front Straight Kick – Elbow Strike in a Horse Stance – Punch Down in a Rest Stance

Preparation Posture: Stand upright with your feet together and clench your fists at your waist. Direct your gaze straight ahead (Figure 12.39).

Figure 12.39

Flash the Palm in a Rest Stance (歇步亮掌)
Movement 1:
Keep your left fist in its current position without moving it. Step to the left with your left foot. Transition your right fist into an open palm. Extend your right arm and swing your right palm from your right side to the upper right, with the palm facing upward. Maintain your focus on your right hand (Figure 12.40).

Movement 2:
Continuing the sequence, cross your right foot behind your left leg and lower your body into a complete squat, assuming a rest stance.

While executing this movement, convert your left fist into an open palm, initiating the motion from your left waist and moving it upward, with the palm and fingers forward. Cross your left palm over the inside of your right forearm, passing it in front of your chest. Then, rotate your left palm inward and circle it to the left until it reaches the back of your body. As it arrives behind you, transition your left palm into a hooked hand with the tip of the hook pointing upward. Simultaneously, maintain the circular motion of your right arm, moving it from the upper right to the left, then downward, and passing it over your abdomen to the right. Keep your palm facing upward. When your right arm returns to the upper right side, snap your right wrist inward to create a flash palm. Position it above your head on the right side, with the palm facing upward and your fingers pointing to the left. Maintain your gaze to the left throughout this sequence (Figure 12.41).

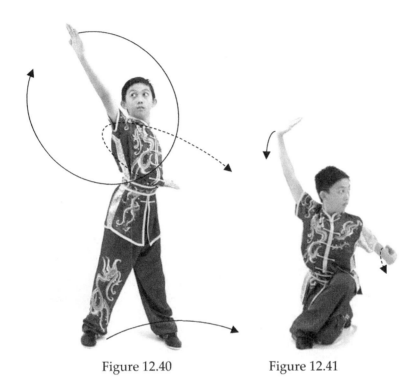

Figure 12.40   Figure 12.41

Important Note: Both arms should move simultaneously without pausing, making a fluid and continuous circular motion in front of your chest.

Turn Around and Swing the Arms and Front Straight Kick (轉身掄臂正踢)
Movement 1:
Stand up and turn your body 90 degrees to the right. Keep your left leg slightly bent and your right leg extended. As you turn, raise your right arm above your head while transforming your left hook hand into a palm and place it behind your body. Stretch both arms as far as possible, one reaching upward and the other reaching downward behind your body (Figure 12.42).

Movement 2:
Turn right 180 degrees, circle your right arm in a complete motion, first backward and then downward and upward, ultimately positioning your right arm above your head to form a flash palm. Simultaneously, circle your left palm from a starting position behind

your body, passing it outside your left thigh and then moving it upward. Continue circling it down behind your body in a full circle. While following the motion of your body's turn, transform your left palm into a hook hand and place it behind your body again, ensuring that the tip of the hook faces upward. As you complete the circular movement with both arms, execute a right front straight kick toward your forehead. Maintain your gaze straight ahead throughout this sequence (Figure 12.43, 12.44).

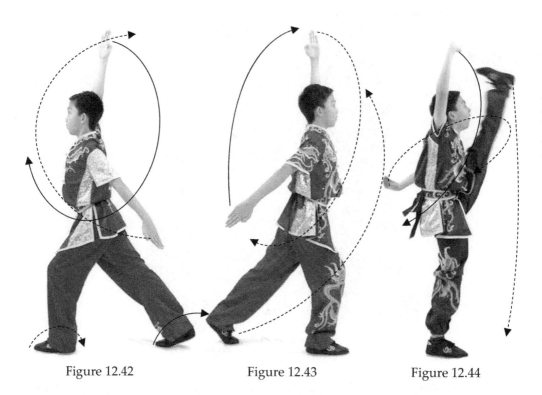

| Figure 12.42 | Figure 12.43 | Figure 12.44 |

Important Notes: Ensure that both arms follow a vertical path as they move. Use your waist as an axis to facilitate the turn of your entire body and arms. Keep your feet flexible to maintain balance and avoid leaning in any direction. Maintain an upright posture with your head up.

Elbow Strike in a Horse Stance (馬步盤肘)

After executing a left kick, land your left foot while simultaneously turning 90 degrees to the right, assuming a horse stance. Place your right fist onto your right waist. Transform your left hook hand into a fist. Bend your left elbow and swing your left arm inward horizontally. As your left arm reaches the left side of your body due to the turn, use the tip and the outside of your left elbow as a pivot point. Strike forward in front of your body with your left elbow, keeping your fist facing downward. Maintain your gaze straight ahead (see Figure 12.45).

Punch Down in a Rest Stance (歇步下衝拳)

Begin by moving your left foot outward and turning your body to the left by 90 degrees. Allow your right foot to follow your left foot, moving forward slightly to create a left rest stance. Simultaneously, execute a downward punch in the front with your right fist while your left fist moves to your left waist. Keep your gaze downward in front. (Figure 12.46).

Hold the Fists on the Waists, with Your Feet Together (并步抱拳)

Step your right foot forward while turning your body 90 degrees to the left. Bring your right foot close to the inside of your left foot, forming a feet-together stance, and place your fists at your waist. Your gaze should be directed to the left (Figure 12.47).

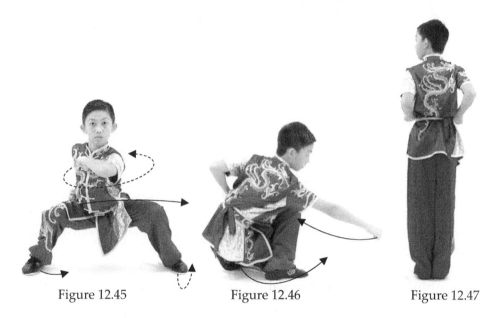

Figure 12.45   Figure 12.46   Figure 12.47

'Rest Stance' and 'Horse Stance' Combination Exercises for Continuous Movement

Important Notes: When performing a 'Rest Stance,' ensure both legs are close together, and the rear leg should tightly touch the outside of your front calf. While swinging your arms and turning your body, use the soles of your feet as the pivot point, and remember that waist movement is crucial for coordination. Execute these movements swiftly. During kicking, stabilize your supporting leg, maintain a chest-out posture, and keep your abdomen in. After kicking and transitioning into a horse stance, continue using the soles of your feet as the pivot point. Slightly move your knee inward while maintaining a chest-out posture and strengthening your waist. Ensure coordination and consistency in your up and down movements.

5. The Combination of 'Cross-Legged Behind,' 'Sitting,' and 'Bow Stance'

Movements: Double Swing Palms with a Cross-Legged Behind Stance – Swing Arms, and Transition to a Sitting Stance with a Burst Fist - Separate the Palms in a Bow Stance.

Preparation Posture: Hold the fists at your waist, with your feet together. Look straight ahead (Figure 12.48).

Double Swing the Palms (插步雙擺掌)

Begin by stepping to the left with your left foot and turn your body to the left. Transform your fists into open palms and push them to the left. Place your left palm in front while the right palm closes to the inside of your left arm. Keep your gaze on your hands (Figure 12.49).

Step your right foot forward over your left foot while turning your body 90 degrees to the left. Strengthen your arms and circle your hands downward to the left, then bring them, upward to the right side of your body. Position your right palm in front at shoulder height with your fingers facing up. Your left palm touches the inside of your right forearm, palms facing up. Simultaneously, cross your left leg behind your right leg. Ensure that your right knee is bent while your left knee is stretched. While swinging your arms and crossing your leg, turn your head to the right to gaze in that direction (Figure 12.50).

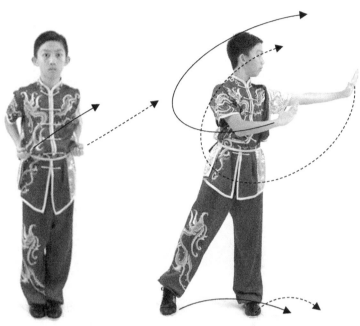

Figure 12.48   Figure 12.49

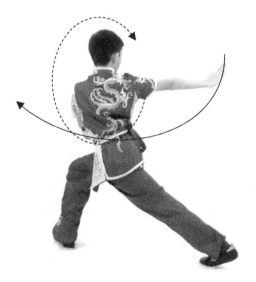

Figure 12.50

Turn, Swing Arms, and Transition to a Sitting Stance with a Burst Fist
（翻身掄臂坐盤崩拳）

Transition smoothly from the previous movement.

Rotate your entire body to the left and perform a flip motion. Then, sit on the ground to create a 'Sitting Cross-Legged Stance.' The left leg is just above your right leg. Simultaneously, swing your left arm downward, upward, and to the left as you turn. Allow your right arm to follow the left arm, moving it downward, and back up. Execute a 'burst fist' to hit your left palm in front of your chest with your palms facing downward. Ensure that your right-hand grips the right wrist tightly. Gaze to the left during this movement (Figure12.51, 12.52, 12.53).

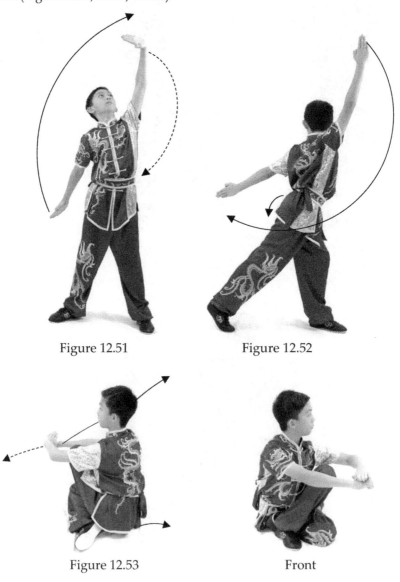

Figure 12.51   Figure 12.52

Figure 12.53   Front

Separate the Palms in a Bow Stance (弓步靠身掌)

Transform your right fist into a palm, drawing it towards your chest. Bend your left elbow and place your palm inside your right arm near your chest.

While transitioning, step your right foot to the right side, forming a right bow stance. Also, rotate your right arm outward, straighten it, and move your right hand to the upper right, raising it above your shoulder with the palm tilted upward. Simultaneously, press your left palm downward to the lower left, with the palm facing downward. Maintain your gaze directed toward the upper right (Figure 12.54).

Figure 12.54

Hold the Fists on the Waists, with Your Feet Together (并步抱拳)

Step your left foot back, return to the preparation position (Figure 12.55).

Figure 12.55

353

'Cross Legged Behind,' 'Sitting Stance' and 'Bow Stance' Combination Exercises for Continuous Movement

6. A Combination of 'Five Types of Stances' or 'Five Stances Fist'

The 'Five Stances Fist,' or 'Wu Bu Quan' (五步拳), is a fundamental routine in Chinese Wushu, primarily designed for beginners. It combines five essential stances, three hand forms, and two variations of footwork. This routine plays a crucial role in developing coordination, mastering key points, refining transitional movements, and enhancing overall technique quality. By regularly practicing the 'Five Stances Fist,' practitioners can establish a strong foundation to advance their skills and delve deeper into the art of Chinese Wushu.

354

Movement Names: Preparation Posture - Punch in a Twist Bow Stance - Punch and Snap Kick - Punch and Block Up in a Horse Stance - Press and Punch with a Rest Stance - Knee-Lift, and Thread the Palm with a Crouch Stance - Tiao Palm with an Empty Stance - Conclude Movement.

Preparation Posture:

Start by standing in an upright position with your feet together. Allow your arms to hang naturally by your sides, with your palms resting gently against the sides of your thighs. Keep your posture straight and maintain a forward gaze, looking straight ahead (Figure 12.56).

After standing in the preparation posture for a brief moment to settle into the practice, which may involve adjusting your posture, regulating your breathing, and centering your mind, proceed to the next movement. Swiftly bring both of your fists up to your waist, clasping them tightly with the knuckles facing upward. Look straight ahead (Figure 12.57).

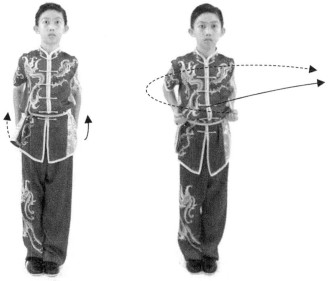

Figure 12.56   Figure 12.57

Key Points:

(1) The movement of 'Holding the Fists on the Waists' is a commonly used starting position in Wushu routines.

(2) The fists should be raised swiftly from the sides to waist level, maintaining a tight grip.

(3) This movement serves as a seamless transition between the preceding and following movements in the routine.

(4) Before initiating the motion, it is important to cultivate a focused and concentrated mindset.

(5) The fundamental posture for the Long Fist style includes a straight head, upright neck, chest slightly protruded, and a well-aligned waist.

(6) The upper body should be straight and stable, while the lower limbs should maintain stability and balance.

(7) The execution of the movement should exhibit symmetry and flow in a rhythmic manner.

Movements:
Punch in a Twist Bow Stance (拗弓步冲拳)

Transition from the previous movement of 'Holding the Fists on Your Waists.'

Keep your right fist stationary while opening your left fist into an open palm. Rotate your left arm inward, turning the palm outward, and extend it to the front of your body. At the same time, rotate your upper body to the left and step your left foot towards the left side, forming a left bow stance.

As your left palm extends forward, sweep it horizontally to the left in a circular motion. Once you have established the left bow stance, transform your left palm into a closed fist and retract it back towards your left waist, with the fist facing upwards. Simultaneously, execute a straight punch with your right fist from your right waist, keeping the fist horizontal. Maintain your focus on your right fist throughout the movement (Figure 12.58).

Figure 12.58

Key Points:
(1) Achieve coordination between pushing the ground, turning to the left, brushing your left hand, and executing the punch with your right fist. These actions should flow seamlessly, showcasing speed and power.

(2) When delivering the punch, extend your right arm straight ahead without bending the elbow or raising the shoulders. Maintain a level head, relaxed shoulders, a flat back of the right fist, engaged left thigh, and a composed mindset.

(3) Generate equal force with your right fist while simultaneously retracting the left fist.

(4) Upon completing the movement, conduct a self-assessment to ensure it aligns with the required standards. Pay attention to factors such as full extension of the back knee, maintaining grounded stability in the right foot, and ensuring the front knee does not extend beyond the front toe, among other considerations.

About the 'Punch' (take the right punch as an example):

The punch is a fundamental and significant 'Hand Technique' in Chinese Wushu. When executing a punch, especially the right punch in this context, there are key principles to consider:

Controlled Power Release: Avoid releasing power too early during the initial phase of the punch. Instead, let the force build up gradually as the arm extends forward. This controlled power release ensures that the punch utilizes its full potential.

Waist Twisting and Arm Rotation: As the arm extends forward, the elbow moves away from the waist while the waist twists to generate rotational power. This twisting motion aids in accelerating the force of the punch. Simultaneously, the right arm rapidly rotates inward, smoothly pushing the shoulder forward. This coordinated movement generates power and contributes to the speed of the punch.

Force Point and Focus: Direct the force point, which is the striking surface of the fist, toward the intended target. Concentrating the force on the fist's face makes the punch more effective and accurate. It is crucial to maintain proper form and alignment to ensure efficient force transfer to the target.

Coordination of Waist and Shoulder: Synchronize the punch with waist twisting and the smooth straightening of the shoulder. By incorporating these movements, the punch gains additional strength and speed. The coordinated action of the waist and shoulder enhances the overall effectiveness of the punch, resulting in greater explosive power.

Punch and Spring Kick (弹踢冲拳)

Transition from the previous movement to initiate the 'Punch and Spring Kick.'

Keep your left foot grounded and stable, providing support for your body. Simultaneously, lift your right knee, using it as an axis, and swiftly kick forward with your right toe. Extend your right knee and fully stretch your toes. Maintain your balance primarily using your left leg. It is essential to slightly curve your left toes to grip the ground but avoid excessive tension.

At the same time, rotate your right arm outward, pulling your right fist back toward your right waist while turning the fist-heart upward. In coordination, rotate your left arm inward and execute a quick straight-line punch with your left fist, maintaining a horizontal fist. Keep your gaze fixed straight ahead (Figure 12.59).

Key Points:

(1) Ensure proper body alignment. Twist your waist, push your left shoulder forward, stretch your chest, and maintain a straight lower back. These movements should be coordinated and consistent throughout the execution.

(2) Coordinate the punch and pulling back of the fists. As you kick with your right leg, punch forward with your left fist and simultaneously pull your right fist back to your right waist. These actions should be synchronized to maintain balance and coordination.

(3) Before executing the kick, shift your weight to the supporting leg (left leg), push the ground with your feet, and then stand up to execute the kick. This sequence of movements ensures stability and power generation.

(4) Focus on force points. When kicking, direct the force to the tips of your right toes, and when punching, focus the force at the face of your right fist. This will enhance the effectiveness and impact of your techniques.

(5) Keep your body upright throughout the movement. Avoid loosening your lower body or protruding your buttocks forward or backward. Keep your head up, shoulders relaxed, and elbows dropped to maintain a strong and balanced posture.

Figure 12.59

About 'Spring Kick'

The 'Spring Kick' is a fundamental 'Leg Technique' that involves flexion and extension. Here are some crucial points to keep in mind when performing the 'Spring Kick':

Maintain proper leg posture: The supporting leg should be straight or slightly bent, providing stability and balance throughout the movement. The leg that performs the kick should raise the knee, with the calf fully relaxed.

Reach waist height with the thigh: As the thigh reaches waist height, maintain a fixed knee angle without further swinging or lifting the leg. This position sets the foundation for the subsequent extension of the knee and toes.

Quick extension of the knee and toes: Once the thigh is at waist height, rapidly extend the knee and toes forward in a straight line. The thigh and calf should align, and the force generated should be directed toward the toes. This ensures a powerful and effective kick.

Relaxation and quick release of the front leg: Prior to the kick, ensure that the front leg and ankle are fully relaxed. This allows for a quick release of strength when the thigh reaches waist level, maximizing the speed and power of the kick.

Maintain fixed knee angle: It is essential to keep the angle and position of the knee fixed during the kick. Use the knee as a lever to extend it forward, avoiding unnecessary swinging or lifting of the leg. This helps differentiate the spring kick from a swinging motion.

Punch and Block Up in a Horse Stance (馬步架打)

Transition smoothly from the previous movement.

After executing the kick and punch, keep your position briefly. Then, step forward with your right foot, pivot your right toes inward, and rotate your body to the left. Squat down to assume a horse stance, ensuring stability and balance.

Simultaneously, transform your left fist into an open palm by turning it upward, bending your left elbow, and raising your left palm over your head to the left. Your left fingers should point to the right. In conjunction with the palm movement, rotate your right arm inward and swiftly punch your right fist in a straight line to the right side of your right waist. Keep your fist at shoulder height with a horizontal orientation. Maintain focus on your right fist as you execute the movement (Figure 12.60).

Figure 12.60

Key Points:

(1) Coordinate the movements of landing your right foot, punching with your right fist, and blocking up with your left palm. These actions should be performed simultaneously, emphasizing synchronization and proper timing.

(2) After landing and forming the half-horse stance, maintain proper body alignment. Extend your shoulders and chest, ensuring your left arm is positioned behind your left ear. Avoid leaning your upper body in any direction, maintaining an upright posture.

(3) Pay attention to the flatness and stability of various body parts. Keep your head flat, shoulders flat, your right arm balanced, and the back of your right fist flat. Additionally, ensure that your thighs are stable and avoid throwing out your buttocks.

(4) Adjust your toes inward and slightly position your knees outward. This alignment contributes to stability and proper weight distribution in the horse stance.

(5) Throughout the movement, maintain a sense of groundedness and stability by directing your Qi to the Dantian, the center of the body in the lower abdomen.

Press and Punch with a Rest Stance (歇步盖打)

Movement 1:

Transition smoothly from the previous movement, maintaining fluidity and control in your body movements.

Now, rotate to the left by 90 degrees, ensuring a smooth and coordinated turn.

Step your left foot back behind your right foot, allowing the sole of your left foot to touch the ground. Simultaneously, turn your right toe inward to facilitate the movement. Transform your left palm into a fist and draw it to your left waist from the left side, preparing for the subsequent motion. Release your right fist and transition it into a palm as you lift it over your head to the left. Bring it in front of your chest, creating a pressing motion. The trajectory of the right arm should resemble a semicircle, with the fingers pointing to the left and the outer edge of your right palm facing forward. Maintain a slight bend in your knees to ensure stability and balance. The height of your right arm should be slightly above your shoulders, creating a visually appealing posture. Direct your gaze toward your right palm, focusing on it (Figure 12.61).

Key Points:

(1) Maintain a seamless flow from the previous actions into the current one, allowing for a smooth transition between postures.

(2) Execute the 90-degree turn to the left while stepping back with your left foot, aligning the sole with the ground and turning your right toe inward. Maintain a stable and balanced stance.

(3) Convert your left palm into a fist, drawing it to your left waist, while simultaneously transforming your right fist into a palm and lifting it over your head to the left. Coordinate the movements of both arms to create a harmonious pressing motion.

(4) Form a semi-circular trajectory with your right arm, with the fingers pointing to the left and the outer edge of your palm facing forward. Maintain a height slightly above the shoulders.
(5) Keep a slight bend in your knees for flexibility and stability.
(6) Direct your gaze toward your right palm, maintaining visual concentration on it.

Figure 12.61

Movement 2:

Proceed seamlessly from the previous movement.

Bend your knees and squat down fully, assuming a right rest stance. Simultaneously, transform your right palm into a fist and swiftly pull it towards your right waist. Execute a punch with your left fist, propelling it forward in a straight line with a horizontal fist. Maintain your gaze on your left fist (Figure 12.62).

Figure 12.62

Key Points:

(1) Ensure a smooth transition from the previous movement to the rest stance. Flow seamlessly into the squatting position, maintaining control and balance throughout.

(2) Bend your knees fully, assuming a right rest stance. This position should provide stability and a solid base for the subsequent movements.

(3) Keep your left fist aligned horizontally as you punch forward, maintaining proper form and technique.

(4) Convert your right palm into a fist, drawing it quickly towards your right waist, while simultaneously delivering a punch with your left fist. Coordinate the movements of both fists for a cohesive and powerful strike.

(5) Direct your gaze towards your left fist, remaining focused on it throughout the movement.

Knee-Lift, and Thread Palm with a Crouch Stance (提膝仆步穿掌)
Movement 1:

Transition smoothly from the previous movement, pushing off the ground with both feet to stand up quickly. Maintain a controlled and balanced movement as you turn to the left.

Release your fists and transform them into palms, with your left palm facing downward and your right palm facing upward. Use your right-hand finger as a force point, extending it out to the right from the back of your left palm.

Raise your left knee as close to your chest as possible while maintaining control and balance. Simultaneously, pull your left palm back to the inside of your right arm. This movement is known as 'the swallow passes through the forest' in Wushu, and it requires coordination and fluidity. Extend your right knee and point down with your left toe, ensuring a stable base. Keep your gaze focused on your right hand to maintain awareness (Figure 12.63).

Key Points:

(1) Seamless transition. Flow smoothly from the previous movement by exerting force with both feet to stand up quickly and executing a swift turn to the left. Transform your closed fists into open palms.

(2) Utilize your right-hand finger as a force point, extending it outward to the right from the back of your left palm. This action creates a dynamic thrusting motion.

(3) Elevate your left knee as high as possible toward your chest while simultaneously pulling your left palm back to the inside of your right arm. This coordinated movement is known as "the swallow passes through the forest" in Wushu.

(4) Extend your right knee and point your left toe downward, establishing a stable crouch stance with a well-grounded position.

(5) Maintain visual focus on your right hand throughout the movement, directing your gaze to enhance precision and concentration.

Figure 12.63

Movement 2:

Transition smoothly from the previous movement, dropping your left foot to the left in a sweeping motion resembling a shovel.

Squat down fully, assuming a left crouch stance. Focus on maintaining stability and balance throughout this movement. Keep your right arm still and stationary, maintaining its position. Extend your left palm forward, with the fingers facing forward. Trace the inside of your left leg with your palm, extending the movement all the way down to your left foot. This action is known as 'the swallow scoops the water' in Wushu, emphasizing the controlled and fluid nature of the movement. Direct your gaze towards your left palm, maintaining visual focus and concentration (Figure 12.64).

Figure 12.64

Key Points:

(1) Maintain a smooth and coordinated transition from the previous movement by dropping your left foot to the left in a sweeping motion.

(2) Squat down fully to assume a left crouch stance, ensuring stability and balance throughout the movement. Completely squat down your right leg so that the back of your right thigh touches your right calf.

(3) Keep your right arm still and steady, maintaining a controlled position while performing the subsequent actions.

(4) Extend your left palm forward, with the fingers facing forward. Begin the movement from your right armpit, tracing along your body, and following the inside of your left leg all the way down to your left foot. Visualize the imagery of 'the swallow scoops the water' in Wushu.

(5) Maintain visual concentration and awareness throughout the movement, directing your gaze towards your left palm.

(6) Ensure that your right toes are tilted about 45 degrees outward, and your left toes are pointed 90 degrees inward. Avoid lifting your right heel and the outside of your left foot off the ground.

(7) Even when leaning forward, keep your upper body straight and avoid shrugging your shoulders or losing your waist. Let your arms form a tilted line while maintaining stability and alignment.

About 'Thread the Palm'

'Thread the Palm,' 'penetrate palm,' 'thrust palm,' or 'pierce palm' are terms used to describe a striking technique commonly found in martial arts. This technique involves extending the arm with the fingers pointing forward, and it is often used to slide underneath the opponent's leading arm to attack vulnerable areas or vital points.

The orientation of the palm can vary depending on the specific technique and application. It can be positioned upward, downward, at an angle, or sideways, depending on the desired target and the martial art style being practiced.

The aim of this technique is to swiftly extend the arm and strike the opponent's vulnerable areas, such as the ribs, solar plexus, chin, or throat. By using proper body mechanics, timing, and precision, this striking technique can be an effective way to penetrate the opponent's defenses and deliver a powerful blow.

It's important to note that the execution of this technique may vary depending on the martial art style and the specific situation. Proper training, practice, and understanding of the principles behind the technique are essential to effectively utilize and apply it in self-defense or combat situations.

Tiao Palm with Empty Stance (虚步挑掌)

Continue the movement sequence from the previous action, maintaining the position of your arms and palms.

Shift your weight forward gradually, bending your left knee as you push your right foot to the ground and step forward, assuming a right empty stance. As your right foot steps forward, rotate your left toe outward at a 45-degree angle. At the same time, pivot around your left shoulder, keeping your left hand positioned forward, upward, and slightly backward in a vertical circular motion.

As your left hand reaches the back, transform your left palm into a hook shape with the tip pointing downward. Ensure that the top of the hook is slightly above your shoulder.

Simultaneously, swing your right palm forward from the back, following a circular trajectory along the outer side of your right thigh. As your right hand moves forward and reaches waist height, use your right finger to flick upward at nose height. This action is referred to as 'Tiao palm' in Chinese. Maintain a forward gaze, focusing your eyes straight ahead (Figure 12.65).

Figure 12.65

Key Points

(1) Shift your weight forward gradually, maintaining stability and control throughout the transition from the crouch stance to the empty stance. Avoid sudden or jerky movements, ensuring a smooth transfer of weight.

(2) Proper alignment of the supporting leg. When stepping forward with your right foot, pay attention to the placement of your left toe, which should be turned outward at a 45-degree angle. The height of the empty stance can vary depending on your flexibility and conditioning but aim to have your supporting leg parallel to the ground. Avoid excessive forward or backward tilting of the hips.

(3) Practice the synchronization of stepping forward with your right foot, flicking your right hand, and forming a left hook with your left palm. Focus on the timing and smooth execution of these movements to create a seamless flow and maximize their effectiveness.

About 'Tiao Palm'

'Tiao Palm' refers to a specific striking technique in Chinese Wushu. It can vary slightly depending on the specific style or tradition. In many traditional styles, 'Tiao Palm' involves a scooping strike with the arm slightly bent and the wrist cocked, targeting with the forearm or palm. This technique is executed by using an upward motion to deliver the strike.

In the Long Fist style, 'Tiao Palm' is characterized by a quick and forceful upward flick of the wrist, presenting the palm as the striking surface. The emphasis is on generating speed and power through the flicking motion of the wrist.

Overall, 'Tiao palm' involves an upward striking action, whether it is performed with a scooping motion or a flicking motion and can be executed with the forearm or palm as the contact point depending on the style and technique being practiced.

Concluding Movement

Ensure a smooth transition from the previous movement to the concluding movement, maintaining the flow and connection between the actions.

Shift your weight to your right leg as you rotate your body approximately 90 degrees to the left. Bring your left foot close to your right foot, assuming a standing position with feet together. Transform your left hook and right palm into fists and position them on both sides of your waist. This signifies the completion of the movement. Maintain a forward gaze to maintain proper alignment and focus(Figure 13.38).

For balanced training and proficiency, repeat the same sequence of movements in the opposite direction, ensuring equal practice on both sides.

The Continuous Motions of the 'Five Stances Fist'

The Combination of 'Leg Technique' Exercises

'Leg Technique' combination exercises are a great way to improve coordination, balance, and overall leg strength in martial arts and other sports. Here are some examples of 'Leg Technique' combination exercises:

1. The Combination of 'Inside (Crescent) Kick' and 'Front Straight Kick'

The Name of the Movements: Preparation Posture - Inside Crescent Kick - Push the Palm with a Bow Stance - Circle Arms and Front Left Straight Kick - Front Right Straight Kick - Stand Up with Feet Together and Hold the Fists on the Waists.

Preparation Posture:
Stand up with the feet together and hold the fists on the waists. Look straight ahead (Figure 12.66, 12.67).

Figure 12.66	Figure 12.67

Inside Crescent Kick (裏合腿)
Movement 1: Swing the Left Arm and Step the Left Foot

Keep your right fist still and maintain an upright posture. Step to the left with your left foot and turn left, forming a left bow stance or high bow stance. Simultaneously, change your left fist into a palm and brush it upward to the upper left corner, with the palm facing out. Maintain your focus on the left hand (Figure 12.68).

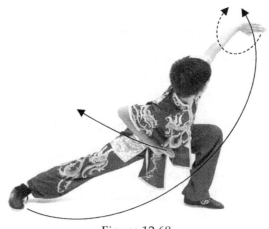

Figure 12.68

Note: As this movement is transitional and not stationary, the bow stance does not need to adhere to a standard posture or be held for a prolonged duration.

Movement 2: Inside Crescent Kick and Turn

Continue from the previous movement.

Stand up and execute an inside crescent kick with your right foot, using your left foot as the pivot point. As you turn your body to the left, perform a 180-degree rotation. Keep your left heel on the ground while executing the kick.

Simultaneously, rotate your left arm outward and strike your right sole with your left palm in front of your face, positioned at 3:00. Release your right fist into a palm, placing it behind your body, and straighten your right arm. Maintain your gaze on the right foot (Figure 12.69).

It's important to practice these movements with proper technique and control. Pay attention to your body alignment, balance, and coordination. As you perform the inside crescent kick, focus on generating power from the hip and maintaining control throughout the movement. Regular practice will help refine your execution and enhance your overall skill in leg technique combination exercises.

Figure 12.69

Push the palm with a bow stance (弓步推掌)

Continue from the previous movement.

After executing the inside crescent kick, bend your left knee and lower your right foot towards 9:00, simultaneously turning to the left and forming a left bow stance. Powerfully push your right palm forward, driving the force from your right waist (3:00 direction). Ensure that your fingers are pointing upward, and the force point is on the outside of your right palm.

At the same time, transition your left palm into a hook and swing it back along the outside of your left hip. The hook tip should be pointing upward, and both arms should be fully extended. The actions of pushing your right palm, dropping your right foot back, and assuming a left bow stance should be synchronized. Maintain a forward gaze (Figure 12.70).

It is crucial to maintain proper body alignment and coordination throughout the movement. Focus on generating power from your core and transferring it through your arms and palms. Additionally, pay attention to the stability and balance of your bow stance, ensuring that your weight is evenly distributed. Practice these movements diligently to improve your leg technique combination exercises. Meanwhile change your left palm into a hook and swing back along the outside of your left hip. The hook tip is upward and stretch both your arms.

Figure 12.70

Circle arms and front left straight kick (抡臂正踢腿)
Movement 1: Circle Arms

Continue from the previous movement. Shift your weight backward, slightly pull your left foot back, and turn 180 degrees to the right.

Simultaneously, perform a vertical clockwise circular motion with your arms to the right. As you turn right, raise your right arm up, move it to the right, and bring it down diagonally behind your body. Your left arm should move downward, to the left, and then up to the front of your head. Prior to the circular motion, your right palm should be facing at 3:00, and your left arm should be in a hook position pointing at 9:00. As you circle your arms, move your right palm up above your head towards 9:00 and then continue down towards 3:00. The movement of your left arm should follow the circular path of your right arm in a straight line. After completing the circular motion, ensure that your arms are aligned in a straight line. Maintain your focus on your left hand (Figure 12.71).

It is important to maintain coordination and fluidity in the movement, synchronizing the rotation of your body and the circular motion of your arms. Pay attention to the positioning and alignment of your arms throughout the circle, maintaining proper form and control.

Movement 2: Left Straight Kick

Continue from the previous movement.

After turning your body, shift your weight forward and support your weight with your right leg. Perform a left straight kick by extending your left leg straight forward. Point your left toes upward and fully extend your left knee. Ensure that your right foot remains grounded for stability.

Simultaneously, transform your left palm into a hook shape and swing it vertically along the outside of your left leg, moving it behind your body. The tip of the hook should be facing upward. Additionally, swing your right arm vertically upward from the back, raising it above your head. Keep a slight bend in your right elbow and orient your palm upward. Throughout the movement, maintain an upright posture and keep your body aligned. Maintain a forward gaze, looking straight ahead (Figure 12.72).

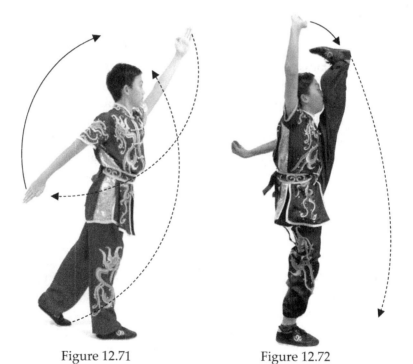

Figure 12.71   Figure 12.72

Key Points:

(1) Maintain proper coordination between the circling of your arms and the vertical swinging motion. Both arms should extend fully in their respective directions, creating a smooth and synchronized movement.

(2) Keep your shoulders relaxed to avoid tension and maintain a straight posture in your waist. Lift your head as you turn to maintain proper alignment and focus.

(3) Maintain flexibility in your feet and ensure good contact with the ground throughout the movement. This will help you maintain balance and stability.

(4) Open your chest and engage your upper body by simultaneously pulling your right arm upward and backward while stretching your left arm and raising it during the kick. This will help generate power and control in your kick.

(5) Straighten your legs fully during the kick and aim to bring your left foot as close to your forehead as possible, showcasing flexibility and control in your kicking technique.

(6) Focus on maintaining proper form and alignment in your entire body. This includes maintaining balance, keeping your core engaged, and focusing on your target.

(7) Practice these movements with precision, gradually increasing the height and speed of your kicks as your technique improves.

Front Right Straight Kick (正踢腿)
Movement 1: Landing

After executing the front left straight kick, smoothly bring your left foot down and land it in front of your right foot. Shift your weight forward onto your left leg, preparing for the next sequence of movements. Lift your right heel slightly off the ground to maintain balance and readiness for the following actions. Simultaneously, swing your right arm forward, bringing it closer to your head. Your arm should move in a fluid and controlled manner, maintaining proper alignment and coordination with your body.

Transition your left hook hand position into a palm, rotating your left arm outward behind your body. Visualize your palms facing upward, resembling the shape of two tiger mouths. Maintain focus on your right hand throughout this landing movement (refer to Figure 12.73).

Remember to maintain stability and balance as you land, ensuring a smooth transition to the next phase of your leg technique combination exercises.

Movement 2: Right Straight Kick

Building upon the previous movements, execute a powerful right straight kick by extending your right leg straight forward. Keep your toes pointed upward, demonstrating control and precision in your kicking technique. Simultaneously, transform your right palm into a hook shape and swing it behind your body. Ensure that the tip of the hook is facing upward throughout the movement.

Additionally, swing your left arm upward in a blocking motion, positioning it above your head. Maintain a slight bend in your left elbow, with your palm facing upward. Maintain a forward gaze, focusing straight ahead throughout the execution of the movement (Figure 12.74).

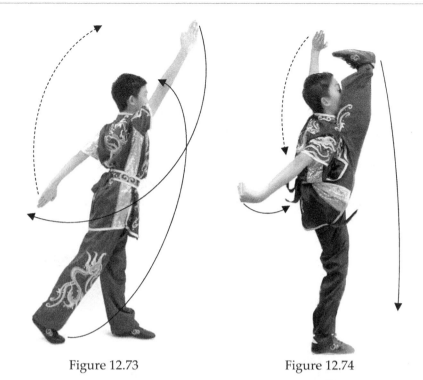

Figure 12.73   Figure 12.74

Hold the fists on the waist, with your feet together (并步抱拳)

Dropping your right foot forward and shifting your weight onto it (Figure 12.75.

Figure 12.75   Figure 12.76

Step your left foot forward, placing it on the inside of your right foot, so that your feet are together. Simultaneously, clench both of your hands into fists and bring them to rest on your waists. Maintain a forward gaze, looking straight ahead throughout the posture (Figure 12.76).

In the concluding posture, ensure that your feet are aligned and touching together, symbolizing stability and unity. Clenching your fists and placing them on your waist represents a sense of power, readiness, and control.
Focus on maintaining an upright posture, relaxing your shoulders, and keeping your body aligned. This concluding posture serves as a moment of stillness and reflection after performing the sequence of leg technique combination exercises.

Continuous Motion of 'Inside Crescent Kick' and 'Front Straight Kick '

2. The Combination of 'Pat Foot' and 'Side Sole Kick'

Movement Names: Preparation Posture - Swing the Arms and Hammer Punch - Single Slapping Kick (pat kick) - Side Sole Kick - Stand Up with Feet Together and Hold the Fists on the Waists.

Preparation Posture: Begin by standing up with your feet together and holding your fists at your waist level. Keep your fists closed and your arms relaxed. Direct your gaze straight ahead, maintaining a focused and attentive posture.

This posture serves as the starting position for the subsequent movements (Figure 12.77).

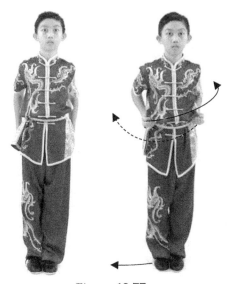

Figure 12.77

Swing the Arms and Hammer Punch (抡臂砸拳)
Movement 1: Swing the Arms 1

Step to the right with your right foot and turn right, forming a high right bow stance. Transform your left fist into a palm and swing it down from your left waist to the right side in front of you. The palm faces inward, with the thumb pointing upward. Simultaneously, release your right fist, open it into a palm, and place it under your left armpit. The palm of your right hand should face outward, with the tiger's mouth facing inward. Direct your gaze towards your left hand (Figure 12.78).

Figure 12.78

Movement 2: Swing the Arms 2

Continue from the previous movement. Turn your body to the left, completing a 180-degree rotation, and swiftly shift your weight to your left leg while raising your right leg to waist height or slightly higher.

Simultaneously, circle your left arm up, backward, and down to the left side of your body at shoulder height, with the palm facing outward and fingers pointing upward. Transform your right palm into a fist, circle it down along the inside of your right leg to the right side until it reaches above your head and extend your arms fully. Ensure the face of your right fist is upward, with the fist-heart inside. Maintain a forward gaze, looking straight ahead (Figure 12.79).

Figure 12.79   Front

Movement 3: Hammer Punch

Continue from the previous movement.

Bend your left knee, assuming a half-squat position, and first hook your right foot before stomping it down close to the inside of your left foot, bringing your feet together. Simultaneously, strike your left palm with the back of your right fist in front of your abdomen. The motion should resemble a hammer pounding downward, while the left palm strikes the back of the right fist upward. The position of the strike is in front of your abdomen, with the distance between the fist and abdomen being approximately 20 cm. Maintain your gaze directed towards your right fist (Figure 12.80).

Single patting foot (单拍脚)
Movement 1: Step Forward and Extend the Arms

Connect to the previous movement.

Push your left foot to the ground, stand up, and step forward with your right foot. Release your right fist into a palm and swing it back behind your body. Meanwhile, extend your left palm forward in front of your head. Two arms should be stretched and tilted in a straight line. Keep your body standing upright. Chest out and tuck your chin and abdomen inward. Look at your left hand (Figure 12.81).

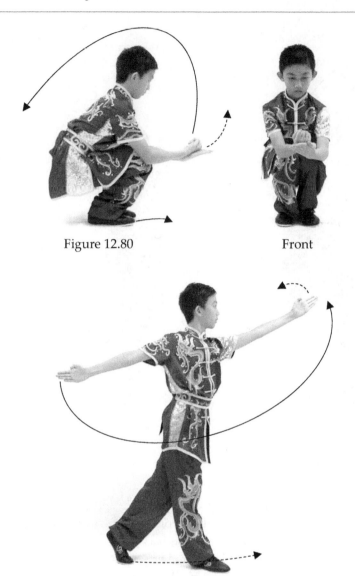

Figure 12.80   Front

Figure 12.81

Movement 2: Pat the Palms

Continue from the previous movement.

Take a big step forward with your left foot while swinging your right arm up from the back of your body. Bring your palms together, with the back of your right palm patting the left palm on the top of your head. Keep your gaze straight ahead (Figure 12.82).

Movement 3: Pat the Foot

Continue from the previous movement.

Push your right foot to the ground and shift your weight onto your left leg. Straighten your right knee, extend your right foot forward, and execute a kick.

Simultaneously, use your right palm to snap the back of your right foot forcefully. Change your left palm into a hook and position it horizontally on the left side, with the hook tip pointing downward. Maintain a forward gaze (Figure 12.83).

Figure 12.82   Figure 12.83

Side Sole Kick (側踹腿)
Movement 1: Cross-Legged Step
Connect to the previous movement and keep your body upright after patting your right foot with your right palm.

Turn right and drop your right foot in front of you, allowing your right toes to point outward to form a cross-legged step. Slightly bend your right knee and straighten your left leg. Cross your hands on your chest, with your right hand on the outside and left hand on the inside. Look at your hands or towards the left (Figure 12.84).

Movement 2: Side kick
Continue from the previous movement. Bend your left knee and lift your left foot forward, moving your left toes inward. Lean your upper body slightly to the right while keeping your right leg straight to support your weight (Figure 12.85).

Then use your left heel as a force point and kick it horizontally to the left. Left toes inward, at shoulder height or higher. Lean right more. Push your palms outward to both sides of your body. Do not let your right palm lower than your shoulder. Look to the left (Figure 12.86).

379

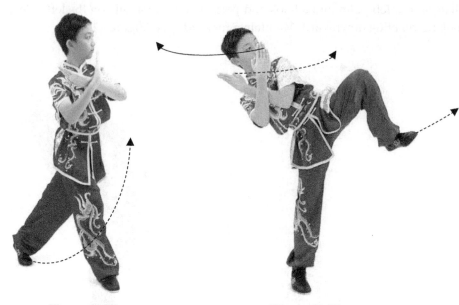

Figure 12.84   Figure 12.85

Hold the Fists on the Waists, with Feet Together (并步抱拳)

Drop your left foot and bring your right foot to the inside of your left foot, aligning them together. Change both hands into fists and hold them at your waist. Look straight ahead (Figure 12.87).

Figure 12.86   Figure 12.87

Continuous Motion of 'Pat Foot and Side Sole Kick'

3. The Combination of 'Front Sweep Kick' and Back' Sweep Kick'

The Movement Names: Split Palm with a Bow Stance - Front Sweep Kick - Double Push Palms with a Bow Stance - Back Sweep Kick - Tiao Palm with a Bow Stance - Stand with Feet Together and Hold the Fists on the Waists.

Preparation posture: Begin by standing up with your feet together and holding your fists at your waist level. Keep your fists closed and your arms relaxed. Direct your gaze straight ahead, maintaining a focused and attentive posture. This posture serves as the starting position for the subsequent movements (Figure 12.88).

Figure 12.88

Split the Palm with a Bow Stance (弓步劈掌)
Movement 1: Hit the Palms above Head

Keep your body upright and focus your Qi in your Dantian. Stand with your left leg, supporting your weight, and lift your right knee in front of your body. Stretch your left foot down. Simultaneously, release both fists and open your palms, raising them above your head. Use your left palm to strike the back of your right palm above your head. Keep your elbows slightly bent. Look straight ahead. (Figure 12.89).

Movement 2: Split Palm with a Bow Stance:

Continue from the previous movement while maintaining your balance.

Place your right foot down to the right side and turn your body to the right, forming a right bow stance. Simultaneously, split your right palm to the right, at shoulder height. Quickly pull your left palm to your left waist. Ensure that both arms move in coordination and at the same time. Look at your right palm (Figure 12.90).

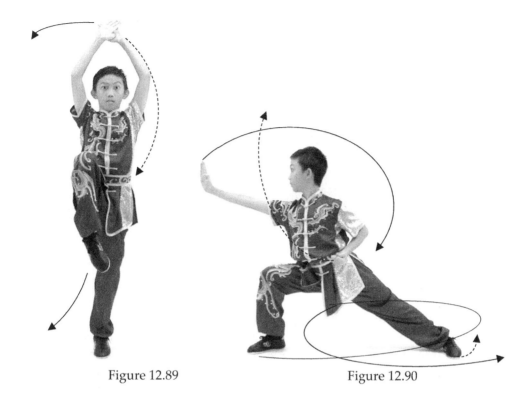

Figure 12.89   Figure 12.90

Front Sweep Kick (前扫腿)

Connect to the previous movement by revolving left in one and a half circles.

Rotate your right hand outward, with the palm facing up, and swing it to the left in front of your chest. Turn your right hand inward and brush it down until it reaches behind your body. When your right hand reaches the back, change it into a hook with the hook tip facing up. Allow your left palm to pass through the inside of your right arm and place it on the upper left side of your head, palm up.

Simultaneously, squat down completely with your left leg, lifting your left heel. Use the sole of your left foot as an axis and grind the ground while stretching your right leg. Move your right toes inward and let the sole of your right foot touch the ground. Perform a sweeping motion forward (to the left) with the sole of your right foot, making one and a half circles around your body (Figure 12.91).

Double Push Palms with a Bow Stance (弓步双推掌)

Movement 1: Cross Hands and Hold a Left Foot Behind the Right Knee:

Push your left foot to the ground and shift your weight to your right leg while turning your body to the right. Bend your right knee and squat slightly. Place your left foot behind your right knee. Change your right hook into a palm and cross both palms in front of your chest, with your right palm facing outward. Look straight ahead (Figure 12.92).

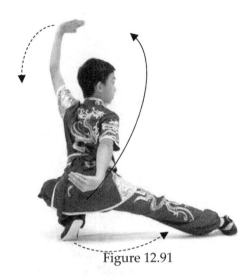

Figure 12.91

Movement 2: Double Push Palms with a Bow Stance

Continue with the previous movement. Take a big step forward with your left foot, extending your right leg to form a left bow stance. Quickly pull your palms to your waists. Then, immediately push forward powerfully, focusing the force on your palms. Keep your arms in line with your shoulders. Look straight ahead (Figure 12.93).

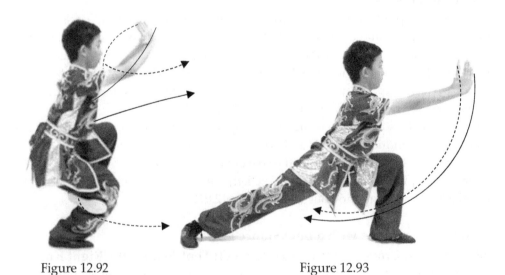

Figure 12.92 Figure 12.93

Back Sweep Kick (后扫腿)

Connect to the previous movement. Quickly turn your upper body to the right, move your left toes inward and squat entirely with your left knee to form a right crouch stance.

At the same time, lean forward and place both palms on the ground inside your right leg, with your right hand near your right foot and your left hand at the back. (Figure 12.94). As your hands touch the ground, twist your upper body to the right, immediately use the sole of your left foot as the axis. With inertial force, sweep your right foot backward in the right-rear direction. The force point of the sweep kick should be on your right heel and the outside of your right foot. Ensure that your entire right foot touches the ground during the sweep. Maintain a vertical axis during the sweep, using the sole of your left foot as the center, and avoid leaning in any direction. (Figure 12.95).

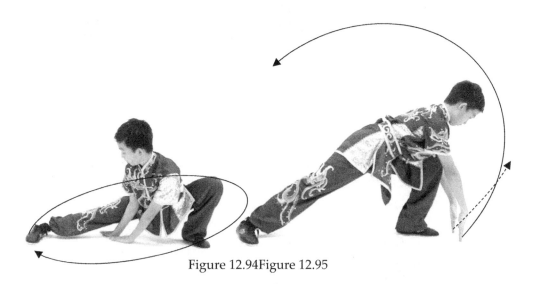

Figure 12.94Figure 12.95

Tiao palm with a bow stance (弓步挑掌)

Continue from the previous movement, maintaining an upright upper body.

Form a left bow stance by positioning your feet accordingly. Simultaneously, swing your right arm upward towards the back, creating a right hook hand. The tip of the hook should be pointing downward. Flick your left palm forward at the height of your shoulder, with your fingers pointing upward and the outside of your little finger facing forward. Look straight ahead (Figure 12.96).

Hold the Fists on the Waist, with Feet Together (并步抱拳)

Continue from the previous movement. Push your left foot to the ground and bring your right foot to the inside of your left foot, aligning them together. Change both hands into the fists, then hold to the waists. Look straight ahead (Figure 12.97).

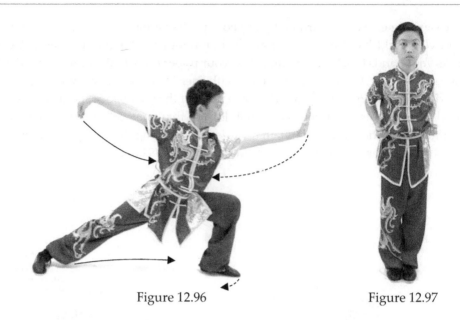

Figure 12.96   Figure 12.97

Continuous motion of 'Front Sweep Kick and Back Sweep Kick'

The Combination of 'Balance' Exercises

1. 'Back Cross-Legged Balance' and 'Swallow Balance'

The Movement Names: Punch with a Back Cross-Legged Balance - Swing the Arms and Hammer Punch - Swallow Balance - Stand up with Feet Together and Hold the Fists on the Waist

Preparation Posture: Stand up with feet together and hold the fists on the waists. Look straight ahead (Figure 12.98, 12.99).

Figure 12.98   Figure 12.99

Punch with a 'Back Cross-Legged Balance' (扣腿冲拳)
Movement 1: Swing Left Arm to the Left in a Left Bow Stance

Begin by turning your body to the right. Step back with your left foot towards the left side, maintaining balance. Bend your right knee, shifting your weight onto your right leg, and create a right bow stance. This means your right foot is firmly planted on the ground, and your right knee is bent while your left leg remains straight.

At the same time, open your left hand and transform it into a palm. Swing your left hand down to the right side from your left waist in a smooth and controlled motion. The palm of your left hand should face inward, and the tiger's mouth (the space between your thumb and index finger) should be facing upward. Maintain your focus on your left hand as you execute the movement (Figure 12.100).

Figure 12.100

Movement 2: Punch with a 'Back Cross-Legged Balance'

Continue from the previous movement.

Turn your upper body to the left, rotating it in that direction. Simultaneously, move your right foot inward, bringing it closer to your body. Keep your right leg in a half-squatting state, maintaining a bent knee position. Push your left foot firmly onto the ground, transferring your weight onto it. Bend your left knee and place your left foot behind your right knee. This position creates a crossed-leg stance.

With power and force, punch your right fist from your right waist to the right side. The fist-eye (knuckles) of your right fist should face upward. At the same time, lift your left palm over your head, with the palm facing up and the fingers pointing to the right side. Maintain your gaze in the direction of the punch, looking to the right (Figure 12.101).

This posture forms a balanced position and belongs to the 'Lasting Balance' category, where you should remain stationary for a while or hold the position for approximately two seconds after its formation.

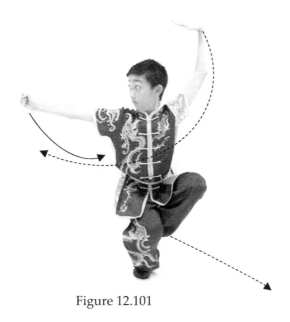

Figure 12.101

Swing the Arms and Hammer Punch (抡臂砸拳)
Movement 1: Swing the Arms with a High Right Bow Stance
Continue from the previous movement.

Turn your body slightly to the right, adjusting your positioning. Put your left foot down to the left side, extending it away from your body. As you place your left foot down, simultaneously swing your left hand down from the top of your head towards the left side and then towards the right in front of your knee. The palm of your left hand should face inward towards your body, and the tiger's mouth should be facing upward.

At the same time, release your right fist and transform it into a palm. Place your right palm under your left armpit, facing outward, with the fingers pointing up. Direct your attention and focus on your left hand as you perform the movement (Figure 12.102).

Movement 2: Raise the Right Arm with a Lifted Knee
Continue from the previous movement.

Turn your body 180 degrees to the left, rotating it in that direction. Push your right foot firmly onto the ground and shift your body weight onto your left leg as you turn. Simultaneously, quickly lift your right leg at the height of your waist or higher, facing to the left side and look straight ahead. Maintain a controlled and balanced posture as you perform this leg lift.

At the same time, circle your left arm in an upward and downward motion to the left side of your body. The left palm should face outward, and the fingers should be pointing upward.

389

Additionally, transform your right palm into a fist. Circle the fist in a downward, rightward, and upward motion, bringing it up to the top of your head. Stretch your right arm fully, and the fist should be facing upward, with the knuckles facing inward (fist-heart inside). Maintain your gaze straight ahead, focusing on your movement (Figure 12.103). Basically, the two arms should be circling in opposite directions with opening your chest and lengthening the arms as much as possible.

Figure 12.102   Figure 12.103

Movement 3: Hammer Punch in a Half Squat

Continue from the previous movement.

Bend your left knee and transition into a half squat position. Hook your right foot by lifting it off the ground and bringing it close to your left foot.

Stomp your right foot down onto the ground, placing it close to the inside of your left foot. This movement results in both feet being together, forming a half squat position.

Simultaneously, perform a striking motion by hitting the left palm with the back of your right fist. The strike should occur in front of your abdomen, at a comfortable distance. Direct your gaze towards your right fist during this movement (Figure 12.104).

Figure 12.104

Swallow Balance (燕式平衡)

After performing the hammer punch movement, take a moment to regulate your breathing and calm down.

Once you feel ready, straighten your right leg to support your body weight. Simultaneously, stretch your left knee and extend your left leg to the back, reaching the highest position possible. As you extend your left leg, lift your palms to both sides of your body, with your fingers pointing upward and your palms facing outward. Lean your upper body forward while keeping your head raised and chest pushed out. Maintain a straight line from your head to your extended left leg. Direct your gaze straight ahead, focusing on a fixed point (Figure 12.105).

Figure 12.105   Figure 12.106

This posture should be held for a while or approximately two seconds after it has been formed. The swallow balance is categorized as a 'Lasting Balance' and requires stability and concentration.

Hold the Fists on the Waist, with Feet Together (并步抱拳)

After completing the swallow balance movement, bring your left foot down and place it inside your right foot.

Ensure that your feet are close together, with the heels touching or nearly touching. Change both hands into fists by curling your fingers inward and closing your palms. Position your fists on your waist, with the knuckles facing upward. Keep your arms relaxed and close to your body. Maintain an upright posture, with your spine straight and your head facing forward. Direct your gaze straight ahead, focusing on a fixed point (Figure 12.106). Take a moment to breathe and relax, preparing for the next sequence or concluding the practice.

Continuous Motion of 'Back Cross-Legged Balance and Swallow Balance'

2. 'Raised Knee Balance,' 'Kick into Sky,' and 'Look at the Moon Balance'

The Movement Names: Raised Knee and Split with the Fist - Kick into Sky - Single Patting the Foot - Look at the Moon Balance - Stand Up with Feet Together and Hold the Fists on the Waists.

Preparation Posture: Stand up with feet together and hold the fists on the waists (Figure 12.107).

Raised Knee and Split with the Fist (提膝劈拳)
Movement 1: Extend the Right Arm in a Left Bow Stance
Turn to the left and step back to the right with your right foot, forming a left bow stance. Simultaneously, release your right fist into a palm and extend it to the left from your right waist in front of your left knee. The palm should be facing inward, and the tiger's mouth should be facing upward. Release your left fist into a palm and thrust it under your right armpit, with the palm facing outward. Look at your right hand (Figure 12.108).

Figure12.107   Figure 2.108

Movement 2: Raised Knee and Split with the Right Fist
Continue with the previous movement.

Push your left foot to the ground and shift your weight to your right leg while lifting your left knee to form a front knee-lifted balance. Change your right palm into a fist and split it to the right, with the fist-eye facing up. At the same time, circle your left palm from the left and up. When your left palm reaches the top of your head, snap your left wrist to form a 'flash palm' with fingers pointing to the right and the palm facing up. Look to the right. (Figure 12.109).

393

In the 'Raised Knee Balance' movement, the one-legged stance is formed with the back and supporting leg straight, while the suspended knee is raised at least to waist height.

Figure 12.109

Kick into Sky Balance (朝天蹬)

Continue with the previous movement.

Release your right fist and transform it into an open palm, raising it above your head with the palm facing upward and the fingers pointing towards the left. Simultaneously, lower your left hand and grasp your left heel from the inside of your calf (Figure 12.110).

Execute a powerful kick with your left foot, aiming for the top of your head. Keep your left knee straight, with the sole of the foot facing upward. If possible, hook the foot, turning the toes inward. Maintain a steady gaze straight ahead (Figure 12.111).

This balance is also classified as a 'Lasting Balance,' which means you should hold the position for a while, ideally for approximately two seconds, after assuming it.

Figure 12.110   Figure 12.111

Single Patting Foot (单拍脚)
Movement 1: Landing and Slapping the Palms Above Head
Continue from the previous movement.
Lower your left foot and turn your body to the left 90 degrees while dropping your hands down to the sides of your thighs. Then, lift them from the front of your body and clap them together above your head, slapping the back of the right hand against the left palm. Keep your gaze straight ahead (Refer to Figure 12.112).

Movement 2: Single Slaps the Foot
Continue from the previous movement.
Push your right foot onto the ground, shift your weight to your left leg, straighten your right knee, extend your right foot forward, and perform a powerful kick. Use your right palm to forcefully slap the back of your right foot. Additionally, transform your left palm into a hook shape and position it horizontally on the left side, with the tip of the hook pointing downward. Maintain a steady gaze straight ahead (Figure 12.113). Typically, as your right foot reaches the highest point of the kick, the speed should increase. The kicking and patting movements should generate the same level of power.

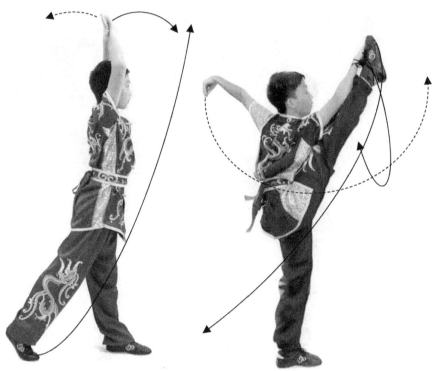

Figure 12.112   Figure 12.113

Look at the Moon Balance (望月平衡)
Movement 1: Cross Hands in front of the Chest
Continue from the previous movement.

After patting the right foot, immediately place your right foot backward and bend your left knee, assuming a left bow stance. Cross your hands in front of your chest, with the right palm on the outside and both tiger's mouths facing inward. The fingers are angled upward. Keep your gaze straight ahead. (Figure 12.114).

Movement 2: Look at the Moon Balance
Continue from the previous movement.

Push your left foot onto the ground and shift your weight to your right leg to maintain balance. Bend your left knee, straighten your left foot, and raise it backward.
Twist your upper body to the right and lean slightly backward.

Simultaneously, circle your arms downward to both sides of your body, then place your right palm on the right side at shoulder height, with the fingers pointing upward. Your left hand should swing upward, forming a 'Flash Palm' above your head, with the palm facing up and the fingers pointing to the right. Gaze to the right. (Figure 12.115).

Figure 12.114   Figure 12.115

Hold the Fists on the Waists with Feet Together (并步抱拳)

Place your left foot inside your right foot to bring your feet together. Transform both hands into fists and hold them at your waist. Keep your gaze straight ahead (Figure 12.107).

The Continuous Motion of
'Raised Knee Balance, Kick into the Sky, and Look at the Moon Balance'

The Combination of 'Jumping' Exercises

1. 'Jump Front Straight Kick' and 'Crouch Stance'

Movement Names: Hit-Heel Step and Tiao Palm – Jump Front Straight Kick – Flash-Palm in a Crouch Stance

Preparation Posture: Assume an upper punch with a left high empty stance, directing your gaze to the left (Figure 12.116).

Hit-Heel Step and Tiao Palm (击步挑掌)

Step your left foot to the left, turn your right fist into a palm, and cross your arms to your chest. Ensure the right arm is positioned on the outside, with fingers pointing upward. Maintain a forward gaze to the left (Figure 12.117).

398

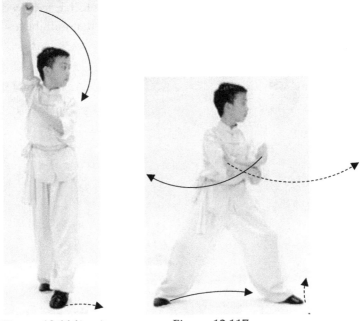

Figure 12.116 ----▶   Figure 12.117

Proceed from the previous movement. Press your left foot into the ground, initiating a jump, and bring your right foot to connect with your left heel mid-air. Concurrently, swing your arms in a circular motion – the right arm swings down to the back of your body, while the left arm flicks forward along your body. Maintain straight palms for both arms. Keep your gaze fixed straight ahead to the left (Figure 12.118).

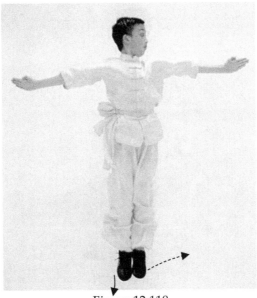

Figure 12.118

Initiate the landing by bringing down your right foot first, followed by your left foot. Keep your eyes following the motion of your left palm, maintaining a straight-ahead gaze (Figure 12.119, 12.120).

Figure 12.119   Figure 12.120

Jump Front Straight Kick (腾空飞脚)

Progress from the preceding movement. As your left foot lands, promptly step forward with your right foot (Figure 12.121).

Figure 12.121

Following this, swing your left leg forward and upward, exert force on your right foot against the ground, initiating a jump. Simultaneously, swing your right arm forward and upward from the back. Complete the movement by bringing the back of your right hand above your head, aiming to connect with your left palm (12.122, 12.123).

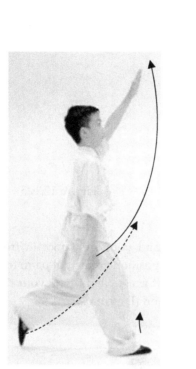 

Figure 12.122   Figure 12.123

While in the air, perform a forward kick with your right foot (you can use a spring or a straight kick) and point your right foot straight. Simultaneously, pat your right foot with your right palm. As you do this, bend your left knee and bring your left foot to the inside of your right leg, pointing your foot downward. Adjust your left palm to the left and transition it into a hook hand. The tip of the hook should be pointing downward and positioned slightly above your shoulder. Slightly lean your upper body forward and keep your gaze fixed straight ahead (Figure 12.124).

Upon landing, your left foot should touch the ground first, followed by your right foot landing in front of your left foot, but exercise control and avoid landing immediately (Figure 12.125).

The action line diagram (solid and dashed lines) resembles the previous 'Jump, Front Straight Kick' movement. If necessary, you can refer back to it for clarification.

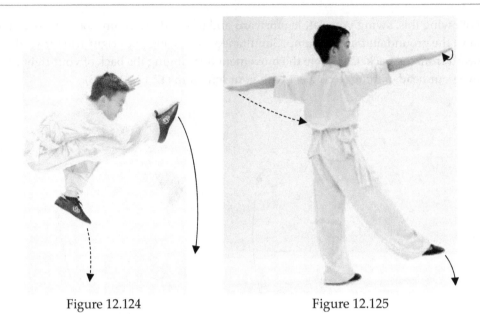

Figure 12.124   Figure 12.125

Flash-Palm in a Crouch Stance (仆步亮掌)

Continue from the previous movement. Land your right foot in front of your left straightly, rotate your right arm outward, and position your right palm to the upper right. Simultaneously, pull your left palm to your left waist. Slightly tilt your right shoulder to the right and focus your gaze on your right hand (Figure 12.126).

Figure 12.126

Progress by swinging your right palm up to the left while gently turning to the left. Subsequently, lower your right arm in a counterclockwise motion in front of your body. As your right palm reaches the upper right again, bend your right elbow, snap your right

402

wrist, forming a 'flash palm' above your head. Simultaneously, guide your left palm through the inside of your right forearm, rotate your left arm inward, and trace your left palm from the chest, forward, left, and to the rear of your body. Transform your left palm into a hook with the tip pointing upward. While executing the wrist snap with your right hand, bend your right knee and assume a full squat, creating a left crouch stance. Swiftly turn your head to the left during the wrist snap (refer to Figure 12.127).

Figure 12.127

Key points:
(1) Ensure that both feet come together with a powerful forward impetus when taking a step forward. The step forward with the right foot should be steady and forceful.
(2) While performing the 'flash palm' in the crouching stance, pay attention to snapping your right wrist inward. Extend your chest, straighten your waist, and lean forward.

Continuous Motion of the 'Jump Front Straight Kick' and 'Crouch Stance'

2. 'Jump Lotus Kick' and 'Split'

Movement Names: A Curve Driving Step Forward – Jump and Blocking the Palm Up –Jump Lotus Kick – Vertical Split.

Preparation Posture: Begin from a left-high empty stance and extend your palms back and forth. Keep your arms at shoulder height and maintain a forward gaze (Figure 12.128).

A Curve Driving Step Forward, Jump, and Palm Blocking Up (弧形纵步架掌)

Take a half step forward with your left foot and slightly lower your hands. Maintain your gaze straight ahead (Figure 12.129).

Figure 12.128   Figure 12.129

Then, take a large step forward with your right foot while bringing your right palm down to your right waist and swinging your left arm from behind, upward, and forward. Point your left finger to the right, with your eyes following the left hand (Figure 12.130).

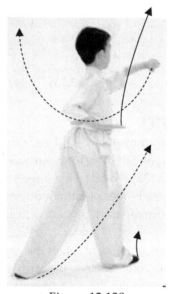

Figure 12.130

Continue from the previous movement. As your right foot lands, immediately push off the ground and jump up. Bend your left knee and hold it in the air in front of your body, at least at waist height. Simultaneously, guide your right hand through the inside of your left forearm and raise it above your head, palm facing upward. Let your left arm swing naturally down towards the left side of your body in a circular motion. Maintain your gaze to the left (Figure 12.131).

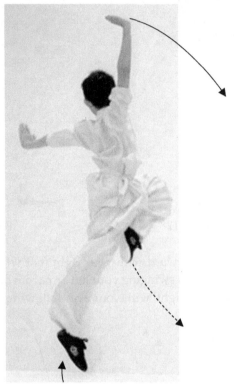

Figure 12.131

Jump Lotus Kick (腾空摆莲)

Continuing from the previous movement, land your right foot first, followed by your left foot in front of your right foot. Slightly shift your weight forward in preparation for the following action (Figure 12.132). Then, take a large step to the right with your right foot (a circular step) with your right toes pointing outward. Simultaneously, lower your right arm and swing your left arm forward, preparing to jump. Maintain a straight-ahead gaze (Figure 12.133).

Continuing from the previous movement, push the ground with your right foot and jump up. Simultaneously, kick your left foot upward, swing your arms forward and upward, and strike your left palm with the back of your right palm while rotating your body to the right (Figure 12.134).

After achieving the jump, execute an outward circular kick with your right leg, patting your right foot with your palms. Then, bend your left knee and bring your leg to the inside of your right leg or extend it to the left side of your body. Lean your upper body slightly forward, and keep your eyes following your hands (Figure 12.135).

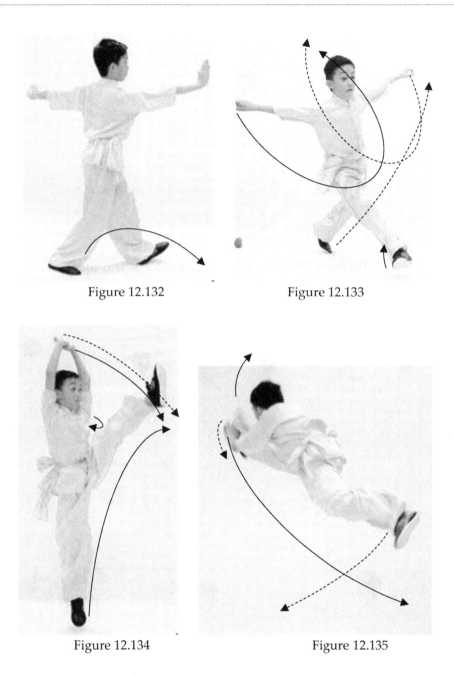

Figure 12.132   Figure 12.133

Figure 12.134   Figure 12.135

The action line diagram (solid and dashed lines) resembles the previous 'Jump, Lotus Kick' movement. If necessary, you can refer back to it for clarification.

Drop Split

After patting, turn right to form a left split down, separate your palms to both sides of your body at the height of the shoulders. Fingers up. Look straight ahead (Figure 12.136).

Figure 12.136

Continuous Motion of 'Jump Lotus Kick and Split'

3. 'Jump Tornado Kick' and 'Horse Stance'

Movement Names: Push Left Palm with a Hit-Heel Step -- Tornado Kick – Punch and Block Up in a Horse Stance.

Preparation Posture: Flash the palm with a high empty stance (Figure 12.136).

Push the palm with a hit-heel step (击步推掌)

Keep your body upright. Step to the left with your left foot and cross both arms to your chest. The right arm should be outside, with the fingers pointing upward. Keep your gaze fixed to the left (Figure 12.137).

Figure 12.136   Figure 12.137

Continuing from the previous movement, push your left foot onto the ground, jump, and strike your left heel with your right foot in the air. Simultaneously, push your left palm through the inside of your right arm to the left, clench your right fist, and swiftly pull it back to your right waist. Maintain your gaze to the left (Figure 12.138).

Figure 12.138

Then place your right foot down first, followed by your left foot landing to the left. Maintain your focus on the left hand (Figure 12.139).

Figure 12.139

Tornado kick (旋风脚)

Continuing from the previous movement, step forward with your right foot and turn your toes inward, preparing to jump. Meanwhile, swing your left arm downward, bend your left elbow, and bring it to your right chest. Simultaneously, the right arm swings up and forward, and the upper body rotates to the left while leaning forward. Maintain your gaze downward toward the right corner (Figure 12.140).

Figure 12.140

Continue with the previous movement. Shift your weight to the right, bend your right knee, push the ground with your right foot, and jump. Simultaneously, lift your left leg and swing it to the upper left while turning your body in the same direction. As you do this, swing your arms down and up to the upper left, allowing your body to spin around. When jumping, retract your right leg inward and strike the sole of your right foot with your left palm in front of your face (Figure 12.141, 12.142, 12.143).

Punch and Block Up in a Horse Stance (马步架打)

Turn to the left and land in a horse stance while extending your right hand downward and executing a powerful punch to the right with your right fist, passing through your right waist. Simultaneously, rotate your left arm inward and raise your left palm, forming a block above your head with the palm facing up and the fingers pointing to the right. Maintain your gaze to the right (Figure 12.144).

The action line diagram resembles the previous 'Jump, Tornado Kick' movement. If necessary, you can refer back to it for clarification.

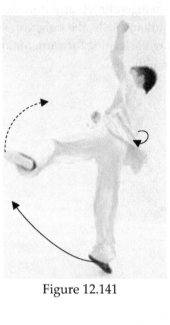

Figure 12.141

Figure 12.142

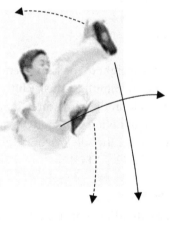

Figure 12.143

Figure 12.144

The Continuous Motion of 'Jump Tornado Kick' and 'Horse Stance'

References:

1. Teaching Materials Committee of the National Institute of Sports, 'General Sports College Teaching Materials,' People's Sports Publisher, ISBN 7-5009-0329-4/G. 314 (課)1989.6, First Edition.
2. Teaching Materials Committee of the National Institute of Sports, 'Specialized Sports College Teaching Materials Volume 1,' People's Sports Publisher, ISBN 7-5009-0329-4/G. 314 (課)1989.6, First Edition.
3. Compiled by the Wushu Training Material Writing Group, National Wushu Training Material Volume 1, Beijing Sports University Publisher.
4. Authorized by the National Sports Committee of the People's Republic of China, Wushu Routine Competition Rules 1996, People's Sports Publisher, ISBN 7-5009-1296-X/G.1200 199.2, First Edition.

About Author

Yajun Zhuang stands as a prominent figure in Chinese Martial Arts (Wushu), with his passion for the art evident from a young age. At just eight years old, he was talented enough to join the Professional Wushu team in Jiangsu Province, China, embarking on an impressive Wushu career.

His journey is marked by significant milestones. By 16, Zhuang was already coaching, having formed his own Wushu team. His academic pursuits at Nanjing Normal University deepened his grasp of Wushu's culture and philosophy. After his studies, he achieved the distinction of being the youngest professor at Nanjing Industrial University. He also played pivotal roles in the Chinese Physical Education Committee and the Wushu Professional Committee and acted as a Senior National Wushu Judge and chief judge at various national and international Wushu tournaments.

Recognized as a scholar in Wushu, Zhuang's extensive research and publications, spanning both Chinese and English, delve into Wushu's practice and philosophy. His expertise led to recognition in the Chinese Wushu community, including being featured in the 'China Wushu Encyclopedia' and appointed as an 'Honorary Consultant' for the Chinese Wushu Hall of Fame.

2003, Zhuang moved to the United States, continuing his Wushu journey. He joined Louisiana State University's Department of Kinesiology, teaching Chinese Martial Arts and researching the therapeutic benefits of Tai Chi and Qi-Gong for conditions such as peripheral neuropathy and Parkinson's disease. His modified Zhuang's Tai-Chi Qi-Gong Therapy is noted for its significant positive impact on patients' functional mobility and life quality.

2011 saw Zhuang establish the 'Zhuang's Tai-Chi & Kung-Fu Academy' in Baton Rouge, Louisiana, where he trains and mentors students, many of whom have excelled in Wushu competitions across America and Pan American. His teachings span a broad spectrum of styles, including both internal and external Kung Fu.

Dedicated to his mission as a practitioner and advocate of Chinese Wushu. He remains a respected mentor, generously sharing his knowledge with students and practitioners and guiding those seeking to understand Chinese Wushu's essence.

The Author has Already Published the Books

Made in the USA
Middletown, DE
17 October 2024

62484800R00245